Convicted

Your Path to Triumph When Life Seems Unfair

Trevon Gross, PhD

Convicted: Your Path to Triumph When Life Seems Unfair

by Trevon Gross, PhD

Copyright © 2024 by Trevon Gross, PhD

All rights reserved. No part of this publication may be reproduced, distributed, or transmitted in any form or by any means, including photocopying, recording, or other electronic or mechanical methods, without the prior written permission of the publisher, except in the case of brief quotations embodied in critical reviews and certain other noncommercial uses permitted by copyright law. For permission requests, write to the publisher, addressed "Attention: Permissions Coordinator," at the address below.

Publisher: That's Gross Productions, LLC

325 E. Jimmie Leeds Road

Suite 7, #210

Galloway, NJ 08205

ISBN: 979-8-218-98808-1

Printed in the United States of America

First Edition, 2024

Scripture quotations are from the Holy Bible, New Living Translation (NLT). Copyright © 1996, 2004, 2015 by Tyndale House Foundation. Used by permission of Tyndale House Publishers, Inc., Carol Stream, Illinois 60188. All rights reserved.

Disclaimer: This is a work of non-fiction. The events are portrayed as accurately as possible, based on the author's memories and experiences. Some names and identifying details have been changed to protect the privacy of individuals.

For more information, please visit: TrevonGross.com

Dedication

To my Heavenly Father, who promised,

"When you go through deep waters, I will be with you. When you go through rivers of difficulty, you will not drown. When you walk through the fire of oppression, you will not be burned up; the flames will not consume you."
(Isaiah 43:2, NLT)

To my wife, Qwynn, who stood by my side and fought with me through the darkest times—I am forever grateful to have married the right woman.

To my children, Trevon Jr., Dianna, and Sarah, who grew up unexpectedly during the fight— I am so proud of each of you.

To my Hope Cathedral family, who trusted my proven character over sensational headlines—our best days are yet to come.

To the men of God, Dr. Raymond Banks Sr., Dr. Leroy Attles Sr., and Apostle I.V. Hilliard—thank you for teaching me what it means to be a man of faith.

And to Tychicus, who was with me every step of the way—I am deeply grateful.

Finding Triumph in the Midst of Trials

Have you ever felt overwhelmed by life's injustices, questioning why adversity seems to target you? In *Convicted: Your Path to Triumph When Life Seems Unfair*, Trevon shares his powerful and inspiring journey of overcoming unimaginable challenges, from the confines of a federal prison camp to the liberating realization of God's grace and purpose.

Through deeply personal stories, Trevon reveals how he transformed his suffering into a platform for growth and resilience. This compelling narrative is more than just a memoir; it is a powerful testament to the unwavering grace of God and His boundless love, which carries us through even the most difficult trials.

"Trevon Gross' Convicted masterfully weaves together the redemptive power of God in the face of unfair situations and challenging seasons. This book, which reads like a gripping movie, brings Romans 8:28 to life in a powerful way. Dr. Gross paints a complex picture of grace, forgiveness, freedom, and trust in God with simplicity and profound depth. Convicted is less about the past and more about God's promise for the future. I'm grateful to have witnessed my friend not only write about these truths but also live them with conviction. Once you start reading, you won't be able to put it down."
— **Pastor Todd R. Bishop, Church Unleashed, Author of Leadership Unleashed, Leveraging Tension, and Human Right**

"I enthusiastically endorse Dr. Trevon Gross' new book, a transparent and profoundly personal account of navigating life's darkest moments. His reflections offer readers not only a glimpse into his resilience but also an invitation to reconsider their own perspectives, providing valuable insights on overcoming adversity and emerging stronger."
— **Bishop Jonathan Briggs, Truth and Fellowship Global Outreach Ministry**

"Dr. Trevon Gross' Convicted is a monumental work that transcends personal testimony—it's a roadmap to resilience, hope, and divine purpose. With raw transparency and profound wisdom, Dr. Gross captures the essence of navigating life's deepest valleys while holding onto faith. This book will not only inspire but equip you to overcome adversity with grace and confidence. It's a must-read for anyone seeking to rise above the challenges life throws their way."
— **Pastor Phil Munsey, Chair of Champions Network, Lakewood Church/ Joel Osteen**

"Though our stories may differ, we all face similar struggles. Dr. Trevon Gross offers a deeply personal and proven roadmap to navigate life's challenges and the unfair circumstances that often trap us in bitterness and ineffectiveness. His story and the principles he uncovered during a dark season will lead you toward developing the character and confidence needed to discover your authentic self in Christ."
— **Bishop Rosie S. O'neal, Senior Pastor, Koinonia Christian Center**

"Dr. Trevon Gross has written a powerful and transformative book that speaks directly to anyone navigating life's toughest challenges. His transparency and deep faith offer a roadmap for overcoming adversity and finding purpose, even in the darkest times. Convicted is a must-read for those seeking hope, healing, and a renewed sense of purpose."
— **Senior Pastor Chad Rowe, Pastor, Destiny World Outreach Center**

"Dr. Trevon Gross' journey through adversity is a masterclass in faith, endurance, and grace. His new book offers readers not only insight into his personal trials but also a roadmap for overcoming life's deepest challenges. With transparency and wisdom, Dr. Gross presents timeless principles that will inspire and empower anyone facing their own battles. His message is both transformative and redemptive, making this a must-read for anyone seeking spiritual growth and victory in tough times."
— **Pastor James McIver, Lead Pastor, Without Limits Christian Center**

TABLE OF CONTENTS

Acknowledgements	11
Foreword	13
Preface	15
Introduction	21
Profile in Conviction: Bishop Richard Allen	29
Chapter 1. The Danger of Asking 'Why Me?'	31
Profile in Conviction: Viktor Frankl	49
Chapter 2. Authenticity Is Key to Freedom	51
Profile in Conviction: Frederick Douglass	67
Chapter 3. Faithfulness Anchors Stability	71
Profile in Conviction: Daniel	90
Chapter 4. Purpose Powers Progress	93
Profile in Conviction: William Wilberforce	111
Chapter 5. Joy Is a Choice Not a Condition	115
Profile in Conviction: Dietrich Bonhoeffer	134
Chapter 6. Trusting God Is Essential	137
Profile in Conviction: George Müller	163
Chapter 7. Community is Crucial	167
Profile in Conviction: Corrie ten Boom	196

Chapter 8. Grace Triumphs Over Injustice	199
Profile in Conviction: Aung San Suu Kyi	221
Chapter 9. Every Loss Teaches a Lesson	223
Profile in Conviction: Horatio Spafford	239
Chapter 10. Forgiveness Frees Us	243
Profile in Conviction: John Wesley	266
Chapter 11. Resilience Redefines Results	271
Profile in Conviction: Winston Churchill	295
Chapter 12. Integrity Guides	299
Profile in Conviction: Immanuel Kant	320
Chapter 13. Greater Things Are Still to Come	323
Profile in Conviction: Richard Wurmbrand	332
Epilogue: D. Qwynn Gross	335
About the Author	343

ACKNOWLEDGEMENTS

To my wife, Qwynn, thank you for your tireless support during the writing of this book. From reading drafts to encouraging me on the hardest days, your love and partnership made this project possible.

To Kristen Santillo, my attorney—God brought you into my life at just the right time. Your unwavering dedication and compassion went beyond legal representation, and your fight for justice meant more to me than words can express. Though it seemed like we lost, I am confident time will prove otherwise. Thank you for standing by me then and continuing to be a friend now.

To the pastors who quietly yet significantly provided encouragement and financial support during my time in the camp—your kindness and generosity made a profound impact. You know who you are, and I want you to know that your prayers, words, and contributions brought light during a very dark season. I am deeply grateful for your unwavering faith and support.

To the men with whom I shared the camp—thank you for sharing your stories and for the once-in-a-lifetime experience we endured together. Your resilience and camaraderie were invaluable during that time, and I carry the lessons we learned with me.

To all the men who have endured or are currently enduring the hardships of prison or camp—may you stand firm on convictions that bring hope, inspiration, and ultimately, transformation. Your strength in the face of adversity is a testament to the power of the human spirit.

FOREWORD

Is it truly possible to live a fulfilled, purposeful life committed to Christ without facing hardships? My teachings have always emphasized that there is glory in suffering wrongfully, that Christ's suffering is the ultimate example for how we are called to suffer. But it goes deeper. Not only are we to suffer as He did, but we are called to endure it patiently. Imagine, if you are a congregational leader seeking a career change, crafting a five-part series on the divine appointment of suffering for Christ's glory. Most would say that you'd shrink a thousand-member congregation to a hundred faster than... well, you get the idea.

The truth remains: we are all called to endure suffering at some point as we labor to bring our Father's kingdom to earth. While not a popular sentiment today, it is especially true for those called to lead. In fact, the early church grew through its suffering. There's no greater testament to one's beliefs than the willingness to lay down one's life for them.

In *Convicted: Your Path to Triumph When Life Seems Unfair*, Trevon Gross masterfully guides us through this difficult terrain. The book is filled with profound examples of courage and the strength to make righteous decisions, even when they come at a personal cost. From moments when you find yourself before God, pleading for Him to take the cup of suffering away, to those times when you are unsure whether the path ahead is best for you but know it is the right one, Trevon's journey serves as a roadmap for how to follow Christ's footsteps.

As I read this book, I was struck by the parallels between his life and my own. The depth of his story is a clear testament to how God chooses each of us for our unique path, and how Trevon embraced his, even when it seemed impossible. His journey reveals the unmistakable presence of the Father, walking alongside him every step of the way.

Terrence Stevenson
Founder & CEO
The Jericho Group

PREFACE

"In the case of the United States versus Trevon Gross," the judge's voice echoed through the courtroom. "We, the jury, find the defendant guilty." The words reverberated in my mind, each syllable feeling like the final blow in a battle I never expected to fight. I had been faithful to God, trusting His guidance every step of the way. Yet, as I stood in that courtroom, condemned for crimes I did not commit, I found myself questioning everything. How had it come to this?

As I walked out of the courtroom that day, the words "guilty" echoed relentlessly in my mind. How had my life come to this point? The events that led me here were far from the battlefield I now faced, but it all began with a single text message—a text I received while attending a church management conference, never realizing that in an instant, my life would change forever.

"Pastor, do you know who Executive-1 is?" That message on my phone, received while I sat in a church management conference, marked the beginning of a journey that would turn my life upside down, ultimately leading to 800 days in a federal prison camp. In that instant, I mentally checked out of the conference, focusing on the attachment about the arrest of a fraudulent bitcoin company trying to take over a small New Jersey credit union. "Bitcoin company? What company is that?" I wondered. It didn't take long for me to realize they were referring to the credit union our church had partnered with for nearly a decade.

This wasn't just any credit union; it was a lifeline for the unbanked in our community, a minority-founded institution that had worked tirelessly to offer financial services to those without access. We started with a seat on the board, and over time, the church assumed full board control, investing both time and resources to keep the credit union operational. We provided loans for college students needing laptops, start-up supplies for small businesses, deposits for apartments, car loans, and emergency funds for unexpected crises. When regulators demanded staff presence during specific hours, the church covered the costs to keep the credit union compliant.

The more we invested, the more our depositor base grew. However, as a credit union, we were bound by ratios that forced us to turn away deposits that would create an imbalance, triggering penalties from banking regulators. Defaults on high-risk loans were covered by the church until they could be brought current. The credit union never lost money on these transactions, but the challenge remained: we needed more deposits to authorize significant loans, yet accepting large deposits would disrupt our ratios.

To navigate this financial dilemma, we applied for a grant, attended training sessions with banking regulators, and sought partnerships to grow deposits sustainably. Despite the operational improvements and incremental growth, we still lacked the critical capital to introduce popular banking features like online banking, debit cards, and extended hours—features essential for attracting more significant, steady business.

Then, a superstorm hit the Jersey Shore, forcing the credit union to relocate to our church campus. The church, true to its commitment, covered the costs of moving, renovation, and staffing. We rebranded the credit union to align more closely with the church's identity, and held membership drives, opening savings accounts and seeing gradual growth. Yet, it wasn't enough to become a primary financial institution for most. Each year, banking regulators assessed our operations, pushing for closure because we hadn't achieved enough growth to warrant ongoing support. They consistently rejected the church's financial support as insufficient because it didn't generate the necessary fee income.

In the winter of 2014, a promising partnership proposal emerged. A collectibles club wanted to join forces, offering to fund the infrastructure needed to support its 10,000 members. While this partnership presented an opportunity, it also raised concerns: would we lose board control and our ability to serve the underserved? After negotiations, we structured an agreement that would facilitate a phased transition of control, allowing us to train the new board members while maintaining our mission.

Initially, the partnership showed promise. We introduced new banking services, attracted more members, and brought in banking expertise. But within months, it was evident that this collaboration couldn't continue. The club failed to honor its commitments, and by November 2014, we severed ties, reverting to the original management structure. It wasn't until I received that fateful text in July 2015 that the full truth came to light.

Unbeknownst to us, this collectibles club was a front for a fraudulent bitcoin scheme targeting banks nationwide. They sought control of our credit union to bypass the regulatory barriers their bitcoin exchange faced. The federal government, upon seizing the club's records, found evidence of their dealings with us. Although we had severed ties, and our association was brief, the authorities saw the church's reimbursement from the club as suspicious, viewing it as a bribe, even though my salary hadn't changed and no money ever came to me personally.

In August 2015, federal investigators appeared, subpoenaing me to a grand jury. My attorney managed to cancel the appearance, but the threats of indictment loomed. Under my attorney's guidance, I participated in an interview, hoping to clarify the situation. It was evident from the outset that the investigators weren't looking for clarity but for a confession. Despite intense questioning, I maintained my innocence. When we left that meeting, I knew this ordeal was far from over.

In March 2016, just as life began to normalize, I received the dreaded call: I was indicted on bribery charges and needed to surrender the next morning. It was supposed to be a formality, a quick process. But after being handcuffed and processed, I returned home with my world forever altered. News of my indictment quickly spread, casting a shadow over my ministry. That Sunday, my wife and I stood before our congregation, sharing the reality of our situation and our resolve to fight the charges. The church rallied around us, and we clung to the hope of a miracle.

The trial, originally set for October 2016, was postponed to February 2017. During the holiday season, a superseding indictment expanded the charges, adding conspiracy and false statements, further reducing the threshold for conviction. The prosecution's tactics aimed to force a plea deal, but I refused. I couldn't admit to something I hadn't done. They threatened me with a maximum sentence of 30 years. Still, I stood firm, holding onto my faith and conviction.

The trial finally began, stretching over five weeks. The prosecution dominated the proceedings, and my defense was limited to just two days. After extensive deliberation, the jury found me guilty on all charges. My sentencing was scheduled for later that year, and in February 2018, I surrendered to a Federal Prison Camp to begin a 60-month sentence.

I wish I could say I faced these challenges with unwavering strength and faith. The truth is, much of the time, I felt numb—trusting and trembling, as my pastor would say. I continued preaching every Sunday, drawing strength from my faith and the support of my church. As I write this book, my purpose isn't to argue my innocence or relitigate the past. God is my Vindicator. My goal is to share how God brought me through this tumultuous season so that others might find strength and hope in their own trials.

This book wasn't easy to write. Re-living these experiences was painful. But I am convinced that my transparent account—the good, the bad, and the ugly—will help others see how God can work even in the darkest times. Life's challenges don't have to defeat or define us negatively. They can be stepping stones to a deeper, more fulfilling existence.

I wouldn't wish my experiences on anyone, nor would I choose to relive them. Yet, I can say with conviction that God transforms trials into testimonies when we stay true to our beliefs. That's what this book is about: personal convictions. These deeply held beliefs guide how we navigate life. Every conviction will be tested. This was my test: Would I stand by the truths I'd preached for so many years, or would I crumble under the weight of false accusations and shifting public opinion? Would I take the easy way out or endure the hard journey of truth?

These moments of trial demand a response that can lead to personal transformation. I invite you to join me on this journey of conviction as I share my story and the lessons I've learned. I emerged better, not bitter, and I hope this book will inspire you to pause, reflect, and prepare for whatever life may bring your way. Together, let's explore what it means to make sense of life, even when it feels profoundly unfair.

INTRODUCTION

The beliefs we hold deeply are not just personal opinions; they are our convictions, guiding us through life's myriad paths. But are they founded on something reliable? Many of us learn our initial beliefs from our caregivers. If you were raised in a tumultuous and abusive environment, your perspectives and convictions might reflect those experiences. Conversely, a nurturing, values-based upbringing instills a set of convictions aligned with positive principles. Thus, we inherit convictions before we truly develop our own. But where do these convictions truly originate? Often, they stem from our earliest environments—imprinted upon us by those who raised us, reflecting their experiences, wisdom, and sometimes, their mistakes.

In my case, the bedrock of my convictions was laid in the loving, disciplined home of my grandparents, Louis and Hattie Gross. Their lives were a testament to their beliefs in hard work, godliness, and the moral duty to instill proper values in the generations that followed. They believed fervently in the power of helping others—a conviction not just preached, but practiced. Growing up, our home was a revolving door for over a dozen foster children, each one a living lesson in compassion and communal responsibility. When social services needed a safe place for a child, my grandparents were always at the top of their list. This was in addition to the 30 or so of my cousins who were already hanging around. These experiences ingrained in me the unshakable belief that if you have the means to help, you must.

However, not everyone comes from this type of environment. You may have experienced abuse or other unspeakable travesties that led you to form defective convictions. Convictions like "Don't trust people," "No one will be there to help you," "People don't really care," or "You don't really matter." These types of convictions chart a path of difficulty. I grew up without a father, and being liked and accepted was a big deal for me. My desire for acceptance was often met with name-calling and put-downs like, "Where is your father?" or "Who's your dad?" Even in the midst of a loving and supportive family, a bitter root of anger took hold in me. When I was mistreated, my response was to plot revenge. It wasn't a hot flash of anger—because I feared being beaten up—it was a methodical and deliberate scheme to get back at a person who had hurt my feelings; and I was willing to wait.

As an adolescent, I became a "tattle-tail." When I knew something, I held onto it until the strategically proper time, and then I told. I was more or less a sophisticated snitch. Those around me grew annoyed because they knew I was always "running my mouth!" One day, as I was walking from church, my godmother beckoned me to her porch and made a simple statement: "Real men are not tattle-tails." From that moment, I changed my actions but not my attitude. I developed a new way to exact revenge on those who hurt me, planning retaliatory strikes when they least expected it.

These experiences, despite the love all around me from my family, ignited a dislike of people because I believed they were mean and couldn't be trusted. I became skeptical of everyone outside my family, and sometimes, I questioned their loyalty too. When our conviction development is skewed, we might live our lives based on flawed beliefs that cause more harm than good. Having convictions doesn't exempt us from life's difficulties, but it's crucial to examine them to ensure they are correct and founded on principles greater than ourselves or our upbringing. I was headed for a collision course based on the unresolved distrust and anger I carried from a young age.

Education is not just about academic achievements or earning degrees. It's about cultivating a mindset that embraces learning and growth, recognizing that education can come in many forms and can unlock doors to a fulfilling life. Growing up in a household where education was revered, it wasn't uncommon to see my grandmother opening her Bible or my grandfather tinkering with a new skill. Though they had limited access to formal education, they believed that one's thirst for knowledge and wisdom should never be quenched. They showed all of us that the pursuit of knowledge was about more than a degree—it was a life-long process.

In retrospect, I realize that education was a deeply rooted conviction in their lives, a belief they passed down to me. They saw education as a way to overcome adversity and create a better life. Throughout history, education has been a catalyst for change, empowering individuals and entire communities to rise above their circumstances. As people two generations removed from chattel slavery, my grandparents knew education carried limitless possibilities. Their actions reinforced that we should never be satisfied with "I don't know" as an answer.

I sought to become knowledgeable about as many topics as I could. It wasn't until I was in college that I learned of Albert Schweitzer, who was considered a Renaissance man. I wanted that: to know a lot about various subjects. This pursuit of knowledge exposed me to lofty philosophical ideas from Socrates, Aristotle, Plato, and Kant, to Aquinas and Nietzsche. In addition to my deepening biblical knowledge, I was introduced to great thinkers who expanded my ability to consider various worldviews and solidify what I wanted my life to stand for.

However, I was not absolved from my deep-seated anger issues. Though I could articulate the source and meaning of the anger I possessed, it was a spiritual encounter that freed me from my unresolved anger. Education gave me the articulation of my problem, but only God could truly expose and heal the root of my anger.

Life has a way of testing our convictions, often brutally, and it is during these moments of trial that our true character is revealed. These tests don't just happen in isolation; they often come at the most inopportune times, when we are least prepared or when the stakes are highest. When convictions are tested, they reveal whether our beliefs are deeply rooted or merely superficial.

One of the most significant tests of my convictions came when I was faced with the possibility of prison time. I was accused of crimes I didn't commit, and the easy path would have been to take a plea deal, admitting guilt in exchange for a lighter sentence. However, my conviction in my own innocence and in the principles of justice was unshakeable. Despite the pressure, the uncertainty, and the fear of what might come, I refused to compromise on my beliefs. This was not just a test of my resolve, but a test of my trust in God and the belief that the truth would eventually prevail.

During these trials, I learned that true convictions might bend under pressure, but they do not break. They are like steel—hardened through fire, capable of withstanding the most intense heat. Every challenge, every accusation, every difficult decision forced me to examine the core of my beliefs, to question what I was willing to endure to uphold them. I came to understand that it is not enough to simply hold convictions; they must be tested, refined, and proven through our actions.

Introduction

In moments of trial, we often find ourselves standing alone, without the support or validation of others. This isolation can be daunting, but it is also where our convictions are most clearly defined. When the noise of the world is stripped away, and we are left with nothing but our own conscience, we must ask ourselves: What do we truly stand for? What are we willing to sacrifice to remain true to ourselves? These are not easy questions, but they are necessary if we are to live lives of integrity and purpose.

The testing of convictions is not just about enduring hardship; it is about emerging from the fire with a stronger, more refined sense of who we are. Each test is a crucible that shapes us, molds us, and prepares us for the challenges yet to come. Through these trials, I learned that while the road of conviction is often lonely and difficult, it is also the path that leads to true fulfillment and peace of mind.

Character is not merely about the values one holds but about the consistency with which one defends and lives those values. Our convictions shape our character, and in turn, our character is what defends those convictions when they are under attack. It's a symbiotic relationship, where each element reinforces the other, creating a resilient structure upon which to build a life of integrity and purpose.

Our character is like a mirror reflecting the convictions we hold dear. When we are faced with ethical dilemmas, personal betrayals, or professional setbacks, it is our character that determines how we respond. Will we stand firm, guided by our principles, or will we waver and compromise? It is in these moments of choice that our true character is revealed. For example, a conviction that honesty is paramount shapes a person who values truth and transparency—traits that define their interactions and choices. Conversely, if our convictions are weak or misguided, our character will reflect that weakness, leading to decisions that we may later regret.

Character is built over time, through the choices we make and the actions we take. It is not something that can be faked or feigned; it is forged in the day-to-day decisions that, cumulatively, define who we are. When faced with adversity, our character acts as a compass, guiding us back to our core beliefs and reminding us of what truly matters. It is what allows us to maintain our integrity even when it would be easier to take the path of least resistance.

In my own life, I've seen how convictions shape character and how character, in turn, reinforces those convictions. My grandparents, for example, lived lives of unwavering integrity, not because it was easy, but because it was who they were. Their actions consistently reflected their deep-seated beliefs in hard work, honesty, and the importance of helping others. This consistency in action and belief is what made their character so strong, and it is what I strive to emulate in my own life.

But character is not static; it must be continually nurtured and developed. Just as our convictions are tested, so too is our character. Each challenge we face is an opportunity to strengthen our character, to prove to ourselves and to others that we are people of integrity, guided by principles that do not change with the tides of circumstance.

In essence, character is the outward expression of our inward convictions. It is what others see and what we rely on when times are tough. A strong character, built on firm convictions, provides the foundation for a life of purpose and meaning. Without it, we are easily swayed, lost in a world of shifting values and uncertain morality.

"No man is an island", and our convictions often need the reinforcement of a like-minded community. The values we hold dear are most often shaped, tested, and strengthened in the context of community. We do not live in isolation; our beliefs are constantly influenced by those around us—family, friends, mentors, and even the broader society. Surrounding ourselves with people who share and support our convictions provides a vital buffer against the challenges that might erode our beliefs.

Community is not just about finding people who agree with us; it's about finding those who challenge us to live up to our highest ideals. In my life, my family has been that community. My grandparents, with their steadfast faith and unwavering commitment to helping others, provided a model of what it means to live a conviction-driven life. Their actions were a daily reminder of the values they held dear, and being part of their community meant that I was constantly being encouraged to adopt and live out those same values.

Beyond family, I've found community in my church, among friends, and in the professional relationships I've built over the years. These communities have been my bulwark, standing with me through trials and triumphs alike. They have provided the support and encouragement I needed to stay true to my convictions, even when the road was difficult. They have also held me accountable, challenging me when I've strayed from the path and reminding me of the standards I've set for myself.

However, community can be a double-edged sword. Just as it can strengthen our convictions, it can also weaken them if we find ourselves in the wrong environment. It is crucial to choose our communities wisely, to surround ourselves with people who will lift us up, rather than drag us down. Negative influences can erode our convictions over time, leading us to make compromises that we would never have considered in a more supportive environment.

In moments of doubt or weakness, it is our community that helps us stay grounded. When we are tempted to give up or give in, it is the voices of those who care about us that remind us of what we stand for. A strong community not only supports us but also serves as a mirror, reflecting our values back to us and encouraging us to live them out more fully.

The importance of community cannot be overstated. We are social beings, and our convictions are often only as strong as the support we receive from those around us. By building and maintaining communities that share our values, we create a network of strength and resilience that can help us weather any storm. In return, we also become part of the support system for others, reinforcing their convictions and helping them stay true to what they believe.

As I reflect on the impact of my upbringing, the trials I've faced, and the lessons I've learned, I am convinced more than ever of the importance of living a conviction-driven life. It is not enough to simply hold beliefs; we must act on them, test them, and allow them to guide our steps. This journey of conviction is not just about adhering to what's been taught; it's about ensuring that those convictions lead to actions that uplift, educate, and inspire both ourselves and those around us.

As I continue to live out the convictions instilled in me, I hope to pass on this legacy of strength, resilience, and moral courage to the next generation. After all, convictions are more than personal guideposts; they are the beacons that light the paths for those who follow. In sharing my story, I invite you to reflect on your own convictions: where they came from, how they have been tested, and how they guide your life's journey.

Conviction Checkpoints

- **Self-Examination Question:** Reflect on a time when you faced an unexpected challenge. How did your convictions influence your decisions and actions?

- **Actionable Step:** Identify one area in your life where your convictions might be tested soon. Write down a plan of action to prepare yourself to stand firm.
- **Conviction Affirmation:** "I am rooted in my convictions, and they will guide me through any adversity."
- **Prayer/Meditation Focus:** Spend a few moments in quiet reflection or prayer, asking for the strength and clarity to uphold your convictions, especially during challenging times. Seek guidance to remain steadfast and true to your beliefs, no matter the circumstances.
- **Goal Setting for Growth:** Set a specific goal related to living out your convictions more fully this week. Whether it's a conversation you've been avoiding, a decision you need to make, or an action you need to take, commit to doing it with integrity and conviction. Revisit this goal at the end of the week to assess your progress.

Profile in Conviction

Bishop Richard Allen: A Pioneer for Self-Determination

Richard Allen was born into slavery in 1760 in Philadelphia, but his deep faith and determination led him to purchase his freedom by the age of 20. Allen became a devoted preacher and was soon recognized for his powerful sermons that resonated deeply with both Black and white congregants. However, his convictions about racial equality were put to the test when he and his fellow Black worshippers were subjected to racial discrimination at St. George's Methodist Episcopal Church.

In 1787, after being forcibly removed from a prayer service and relegated to the gallery seats, Allen, along with Absalom Jones and other Black congregants, walked out of St. George's in protest. This act of defiance led Allen to found the Free African Society, a mutual aid organization dedicated to helping newly freed Blacks in Philadelphia. His commitment to self-determination and equality did not stop there.

In 1794, Richard Allen established the Bethel African Methodist Episcopal (AME) Church, the first independent Black denomination in the United States, where he became the first bishop. Under his leadership, the AME Church grew rapidly, becoming a beacon of hope and empowerment for Black people during a time of pervasive racial oppression. Allen's conviction that Black people should worship freely and govern their own churches laid the foundation for the growth of independent Black churches across the nation.

Throughout his life, Allen's convictions were tested in various ways, but he remained steadfast in his belief in the dignity, equality, and self-determination of Black people. His legacy continues to inspire, as the AME Church remains a significant religious institution in the United States and beyond.

CHAPTER 1
THE DANGER OF ASKING 'WHY ME?'

Life often presents us with challenges that seem insurmountable. During the early stages of my legal battle, I found myself repeatedly asking, "Why me?" This question, rooted in a sense of victimhood, can trap us in a cycle of self-pity and hinder our growth. It was through faith, reflection, and historical wisdom that I learned to navigate this treacherous mindset.

When I first received the news of my impending legal troubles, it felt like the ground beneath me had vanished. The shock and disbelief were overwhelming. I had always tried to live my life with integrity, making decisions that reflected my values and faith. Yet, here I was, facing accusations that threatened to unravel everything I had worked so hard to build. The question "Why me?" became a constant refrain in my mind, echoing through the sleepless nights and anxiety-filled days.

Scriptural Guidance for Adversity

The Bible recounts the story of a man who lost everything in a satanic attack, and in the aftermath of that horrendous situation, Job asked, "Shall we indeed accept good from God and not accept adversity?" (Job 2:10) Job mistakenly assumed that God was the author of both good and bad. But this was flawed theology. Nevertheless, Job remained faithful to God and expressed unwavering faith in the face of unimaginable suffering. The story of Job instructed me during this crucial time because everything Job went through was not hidden from the sovereign God. And even though I had too many questions to enumerate, I trusted the goodness of God. Life is truly filled with both good and bad, blessings and hardships, but God is always good. Life may seem unfair but God is still good!

"God is too good to be unkind and He is too wise to be mistaken. And when we cannot trace His hand, we must trust His heart." - CHARLES SPURGEON

Regardless of the outcome, I determined just like David, "Yet I am confident I will see the Lord's goodness while I am here in the land of the living." (Psalm 27:13) I had to spend time building my confidence in God's goodness when my mind descended into the depths of despair, questioning His intentions.

The Struggle with Romans 8:28

I had grown up quoting Romans 8:28, "And we know that in all things God works for the good of those who love him, who have been called according to his purpose." But honestly, I had never experienced any challenge like this, and I wrestled with quoting it and even believing it was true. Did that verse really mean all things—even legal things? I wasn't sure! I wanted to believe, but how in the world could there be a greater purpose in this? Yet, I had believed and preached this verse because it underscores the belief that every experience, no matter how painful, contributes to a greater divine plan. Now, I questioned if this was true by asking, "Why me?" I needed to trust that my struggles had purpose and meaning, even when they were not immediately apparent. During many of my dark moments, this verse took on new meaning and provided a glimmer of hope. It reminded me that my life was part of a larger tapestry, one that I could not fully see or understand but had to trust was being woven for a greater good.

As you recall, I was raised by those one generation (my grandparents) before me. Because of this upbringing, I've often been described as having an "old soul." One of the songs I learned early on was "We'll Understand It Better By and By." This song was part of a cadre of hymns that celebrated the clarity heaven would bring to the life we are living. As hopeful as this song had always been, it hit me differently during this season because I needed answers now. But I pressed forward into uncharted territory.

Reflecting on Romans 8 during my trial, I was reminded of the lessons instilled in me from a young age, lessons that seemed even more relevant as I navigated this dark season.

Biblical Insights on Suffering

Here's what's strange: the Bible, which I was taught to trust and build my life upon, speaks a lot about the difficulties in life and how we should respond. Did you know that Jesus' brother wrote one of the books in the New Testament? Here is how he describes our response to life's difficulties: "Consider it pure joy, my brothers and sisters, whenever you face trials of many kinds, because you know that the testing of your faith produces perseverance. Let perseverance finish its work so that you may be mature and complete, not lacking anything." (James 1:2-4) My trials were not punishments but opportunities for personal growth and spiritual formation. They inspired me to embrace resilience and to see each challenge as a step toward spiritual and personal maturity. It wasn't easy to find joy in such painful circumstances, but these words encouraged me to look beyond the immediate pain and see the potential for growth and strength that lay within the struggle.

Questioning God's Sovereignty

Questioning "Why me?" also brings into focus a significant theological point: it can supplant the sovereignty of God. When we ask this question, we may inadvertently suggest that we know better than God about how our lives should unfold. This mindset challenges the divine wisdom and plan that God has for us. The trajectory of success that we lay out is far different from the one God designs. The foundation of "why me" comes from our ignorance of that larger, God-designed plan. Though we want to know "why" and "what", we really couldn't handle knowing this information in advance.

The Defeat of Israel and its Lessons

The children of Israel suffered a devastating defeat with huge ramifications.

1. And Samuel's words went out to all the people of Israel. At that time Israel was at war with the Philistines. The Israelite army was camped near Ebenezer, and the Philistines were at Aphek.
2. The Philistines attacked and defeated the army of Israel, killing 4,000 men.
3. After the battle was over, the troops retreated to their camp, and the elders of Israel asked, 'Why did the Lord allow us to be defeated by the Philistines?' Then they said, 'Let's bring the Ark of the Covenant of the Lord from Shiloh. If we carry it into battle with us, it will save us from our enemies.'
4. So they sent men to Shiloh to bring the Ark of the Covenant of the Lord of Heaven's Armies, who is enthroned

> between the cherubim. Hophni and Phinehas, the sons of Eli, were also there with the Ark of the Covenant of God.
> 5 When all the Israelites saw the Ark of the Covenant of the Lord coming into the camp, their shout of joy was so loud it made the ground shake!
> 6 'What's going on?' the Philistines asked. 'What's all the shouting about in the Hebrew camp?' When they were told it was because the Ark of the Lord had arrived,
> 7 they panicked. 'The gods have come into their camp!' they cried. 'This is a disaster! We have never had to face anything like this before!
> 8 Help! Who can save us from these mighty gods of Israel? They are the same gods who destroyed the Egyptians with plagues when Israel was in the wilderness.
> 9 Fight as never before, Philistines! If you don't, we will become the Hebrews' slaves just as they have been ours. Stand up like men and fight!'
> 10 So the Philistines fought desperately, and Israel was defeated again. The slaughter was great; 30,000 Israelite soldiers died that day. The survivors turned and fled to their tents.
> 11 The Ark of God was captured, and Hophni and Phinehas, the two sons of Eli, were killed. (1 Samuel 4:1-11)

The Israelites asked, "Why has the Lord brought defeat upon us today before the Philistines?" They questioned God's plan and took the Ark of the Covenant into battle, thinking it would ensure victory. This sounded a lot like where I was. I was in my late 40s; my family and ministry were thriving. My children were maturing into adulthood and preparing for college; our growing, healthy ministry had three full services each Sunday. It was a good season, and surely, only great things were in store. Then suddenly, the bright future I had envisioned was in question. This was Israel's story. They expected victory, but instead, they suffered a devastating loss, and the Ark was captured. It's one thing to lose a battle, but to lose the presence of God and the most cherished part of their faith was unbearable. This story reminds us how easy it is to fall into the trap of questioning God's intentions in order to manipulate His will to fit our desires.

A Deeper Theological Reflection on Suffering

When we face adversity, it's a natural human response to ask, "Why me?" This question is often born from the depths of our pain, confusion, and disillusionment. It's a question that echoes through the ages, reverberating in the hearts of those who have walked through the valley of suffering. As a theologian, I find this question not only understandable but deeply human. Yet, as a pastor, I urge us to consider its implications on our spiritual journey.

The question "Why me?" often carries with it an underlying assumption that life should be free from suffering, especially for those who have strived to live righteously. We may feel that our good deeds, our faithful service, and our devotion to God should somehow shield us from the harsh realities of a broken world. However, Scripture presents a different narrative—one that invites us to view suffering not as a punishment or a sign of God's absence, but as a profound opportunity for spiritual growth and deeper communion with our Creator.

Consider the life of Job, a man described as "blameless and upright, one who feared God and shunned evil" (Job 1:1, NLT). Despite his righteousness, Job endured unimaginable loss and suffering. His livestock were stolen, his servants were killed, his children perished, and his own health was struck down. In the midst of his anguish, Job cried out, "Why is life given to those with no future, those God has surrounded with difficulties?" (Job 3:23). His question is one that many of us have asked in our darkest moments. Yet, the book of Job teaches us that our suffering does not negate God's goodness or His sovereign plan for our lives. Rather, it challenges us to trust in God's wisdom and timing, even when we cannot comprehend the reasons behind our trials.

The Role of Faith in the Midst of Trials

Faith, by its very nature, requires us to trust in what we cannot see or fully understand. The apostle Paul reminds us that "we walk by faith, not by sight" (2 Corinthians 5:7, NLT). When we encounter suffering, our faith is put to the test. Do we trust that God is still good, even when life feels anything but? Do we believe that He is still in control, even when our world seems to be falling apart? These are not easy questions to answer, but they are essential to our spiritual growth.

During my own trials, particularly during the legal battle that threatened to unravel everything I had built, I found myself wrestling with these very questions. I had preached countless sermons on the sovereignty of God, on His unfailing love, and on His ability to bring good out of even the most dire circumstances. But now, I was faced with the challenge of living out those beliefs in real time, under immense pressure.

There were moments when I, like Job, questioned God's plan. I wondered how He could allow such injustice to befall me, especially when I had dedicated my life to serving Him. But as I spent time in prayer and reflection, I began to see my situation through a different lens. I realized that my suffering was not a sign of God's abandonment, but rather, an invitation to deeper trust and greater reliance on Him.

Romans 8:28 took on a new meaning for me during this time: "And we know that God causes everything to work together for the good of those who love God and are called according to his purpose for them" (NLT). I had always believed this verse to be true, but now I was being asked to live it out in the most challenging of circumstances. It wasn't easy, and there were days when I struggled to believe that any good could come from my situation. But as I continued to lean into my faith, I began to see glimpses of God's purpose in my pain.

Modern Misinterpretations of Suffering

In our contemporary culture, it's not uncommon to encounter various interpretations of suffering that, while well-intentioned, can lead to an incomplete understanding of the Gospel. These interpretations often arise from a desire to reconcile the presence of pain and adversity with the goodness of God. However, when these explanations are taken in isolation, they can sometimes paint an incomplete picture of who God is and what the Gospel truly offers. In essence, our understanding of suffering must be rooted in the full narrative of the Gospel, which calls us to trust in God's presence and purpose even in the midst of our deepest trials. It is through this lens that we find true comfort and meaning.

The Incomplete View of Transactional Faith

One such interpretation is the view that our relationship with God operates on a kind of spiritual transaction: if we live righteously and adhere to God's commandments, we will be rewarded with a life free from hardship. Conversely, when we face trials, we might conclude that we've somehow failed or that God's favor has been withdrawn.

While it is true that God blesses obedience and that our actions have consequences, this view oversimplifies the Gospel message. The life of Jesus and the teachings of Scripture make it clear that righteousness does not guarantee a life devoid of suffering. In fact, Jesus tells us, "In this world, you will have trouble" (John 16:33). The Gospel does not promise us a life without pain; rather, it assures us of God's presence with us in the midst of our pain.

When we reduce our faith to a transactional relationship, we risk missing the richness of God's grace, which sustains us even when life does not go according to our plans. The Gospel calls us into a relationship with God that is based not on what we can get from Him, but on who He is—a loving Father who walks with us through every trial, offering comfort, strength, and hope.

Misreading God's Character Through Suffering

Another common conclusion drawn from suffering is the belief that it reflects a flaw in our relationship with God, or worse, that it signifies God's displeasure with us. This perspective can lead us to question God's goodness or to believe that our suffering is a sign that we've somehow fallen out of His favor.

However, this interpretation does not capture the full picture of the Gospel. The Bible teaches us that suffering is a part of the human experience, even for those who are deeply loved by God. The story of Job, for example, reminds us that suffering can happen to the righteous, not as a punishment, but as a part of the mysterious and sovereign plan of God, a plan that we might not fully understand but can trust is ultimately for our good.

God's character is not defined by our circumstances. He is good, faithful, and just, regardless of the trials we face. The Gospel assures us that God's love for us is steadfast and unchanging, even when we are walking through the darkest valleys. Rather than seeing suffering as a sign of God's displeasure, we are invited to see it as an opportunity to draw closer to Him, to rely on His strength, and to experience His grace in new and profound ways.

Embracing the Fullness of the Gospel

To fully embrace the Gospel, we must recognize that it encompasses both the joy of God's blessings and the reality of suffering. The good news is not that we will be spared from hardship, but that through Christ, we have been given the strength to endure it. Jesus Himself experienced the deepest suffering on the cross, and through His resurrection, He demonstrated that suffering is not the end of the story—it is the pathway to new life.

The Gospel invites us to trust in God's goodness, even when our circumstances suggest otherwise. It calls us to look beyond the immediate pain and to see the greater story that God is writing in our lives. In this story, suffering is not meaningless; it is a tool that God uses to shape us, to refine our faith, and to draw us closer to Him.

By embracing the full message of the Gospel, we can resist the temptation to view suffering through a limited lens. Instead, we can see it as part of the larger narrative of God's redeeming work in our lives—a narrative that is rich with hope, purpose, and the assurance of His unfailing love. Having explored the potential pitfalls in our understanding of suffering, it's crucial to recognize the deeper purpose that trials can serve in our spiritual journey.

The Gift of Suffering

As paradoxical as it may sound, suffering can be a gift. It strips away our illusions of control, humbles us, and brings us to our knees before God. It forces us to confront the reality of our human limitations and our deep need for divine grace. In this way, suffering can be a powerful catalyst for spiritual transformation. It invites us to view our trials through the lens of faith, recognizing that they can produce in us a resilience and maturity that we would not otherwise attain.

In my own journey, I found that the more I leaned into God during my times of trial, the more my faith was strengthened. It was in the crucible of suffering that I discovered a depth of trust and reliance on God that I had never known before. My suffering became a place of encounter with God—a place where I experienced His presence, His comfort, and His guidance in profound ways.

Finding Greater Glory in Suffering

Jesus' interactions with His followers reveal another instance where the question "why" arises. Jesus received news that His dear friend, Lazarus, was ill. "When he heard this, Jesus said, 'This sickness will not end in death. No, it is for God's glory so that God's Son may be glorified through it.'" (John 11:4) His followers had seen Him perform incredible miracles, so they had no doubt about what Jesus said. But instead of Lazarus getting better, he actually died! The disciples and Lazarus' family could not understand why he had to suffer and die. Surely, God's glory would be seen in Lazarus' healing! Why would he have to die in order for God's glory to be seen?

I learned that there is glory, but also greater glory! Yes, God would have gotten glory from the miraculous healing of Lazarus; this had occurred many times in Jesus' ministry. However, when Lazarus died, there was an opportunity for greater glory for God! To be honest, God's purposes don't involve our comfort or ease. It's all about Him. The way that God would get the greater glory from Lazarus' sickness and death was through resurrection—or more accurately, resuscitation. (I differentiate between these two words because resurrection restores life to one who was dead, never to die again. Jesus resuscitated

Lazarus, but he was not immortal.) Thus, one of the reasons we go through situations that seem unfair is because there is a greater glory to be shown. This revelation gave me hope for what God would do through my life and future. I believe the same is true for you.

This realization aligns with the wisdom shared by many great thinkers throughout history, who have recognized the inner strength that emerges from adversity.

> *"What lies behind us and what lies before us are tiny matters compared to what lies within us."* - RALPH WALDO EMERSON

The Role of Scripture in Adversity

In fact, scripture is not silent on the presence of challenges in our lives.

Psalm 34:19 provides further comfort: "The righteous person may have many troubles, but the Lord delivers him from them all." This verse reassures us that while trials are inevitable, divine deliverance is always at hand. It encourages us to maintain faith in God's ability to guide us through even the most daunting circumstances. There were days when it felt as though the troubles would never end, but this verse helped me hold onto the belief that deliverance was possible, that my faith would see me through.

Week after week, I followed the same schedule. I preached at three services. I returned home to pack, then one of the brothers in the church drove me to a hotel in Manhattan. Monday, I would be in court, and by Thursday night, I was heading back home. I never missed preaching one Sunday during the trial. While I stood strong and welcomed all the best wishes and supportive words, I gained a keen appreciation of suffering. Each Thursday on the ride home, I felt some relief, only to take it back up again as I entered through the Lincoln Tunnel into New York City. The question of "Why?" never left. It was muted, and sometimes it felt like I was done with the question, but unexpectedly, and usually at a time when I felt some momentary joy, the question came screaming back into my mind!

Rejoicing in Suffering

"Dear friends, do not be surprised at the fiery ordeal that has come on you to test you, as though something strange were happening to you. But rejoice inasmuch as you participate in the sufferings of Christ, so that you may be overjoyed when his glory is revealed." (1 Peter 4:12-13)

I had to amend my understanding of suffering and its causes. Suffering is an unavoidable, shared human experience. No one gets through life unscathed by it. The difference is that when one has faith, that suffering takes place in a larger spiritual narrative authored by God. By participating in these trials, we partake in a journey that ultimately leads to greater joy and fulfillment. This perspective helped me see my struggles not as isolated incidents but as part of a collective human experience, one that brought me closer to understanding the depth of faith, resilience, and the goodness of God. There were days when the fear of the future held a stranglehold around my neck, but I refused to allow fear to win. Similarly, the words of Nelson Mandela offer a profound perspective on how we should approach the challenges that threaten to overwhelm us.

"I learned that courage was not the absence of fear, but the triumph over it. The brave man is not he who does not feel afraid, but he who conquers that fear." - NELSON MANDELA

If I allowed fear to drive me, the end would be bitterness and defeat, not triumph. I soon realized that my triumph might not lie in the avoidance of the trial but in the grace to go through to the end. Fear wouldn't get me there, but faith would.

A Night of Deep Despair

One particular night stands out vividly in my memory. I had spent the day in court, surrounded by people who seemed determined to see me fall. The weight of their accusations, the hostile glares, and the relentless misrepresentations had left me drained and despondent. I came home emotionally exhausted. "Why me?" screamed in my mind so loudly, I couldn't entertain any other thought! There was nothing anyone could do to get me out of this state. I never allowed my family to see me in these moments of weakness. You can criticize me for this, but there was enough trauma going on in and around my family that I didn't want to add to their burden. Moreover, when I sunk to these depths—from time to time—there was no human interaction that could help me. Thankfully, God could handle me in these moments. I needed quiet and a space to just sit before God. While I never got all the answers to "why me," God met me with comfort and compassion.

At this moment of deep hopelessness, I was in a bad place. But God met me. He reminded me of a strange image (vision) I had seen throughout my life and never understood. It was the image of a dark brown wooden room with a green marble desk in the middle. At intrusive moments, this image would appear in my thoughts and then disappear. I never understood it. At that moment, I realized this image was the exact replica of the courtroom where my trial was held. You see, during the preliminaries of the trial, the courtroom where we met was an oak wood room. Right before the trial was to commence, the judge decided to move the trial to a larger courtroom. I hadn't made the connection, but here I sat in the exact room I had seen years prior.

When I say years prior, I mean since my teen years through my adult life. In this moment, it all became clear. This legal situation was not a surprise to God—even though it was to me! God cared enough about this season of my life that He prepared me decades before. But it also meant that God was not only knowledgeable about this but that it was part of His Master Plan for my life. It all came into perspective at that moment. God was on my side, and while significant questions remained, I knew I wasn't alone and that there was a purpose in all of this. Finally, consider the ancient wisdom of Confucius, which echoes the transformative power of trials in shaping our character.

> *"The gem cannot be polished without friction, nor man perfected without trials."* - CONFUCIUS

Gaining Perspective and Strength

Another personal anecdote that stands out is a conversation I had with an old friend who had also faced legal troubles. He shared his experience of being falsely accused and the subsequent ordeal that followed. His advice to me was simple yet profound: "Don't let this define you. You are more than this moment. Keep your faith and let it guide you." His words resonated deeply, reminding me that my identity and worth were not tied to my current circumstances but to the broader journey of my life and faith.

As I continued to navigate the legal battle, I began to understand that asking "Why me?" was not just a question of seeking answers, but a reflection of a deeper struggle with faith and identity. It was about reconciling the image I had of myself with the harsh reality I was facing. Through prayer, reflection, and the support of loved ones, I gradually shifted my perspective. Instead of asking "Why me?" I started to ask, "What can I learn from this?" and "How can this experience shape me into a better person?"

This shift in mindset did not happen overnight. It was a gradual process, one that required constant reinforcement through scripture, prayer, and reflection. I began to see my struggles as a crucible, a means through which my faith and character were being tested and refined. Each day presented new challenges, but with each challenge came an opportunity to grow stronger and more resilient.

Strategies for Overcoming the "Why Me?" Mindset

As a pastor, I understand that the "Why me?" question is often the first step in a journey of faith. It's a starting point, not a destination. While it's natural to ask this question, we must not allow ourselves to get stuck there. Instead, I encourage you to take the following steps to move beyond the "Why me?" mindset and embrace the spiritual growth that your trials can bring.

1. **Reframe Your Perspective:** Begin by acknowledging your pain and your questions, but don't stop there. Ask God to help you see your situation from His perspective. Pray for the grace to trust that He is at work, even in the midst of your suffering.
2. **Anchor Yourself in Scripture:** Immerse yourself in the promises of God's Word. Allow scriptures like Romans 8:28, James 1:2-4, and Psalm 34:19 to become your anchor in the storm. Meditate on these verses and let them strengthen your faith.

3. **Lean on Your Community:** Don't try to go through your trials alone. Reach out to your church family, your small group, or trusted friends who can pray with you, encourage you, and remind you of God's faithfulness.
4. **Embrace the Process:** Understand that spiritual growth is a process, and it often involves enduring hardships. Trust that God is using your current challenges to shape you into the person He has called you to be.
5. **Look for the Greater Glory:** Remember that God's purposes are often bigger than we can imagine. Just as Jesus allowed Lazarus to die so that God's greater glory could be revealed through his resurrection, so too may God be allowing you to go through this trial for a greater purpose. Ask Him to show you how He is working all things together for good, even when you can't see it yet.

In retrospect, the question "Why me?" was a natural response to an overwhelming situation. It was an expression of confusion, hurt, and a deep sense of injustice. However, by reframing the question and seeking meaning in the midst of adversity, I was able to move beyond victimhood and embrace a path of growth and resilience.

Asking "Why me?" can lead us down a path of despair and stagnation. Instead, by embracing adversity with faith, wisdom, and resilience, we can transform our struggles into powerful catalysts for growth. I understood, in living color, that challenges are an integral part of my journey, shaping me into a stronger, more compassionate individual. It is through these trials that we discover the depth of our faith and the strength of our spirit. So, in essence, and I know you've heard this before, it's never a question of "why me?" but rather, "What now?" How do I comport myself while I walk through this uncomfortable time in my life?

Conviction Checkpoints

- **Self-Examination Question:** Reflect on a time when you questioned your purpose in the face of adversity. How did you navigate that challenge? What did you learn about your inner strength?
- **Actionable Step:** Identify a current challenge in your life where you feel overwhelmed. Take one small step today toward reframing that challenge as an opportunity for growth.
- **Conviction Affirmation:** "In every challenge, I find strength and wisdom. My trials are the forge that shapes my resilience."
- **Prayer/Meditation Focus:** Spend time in prayer or meditation, seeking clarity on the lessons within your current struggles. Ask for the courage to embrace the growth opportunities hidden within adversity.
- **Goal Setting for Growth:** Set a goal to deepen your faith and resilience this month. Whether through regular prayer, meditation, or journaling, commit to practices that help you reflect on and grow from your challenges.

As you reflect on these checkpoints, consider how your own journey through adversity can be a testimony to others. Your resilience and growth are not just personal victories; they are a beacon of hope for those who may be walking a similar path.

Profile in Conviction

Viktor Frankl: Finding Meaning in Suffering

Viktor Frankl, an Austrian neurologist and psychiatrist, endured unimaginable suffering as a Holocaust survivor. Imprisoned in Nazi concentration camps, Frankl lost his wife, parents, and brother to the atrocities of the Holocaust. Despite these profound losses, Frankl emerged from the camps with a deep understanding of the human capacity for resilience and meaning-making.

In his seminal work, *Man's Search for Meaning*, Frankl explores the idea that even in the most harrowing circumstances, we have the power to choose our response. He observed that those who found meaning in their suffering were more likely to survive the brutal conditions of the camps. Frankl's philosophy, known as logotherapy, posits that the primary drive in human beings is not pleasure or power, but the pursuit of meaning.

Frankl's insights have inspired millions to find purpose in their own struggles. His life and work remind us that, no matter how dire our circumstances, we can choose to find meaning and hope. Frankl's journey is a testament to the resilience of the human spirit and the transformative power of faith and purpose.

CHAPTER 2
AUTHENTICITY IS KEY TO FREEDOM

Authenticity is the cornerstone of a conviction-driven life. It's easy to espouse beliefs, but living them out consistently, especially under scrutiny and misunderstanding, is where true conviction is tested. The journey toward authenticity demands a commitment to truth, transparency, and integrity, regardless of the consequences.

Before diving into the strategies for living authentically, it's important to clarify the distinction between authenticity and integrity. While integrity refers to adhering to moral and ethical principles, authenticity is about being genuine and true to who you are. Both are crucial in living a life of conviction, but this chapter will focus specifically on how to live authentically, staying true to your values, beliefs, and identity, even in the face of challenges.

Ephesians 4:25 urges us to "stop telling lies. Let us tell our neighbors the truth, for we are all parts of the same body." This scripture underscores the importance of honesty, not just as a moral duty, but as a fundamental aspect of our interconnected lives. Honesty breeds trust, and trust is essential for any community or relationship to thrive. Without trust, the very fabric of our relationships unravels, leaving us isolated and disconnected from others and even from our true selves.

The Example of Joseph

One of the most powerful examples of living authentically in the face of adversity is the story of Joseph from the Book of Genesis. Joseph's life is a testament to the power and cost of authenticity. From a young age, Joseph was given dreams by God—visions that revealed his future as a leader over his family. In Genesis 37:5-7, Joseph tells his brothers about his dream: "Listen to this dream I had. We were binding sheaves of grain out in the field when suddenly my sheaf rose and stood upright, while your sheaves gathered around mine and bowed down to it." His brothers, already jealous of the special treatment Joseph received from their father, reacted with anger and hostility to his honesty. Yet, Joseph did not let the potential fallout stop him from sharing his dreams, demonstrating a deep commitment to being true to what God had shown him.

Joseph's authenticity in sharing his dream set off a chain of events that would lead him into the darkest periods of his life—betrayed by his brothers, sold into slavery, and later imprisoned on false charges. But through it all, Joseph never wavered in his integrity or his trust in God. Even when he was tempted, as in the case of Potiphar's wife, Joseph remained true to his values, saying in Genesis 39:9, "How then could I do such a wicked thing and sin against God?" His refusal to compromise his principles, even in the face of severe consequences, highlights the strength that comes from living authentically.

Joseph's journey is not just a story of personal integrity; it's a profound illustration of how authenticity aligns with the broader principles of God's kingdom. Authenticity is deeply connected to the fruit of the Spirit—especially truthfulness and faithfulness. When we live authentically, we are embodying the truth of God's Word, allowing His Spirit to work through us. Joseph's refusal to compromise his values, even when it led to personal suffering, is a reflection of how God calls us to live in truth and integrity, trusting that His plans are greater than our immediate circumstances. Just as Joseph's authenticity eventually led to his elevation in Egypt, our commitment to living authentically opens the door for God to work powerfully in our lives.

My Struggle for Authenticity

In my own life, there were numerous occasions where standing firm in my convictions meant facing misunderstanding and false accusations. These moments were not just tests of my beliefs, but of my willingness to remain true to myself despite external pressures. John 8:32 offered solace during these times: "And you will know the truth, and the truth will set you free." This verse reminded me that authenticity, while challenging, ultimately leads to freedom. The freedom that comes from living authentically is not just a release from external pressures but an internal peace that transcends circumstances.

One poignant example of this was during the height of my legal battles. The accusations against me were severe, and the temptation to bend the truth or adopt a defensive façade was strong. However, I chose to remain transparent, trusting that my integrity would eventually shine through. This decision was not easy, but it was rooted in the belief that true freedom comes from living authentically. I was reminded of Proverbs 12:19, *"Truthful lips endure forever, but a lying tongue lasts only a moment."* This verse reinforced the idea that truth, though often difficult, has an enduring power that outlasts deceit and manipulation.

Remaining authentic was not only a personal journey but one that deeply affected my relationships with others. Inside the prison, my commitment to authenticity allowed me to build genuine connections with other inmates and even with the prison staff. Outside, my authenticity was a source of strength for my family, who needed to see that despite the challenges, I remained true to my beliefs. The consistency in my actions provided a sense of stability for those who were watching my response to the trials I faced. This experience reinforced the truth that authenticity is not only about self-preservation but also about serving as a beacon of hope and integrity for those around us.

Joseph's journey did not end in despair; instead, his authenticity and faithfulness to God's plan eventually led to his rise as the second most powerful man in Egypt. Through a series of divine appointments, Joseph was elevated from the prison to the palace, demonstrating that living authentically, even when it seems to lead only to hardship, ultimately positions us for God's greater purpose. In Genesis 50:20, Joseph reflects on his journey with his brothers, saying, *"You intended to harm me, but God intended it for good to accomplish what is now being done, the saving of many lives."* This powerful statement underscores how authenticity aligns us with God's greater plan, even when the path is fraught with difficulties.

However, living authentically comes with its own set of costs. The decision to remain true to my values meant enduring misunderstandings, facing false accusations, and even losing relationships that couldn't withstand the pressure of my convictions. There were times when the cost of authenticity felt almost too high to bear, yet I knew that compromising my values would have resulted in an even greater loss—losing my sense of self and my connection with God. Authenticity often requires sacrifice, but it is a sacrifice that ultimately leads to a deeper, more meaningful life.

Chapter 2: Authenticity Is Key to Freedom

Entering the Prison Camp

As I entered the prison camp, the reality of my situation hit hard. The environment was harsh, the routines rigid, and the social dynamics complex. My initial days were filled with a mix of fear, confusion, and a strong desire to prove my innocence. It was a test of my ability to maintain authenticity in the face of extreme adversity.

On the three-hour ride to the prison camp, I felt a foreboding sense of uncertainty. The only thing I was certain about was that I was not going to let the experience change me—I was going to stay true to who God had created and called me to be. One of the young men I had mentored called me the night before I surrendered to prepare me for being locked up. He gave me helpful tips and taught me the lay of the land. He understood the prison hierarchy and gave me advice on how to engage with those who were perceived as the power brokers. He also suggested places to work so that "I would do the time and the time wouldn't do me." It was surreal having this conversation, but it was necessary, and I saw it as God's favor on my life.

He was very detailed in his advice, even down to what I should take with me when I surrendered. He was adamant that I take cash to put on my books so my family could be immediately in touch with me, and to write out all my important names, email addresses, and phone numbers. I said, "But I need my Bible." He responded, "They won't allow it. You can only get items from Amazon." His last piece of advice was to make sure to bring my license—though I thought this a strange request. There was so much wisdom in his words, and I was determined to follow all of it. Even when I asked why I should do this, he just said he "felt like" I should. You'll learn later how vital it was that I had my license.

As I sat in the car with Qwynn, every fiber of my being wrestled with the situation. The weight of betrayal, not just by those who had wronged me but by the very God I had served my entire life, bore down on me. In that moment, I remembered Psalm 13, where David cries out, "How long, Lord? Will you forget me forever? How long will you hide your face from me?" Like David, I felt forgotten and abandoned. But just as David's psalm ends with a declaration of trust in God's unfailing love, I felt a small, quiet voice in my heart urging me to hold on. This moment became a pivotal point in my journey, where I realized that authenticity doesn't mean having all the answers; it means being honest with God about our pain while still clinging to the belief that He is with us, even in our darkest hours.

The Challenge of Self-Surrender

As my wife, Qwynn, and I drove up to the prison camp, it was awkward. We were "trusting and trembling." Through the uncomfortable silence, we could see the pain on each other's faces and wanted to blurt out, "This is so unfair," and "God, how could you let this happen?" but we knew better. There was a plan at work greater than our understanding. I would periodically say a phrase I can never remember saying before, "We got this!" When we finally saw the sign for the prison camp, it was called USP Canaan. I immediately knew the significance of this term biblically, but I had no idea how it would play into my real-life story. As we took one more desperate look at each other, we exited the car so I could self-surrender.

At the entrance of the prison, there was a huge rock, and it said, strangely, "WE GOT THIS!" What a strange phrase to have in front of a maximum security prison. (I learned it was a message for those who worked there as a way to encourage them.)

I approached the front desk where a correctional officer was seated, and he asked what I was there for. I told him that I was supposed to self-surrender today and gave him my name. He checked the computer and said, "I don't see your name." For a moment, I really thought that my deliverance had come. It took a long time, but could it be that at this very moment, before I was supposed to self-surrender, God had brought me deliverance?

The corrections officer said he was going to find out what was going on. After a period of time, he came back and said, "We still can't find any paperwork for you. However, if you know you're supposed to self-surrender, it's best to go ahead and do it because if not, the Marshals will come and get you and bring you here by force. And you don't want that." At that very moment, when he said that, a rage rose in me that I had never felt before against God. In my mind, I thought of everything that I had sacrificed, everything that I had given up, every righteous option I took instead of taking an unrighteous option. My mind was reeling over the situation, wondering how God could fail me. How could He let this happen to me? I had been serving God my whole life since nine years old. How could He leave me like this at 48 years old?

I purposed in my heart—I'm not proud of this—but I decided that I would never say another word on His behalf. The joy I got from preaching, I was fine with giving it all up because God had betrayed me by allowing all of this to happen to me. I hope that you are okay with me being transparent because every feeling that you could possibly imagine was going through my mind. The whole time, I was looking at this CO, wondering if he could read my mind or if my face was showing the internal anguish that I was feeling.

The Unexpected Kindness

A few seconds later, I could hear the thunderous clang of the prison door unlocking, and the squeaking steel against unoiled steel as the door opened to allow the CO who was coming to retrieve me to take me into custody. I was literally going to be in federal custody for at least 60 months. As the CO made pleasantries with the other CO, I tried desperately to calm myself down so I did not show the rage that was boiling inside of me. As the CO approached me, I could hear the jangling of his keys, a sound I would become very familiar with at midnight, 3 AM, 5 AM, 4 PM, and 9 PM on weekdays. On weekends, we had a 9 AM count. (The count is when the CO walks through the unit making sure everyone is still in the unit, like taking attendance.) He was ready to take me into custody, and in a very kind gesture, he said, "You should say goodbye to your wife and not allow her to see this next part."

With all the strength I could muster, I hugged my wife and kissed her goodbye for the first time in over 25 years, not knowing what the next day was going to hold. I asked her to please leave because I didn't want her to see me taken into custody. As I write this, I still feel the emotions as if it's happening right now. Qwynn was very reluctant to leave, and out of an act of kindness, the CO did not rush the situation. He stood and waited. He even said, "I understand, I understand," and I kept begging her to please leave, please leave. She was reluctant for obvious reasons, but I had a determination that I needed to get this over with and to get this started. As soon as she left the building, the officer gave me reassurance that everything was going to be okay. He even said something to the effect of, "You don't have to worry, she'll be right here when it's your time to leave." I was appreciative of his kindness. He, then, whispered to me, "I'm supposed to put cuffs on you to pass by security, but I don't feel comfortable doing that to you—and honestly, I don't think our cuffs would fit you. Just lay them on your wrists while we go through security."

At that moment, the CO gave my name to the control officer behind the tinted glass, and the door unlocked with its all-too-familiar sound and the creaking of the chain that pulled the door open. Once the first security door closed, I had to present myself to the next security officer and give my name and social security number to validate that I was the right person. Then another door opened. As we walked down the long hallway toward inmate intake, he made small talk. He asked what I was in for and what my profession was. It was surprisingly pleasant. As soon as we hit the door to enter the area where inmates were processed into the facility, his general demeanor changed—not toward me, but toward the other inmates who were already in the receiving area in cells.

He started using foul language at a level I had not experienced—ever! Little did I know this was a foretaste of what I would hear for the next 800 days. Guys called out from the holding areas and asked questions. Each question received a terse, profanity-laced response as a longer way to just say, "no." I was struck with fear and confusion. I did not understand what was going on. Was this the same guy that just walked with me down the hall and showed me great respect and kindness? What in the world was going on?

Little did I know God was showing me His favor. These guys didn't ask for anything unreasonable: "Can I get something to eat or drink? Do you know when we will go to the unit?" No matter the request, it was met with a barrage of profanity.

As he responded to the other inmates, everything he said to me was respectful and in a regular tone. I thought he was going to put me in the cell with one of the other guys, which is standard protocol, but instead, he let me sit on a bench free from any kinds of shackles or cells. He even asked me, "Would you like something to eat? Can I get you a sandwich or would you like some water?" to which I declined. But everything he said was very kind, even to the point where, when it was time for the strip search, he apologized that he had to do it, but we went ahead and got through it as quickly and as painlessly as possible. Another amazing thing happened—and you'll probably hear the word amazing a lot of times throughout this story because as I look back on it, much of these things really just blew my mind. Once I was finally processed and ready to become a new camper, they gave me a uniform, which is your transport uniform until you're able to get the full uniform, which wouldn't be until the next day.

They called for a driver to come and take me down to the camp because all the processing was done up at the penitentiary. USP Canaan was known for its security level, which was the highest outside of Supermax, which was in Colorado. Some of the worst of the worst inmates were housed in that facility, and if they weren't housed there, they at least passed through there because it was also one of the main transportation hubs for the prison system where inmates from New York and all over the East Coast were processed as they were sent to most likely the Supermax. In fact, even El Chapo, when he was arrested and finally lost his case, came through USP Canaan on his way to the Supermax. But there were many others who came through as well—very popular names. I never saw them or met them. But one thing you know about prison culture is there is a lot of gossip and there's always information flowing around.

So, lo and behold, I sat and waited for the driver to come and pick me up. While the CO was waiting with me, he said, "You must be royalty because I've never seen this guy come and pick up anybody. He always sends another camper to pick up someone who's a new inmate." As a new person, I had no idea how strange and yet remarkable this was. Because in my time there, I had never known this person to go pick up anybody and bring them down to the camp. We exchanged pleasantries, and usually the first question when you're inside is, "What are you in for, and what did you do on the outside?" Having answered all those, he asked me what I wanted to do and where I wanted to work; thankfully, all of those questions I already had answers for because I had been prepped by the young man the night before. I had been prepared to navigate this new reality by remaining true to myself, even in a place where authenticity is often a rare commodity.

This experience reminded me that when we hold onto our authenticity, even in the most challenging circumstances, it often invites unexpected grace. The kindness shown by the CO was not something I could have anticipated, but it was a powerful testament to how God's favor can manifest through others when we stay true to our values. It was as if God was reassuring me that, despite the overwhelming injustice of the situation, He had not abandoned me. Instead, He was working through the details, providing moments of grace that would sustain me through the difficult journey ahead. This reinforced my belief that living authentically, even when it seems to lead to hardship, ultimately aligns us with God's purposes and opens the door for His unexpected blessings.

Holding on to Authenticity

As we made our way to the camp, I realized how vital it was to maintain my authenticity in this environment. Prison, by its very nature, is designed to strip away individuality and reduce everyone to a number. But I knew that if I allowed this system to change who I was at my core, I would lose far more than my freedom. I would lose my identity, my faith, and the convictions that had guided me throughout my life.

Psalm 139:14 came to mind: "*I praise you because I am fearfully and wonderfully made; your works are wonderful, I know that full well.*" This verse was a reminder that no matter where

I was or what I was going through, I was created with purpose and dignity. Holding onto that truth gave me the strength to stay authentic, even in the face of overwhelming pressure to conform.

As I navigated the complexities of this challenging period, I learned valuable lessons about the power of staying true to oneself. These experiences have informed the following strategies, which I believe can help anyone seeking to live an authentic life.

The Role of Faith in Authenticity

Faith plays a pivotal role in the journey toward authenticity. In moments of doubt or external pressure, it is often our faith that anchors us, reminding us of the importance of staying true to our values and beliefs. Throughout the Bible, we see examples of individuals who remained authentic despite significant risks. For instance, Daniel chose to maintain his devotion to God even when it meant facing the lion's den, and Esther risked her life to reveal her true identity in order to save her people. These stories serve as powerful reminders that living authentically is not just a personal choice but a spiritual act of trust in God's plan. Faith assures us that when we live in alignment with our true selves, we honor God, and He, in turn, honors our commitment to truth.

Building upon the example of Joseph and the role of faith in maintaining authenticity, let's explore practical strategies for living authentically in our daily lives.

Strategies for Living an Authentic Life

Integrity is about staying true to moral and ethical principles; authenticity is about being true to your unique self. While integrity and authenticity are closely related, it's important to understand that they play different roles in our lives. Integrity is about adhering to moral and ethical principles consistently, and authenticity is about being true to who you are—living in alignment with your own values, beliefs, and identity. Authenticity is the foundation upon which integrity is built; without knowing and accepting your true self, it is difficult to consistently live with integrity. Together, they form the bedrock of a conviction-driven life, where one's actions are consistently aligned with both personal truth and Biblical moral standards. Living authentically means aligning your actions, words, and choices with your true self—your values, beliefs, and identity. While integrity involves adhering to moral and ethical principles, authenticity is about being genuine and true to who you are. Here are strategies to help you cultivate authenticity in your daily life:

1. **Know Yourself Deeply**

    Authenticity begins with self-awareness. Reflect on your core values, beliefs, passions, and strengths. Identify the non-negotiables in your life and recognize what brings you true joy and fulfillment. This self-knowledge lays the foundation for living in alignment with your true self.

2. **Embrace Your Uniqueness**

    Authenticity is about embracing your uniqueness, rather than conforming to the expectations of others. Celebrate what makes you different and resist the urge to fit into molds that don't reflect who you are. Your unique qualities, experiences, and perspectives are valuable and contribute to the richness of your life and the lives of others.

    Understanding who you are at your core is the first step; from there, the journey to authenticity involves embracing that identity and living it out fully.

3. **Align Your Actions with Your Values**

    Living authentically means ensuring that your actions align with your values and beliefs. It's not just about what you say or think, but how you live. When your actions are consistent with your values, you experience a sense of coherence and harmony in your life.

4. **Be Honest with Yourself and Others**
Authenticity requires honesty, especially with yourself. Acknowledge your true feelings, desires, and limitations, even when they are uncomfortable. Being honest with yourself allows you to live a life that is true to who you are, rather than one based on pretense or denial.

5. **Build Relationships that Encourage Authenticity**
Surround yourself with people who value and encourage your authenticity. Authentic relationships are built on mutual respect, trust, and openness, where both parties feel free to be themselves without fear of judgment.

6. **Accept and Learn from Mistakes**
Authenticity is not about perfection; it's about being real. Accept that you will make mistakes along the way, and use them as opportunities to learn and grow. Being authentic means acknowledging your imperfections and being open about your struggles, rather than hiding them.

7. **Live with Purpose**
Authenticity is closely tied to living a purposeful life. When you are clear about your purpose, it guides your decisions and helps you stay true to yourself, even in challenging situations. Your purpose acts as a compass, keeping you aligned with your true self.

8. **Embrace Vulnerability**
Authenticity requires vulnerability, the willingness to be seen as you truly are, with all your strengths and weaknesses. It means sharing your true self with others, even when it's uncomfortable or when there's a risk of rejection. Embracing vulnerability is a powerful step toward living au-

thentically because it allows you to connect with others on a deeper level.

9. **Practice Consistent Self-Reflection**
Regular self-reflection is essential for maintaining authenticity. It's easy to drift away from your true self when life gets busy or when you face external pressures. Self-reflection helps you stay grounded and ensures that your actions continue to align with your core values.

10. **Cultivate Resilience in the Face of Opposition**
Living authentically often means standing out or going against the grain, which can invite criticism or opposition. Cultivating resilience helps you stay true to yourself even when others challenge your authenticity. Remember, the goal is not to please everyone but to live in a way that is true to who you are.

By incorporating these strategies into your daily life, you can cultivate a deeper connection with your authentic self and live in harmony with the values and beliefs that define you. This alignment is not only key to personal fulfillment but also to living out the purpose God has designed for you.

Living an authentic life is a continuous journey that requires self-awareness, courage, and a daily commitment to being true to yourself. Authenticity is not just about making one-time decisions but about consistently aligning your actions with your true values and beliefs. By embracing these strategies, you cultivate a life that is genuine and fulfilling, allowing you to live with a sense of freedom and peace, knowing you are walking in the truth of who you are and who God created you to be. Authenticity frees you from the chains of fear and falsehood, allowing you to walk confidently in your truth and inspire others to do the same. As you navigate this journey, remember that every step toward authenticity is a step toward a life of greater freedom, purpose, and impact.Living an authentic life is a continuous journey that requires self-awareness, courage, and a daily commitment to being true to yourself. Authenticity is not just about making one-time decisions but about consistently aligning your actions with your true values and beliefs. By embracing these strategies, you cultivate a life that is genuine and fulfilling, allowing you to live with a sense of freedom and peace, knowing you are walking in the truth of who you are and who God created you to be. Authenticity frees you from the chains of fear and falsehood, allowing you to walk confidently in your truth and inspire others to do the same. As you navigate this journey, remember that every step toward authenticity is a step toward a life of greater freedom, purpose, and impact.

Conviction Checkpoints

The journey toward authenticity is one that has been walked by many before us. Throughout history, individuals who lived authentically have not only transformed their own lives but have also left a lasting impact on the world. One such figure is Frederick Douglass, whose commitment to truth and integrity serves as a powerful example for us all.

- **Self-Examination Question:** Reflect on a time when staying true to yourself tested your integrity. How did you respond, and what was the outcome? What did you learn about the importance of authenticity?
- **Actionable Step:** Commit to making choices that reflect your true self, even when it's difficult. Identify one area in your life where you've been tempted to compromise your authenticity, and take steps to align your actions with your core values.

- **Conviction Affirmation:** "I am uniquely crafted with purpose, and I will embrace authenticity, living true to who I am in every situation."
- **Prayer/Meditation Focus:** Spend time in prayer or meditation, asking for the strength to remain authentic in all situations. Seek God's guidance in areas where you feel pressured to conform, and ask for the courage to stand firm in your convictions.
- **Goal Setting for Growth:** Set a goal to practice authenticity in your interactions this week. Whether at work, with family, or in social settings, commit to speaking and acting in ways that reflect your true self.

Profile in Conviction

Frederick Douglass: The Power of Authenticity in the Fight for Freedom

Frederick Douglass, born into slavery in 1818 in Talbot County, Maryland, would go on to become one of the most influential abolitionists, orators, and writers in American history. His early life was marked by the brutality and dehumanization of slavery, but Douglass's spirit remained unbroken. At the age of 20, he escaped from slavery, risking everything for the chance to live as a free man.

Douglass's authenticity and commitment to truth were evident in his powerful speeches and writings. In 1845, he published his first autobiography, *Narrative of the Life of Frederick Douglass, an American Slave*, which detailed his experiences and exposed the horrors of slavery to a wide audience. This act of truth-telling was revolutionary; Douglass risked his newfound freedom by publicly acknowledging his status as a fugitive slave. Yet, he understood that only by being completely authentic—by telling his own story—could he effectively fight for the liberation of others.

His dedication to authenticity did not end with his personal narrative. Douglass was an unwavering advocate for the rights of all oppressed people, including women and Native Americans. He often spoke out against the hypocrisy of a nation that claimed to value liberty while upholding the institution of slavery. His famous ante-bellum speech, "What to the Slave Is the Fourth of July?" delivered in 1852, is a powerful indictment of American society's failure to live up to its ideals.

Douglass's life and work demonstrate that authenticity is not just about personal integrity; it is a powerful tool for social change. By living and speaking truth, Douglass challenged the conscience of a nation and helped to lay the groundwork for the abolition of slavery. His legacy is a testament to the transformative power of living authentically in the pursuit of justice and freedom.

Frederick Douglass's commitment to truth and authenticity serves as a powerful reminder that our personal integrity can have a profound impact on the world around us. Just as Douglass's refusal to hide his past as a fugitive slave fueled his fight for freedom, our willingness to live authentically can be a catalyst for change, both in our own lives and in the lives of those we influence. This connection between personal authenticity and social transformation is a testament to the power of living in alignment with our true values. As we embrace authenticity in our own journeys, we become part of a larger narrative—one that challenges injustice, promotes freedom, and inspires others to live with integrity and courage.

Both Frederick Douglass and Joseph exemplify the power of authenticity in the face of adversity. Douglass, by embracing his unique voice and standing firm in truth, aligned his actions with his deeply held beliefs, embodying the strategy of 'Embrace Your Uniqueness.' Similarly, Joseph's unwavering commitment to his identity and faith, even in the most challenging circumstances, illustrates the importance of 'Living with Purpose' and 'Being Honest with Yourself and Others.' Their lives serve as powerful examples of how authenticity, when paired with resilience, can lead to profound impact and legacy.

As you continue your journey toward authenticity, remember that every choice you make in alignment with your true self brings you closer to living a life of purpose, integrity, and freedom. Start today by reflecting on one area of your life where you can embrace authenticity more fully, and take a step forward with courage and faith.

CHAPTER 3
FAITHFULNESS ANCHORS STABILITY

In the ever-changing currents of life, faithfulness acts as a steady anchor, grounding us when everything else feels uncertain. It's not just about loyalty or consistency; it's about a deep-rooted commitment to the principles and truths that guide us, even when we face storms that threaten to tear us apart. Faithfulness goes beyond mere loyalty or habitual consistency. It is an active and deliberate commitment to uphold one's beliefs, values, and responsibilities, regardless of external circumstances. It demands not only perseverance but also courage and unwavering dedication to what one knows to be true. Faithfulness is more than just a virtue; it is the bedrock of trust, reliability, and perseverance. In every aspect of life—whether in our relationships, our work, or our spiritual journey—faithfulness ensures that we remain steadfast in our commitments, even when faced with challenges. This chapter explores how faithfulness shapes our character and guides our actions, helping us to live lives of purpose and integrity.

In a world where circumstances and situations are constantly shifting, our commitment to faithfulness provides a solid foundation. It is this steadfastness that allows us to navigate the ups and downs of life with purpose and grace. Faithfulness is the quiet force that strengthens our resolve, helping us navigate through adversity with a sense of purpose and stability. It's the ability to hold on to what is true and right, even when the world around us is in chaos.

The Value of Faithfulness Over Success

> *"I do not pray for success; I ask for faithfulness."* - MOTHER TERESA

Mother Teresa's words echo the profound truth that faithfulness is more valuable than success. Success can be fleeting, but faithfulness endures, providing the stability and direction needed in life's most challenging moments. This understanding is crucial, especially when everything else seems uncertain or out of control.

Romans 5:3-4 offers a similar perspective: "We can rejoice, too, when we run into problems and trials, for we know that they help us develop endurance. And endurance develops strength of character, and character strengthens our confident hope of salvation." This scripture illustrates how faithfulness, particularly during trials, is not just about surviving but about growing—developing the endurance and character that deepen our faith and anchor our lives in stability.

Faithfulness Tested in Adversity

Faithfulness was something I clung to in the most difficult season of my life, a time when everything I knew and believed was put to the test. You'll remember that I had promised God upon surrendering that I would never speak for Him again. Though spoken in a moment of anger and profound disappointment, I meant it. I was resolved that if this was the path God allowed for me, after all I had sacrificed, I wouldn't serve

Him any longer. But life has a way of challenging our declarations, and faithfulness, even in our weakest moments, has a way of pulling us back to the truth.

That first night in prison, as I lay on my bunk, tears of anger ran down my face. The cold reality of my situation was sinking in. When I awoke the next morning, I realized that I had to face this new reality head-on. The practicalities of prison life began to take over—I needed to get my uniform, boots, and other essentials for the cold winters in Northeastern Pennsylvania. I started to meet the other inmates, feeling out this new environment that would be my home for the next several years.

Despite the challenges, there was a surprising sense of freedom within the camp. It was a minimum-security facility with amenities that included a baseball field, soccer area, fully functional gym, greenhouse, putting green, and even a horseshoe/Bocce court. But the real test came when I needed to secure a job. In a prison camp, every inmate must work, and finding the right job became a priority.

This principle of faithfulness being tested in the crucible of adversity is not new. Throughout history and scripture, we see countless examples of individuals who chose to remain faithful even when everything seemed to be against them. One such powerful example is the story of Joseph.

Seeing Trials as Opportunities for Growth

As you might recall, the camp I was at was attached to a high-security prison, notorious for housing some of the most dangerous inmates on the East Coast. When the prison went into lockdown, campers were required to work in the kitchen to prepare meals for the 1,500 inmates in the high-security facility. This was no small task, and the environment was intense. My early days in prison were marked by this kind of grueling work, which, in an odd way, became a useful distraction from the emotional turmoil I was experiencing.

One of the most challenging aspects was adjusting to the stringent security measures that were foreign to us in the camp. Strip searches before and after entering the high-security facility, following strict protocols, and dealing with the stress of working under constant supervision—all of these were part of the new reality I had to navigate.

Despite the physical and emotional strain, I chose to approach my work with a mindset of faithfulness. I decided to take the least desirable job in the kitchen—the prep room—where I would open and prepare hundreds of cans of vegetables or fruit. The work was tedious, but it allowed me time to think and reflect even cry and worship.

I recall one instance when I had finished early from the prep room and was asked to assist with cutting vegetables. You can imagine that in the cutting room there are strict guidelines because inmates with knives is dangerous. All knives were anchored to the table and a CO had to give you permission to use each item. For added security, they would lock the door so if something did go wrong, it could be contained. However, as campers, there was no violence associated with us and in our own kitchen in the camp, we used all types of cutting utensils in the preparation of the food. (They even used campers as waiters when they had big events with prison hierarchy.) As the CO started to close the door, uncharacteristically, I called out, "Hey! We are campers. We are non-violent. No locked doors please!" I laugh when I think of this because I had no right to make such a request! But, the CO honored the request and the other campers expressed gratitude that they were not locked in.

The Importance of Character

"When wealth is lost, nothing is lost; when health is lost, something is lost; when character is lost, all is lost." - BILLY GRAHAM

Billy Graham's words serve as a reminder of the importance of maintaining character—something deeply tied to faithfulness. In prison, where everything was stripped away, it became clear that the only thing I truly had was my character. Faithfulness meant holding on to that character, even when it would have been easier to let it slip.

Faithfulness in daily life serves as a safeguard, protecting us from the subtle erosion of integrity. It's the consistent, small choices that fortify our character and build internal resilience, preparing us to stand firm in the face of larger ethical challenges. Just as a stonecutter's repeated blows eventually split a rock, our consistent faithfulness chips away at our own flaws, gradually shaping us into people of strong character. This commitment to faithfulness, even in the mundane aspects of life, cultivates spiritual maturity and strengthens our resolve, making us less likely to compromise when faced with significant temptations or pressures.

Just as I found myself wrestling with the challenges and temptations within the confines of the prison camp, Joseph, too, faced immense trials that tested his character and faithfulness. His story, much like my own, illustrates how faithfulness can transform our circumstances and prepare us for a greater purpose, even when we are surrounded by adversity. While my personal experience in the camp challenged my faithfulness, it was the story of Joseph that continually reminded me of the importance of staying true to one's principles, regardless of the circumstances.

Joseph: A Model of Faithfulness

This idea of faithfulness leading to stability is powerfully illustrated in the story of Joseph. Joseph, who was sold into slavery by his brothers, found himself in Egypt serving in the house of Potiphar, a high-ranking official. Despite being in a foreign land and far from his family, Joseph remained faithful to God and to the duties assigned to him. Genesis 39:2-4 says, *"The Lord was with Joseph so that he prospered, and he lived in the house of his Egyptian master. When his master saw that the Lord was with him and that the Lord gave him success in everything he did, Joseph found favor in his eyes and became his attendant. Potiphar put him in charge of his household, and he entrusted to his care everything he owned."*

Joseph's faithfulness in Potiphar's house was evident in his diligent work and his commitment to doing what was right, even when no one was watching. His integrity brought him favor with Potiphar, who entrusted him with everything in his household. Yet, this same faithfulness led to one of his greatest tests when Potiphar's wife attempted to seduce him. Joseph's refusal to sin against God, even at the cost of his freedom, demonstrated his unwavering commitment to his convictions.

When Potiphar's wife falsely accused Joseph, leading to his imprisonment, Joseph's faithfulness did not waver. Even in the dark, confining space of a prison cell, he remained steadfast. Genesis 39:20-23 tells us, *"But while Joseph was there in the prison, the Lord was with him; he showed him kindness and granted him favor in the eyes of the prison warden. So the warden put Joseph in charge of all those held in the prison, and he was made responsible for all that was done there. The warden paid no attention to anything under Joseph's care, because the Lord was with Joseph and gave him success in whatever he did."*

Despite his unwavering faithfulness, Joseph likely experienced a range of complex emotions during his years in prison. Being unjustly confined would naturally bring feelings of frustration, confusion, and doubt. Joseph, known for his integrity and diligence, faced the harsh reality that his commitment to doing what was right had led to false accusations and imprisonment. The sense of injustice could have been overwhelming, knowing that he was being punished for a crime he did not commit.

In the silence of the prison, Joseph's mind might have wandered back to the betrayal of his brothers and the accusations that landed him behind bars. It would not be unreasonable to assume that Joseph felt the weight of isolation, perhaps wondering why his faithfulness was met with such hardship. The path that once seemed so clear, filled with dreams of leadership and purpose, now appeared obscured by the shadows of uncertainty.

Yet, it was precisely in these challenging circumstances that Joseph's faithfulness became a beacon of resilience. While he might have grappled with inner questions and the natural human desire to understand "why," Joseph remained steadfast. His trust in God's overarching plan provided a sense of stability and purpose, even when external signs were absent. The stories of his ancestors—how God had been faithful to Abraham, Isaac, and Jacob—likely offered Joseph the reassurance that God was still present, even in the depths of a prison cell.

Joseph's faithfulness wasn't a denial of his difficult reality; it was an acknowledgment that his life was part of a larger narrative that God was orchestrating. This perspective enabled Joseph to endure with patience, finding ways to serve and excel even in his confined circumstances. By committing to do his best in every task given to him, no matter how menial,

Joseph demonstrated that faithfulness is not contingent on favorable conditions. His consistent actions spoke louder than words, reflecting a deep-seated belief that God had not abandoned him.

Joseph's enduring faithfulness eventually earned him the trust of the prison warden, who recognized his integrity and granted him responsibilities. This shift not only provided Joseph with a sense of purpose but also prepared him for the greater role he would play in the future. Through his daily choices to remain faithful, Joseph's life illustrated a profound truth: that maintaining one's integrity and commitment to God, even in adversity, can lead to unexpected opportunities and blessings.

Joseph's story serves as a powerful reminder that faithfulness can sustain us through our darkest moments. While he may not have seen the immediate outcome of his suffering, Joseph's steadfastness paved the way for his future rise to power and the fulfillment of God's promises. His life teaches us that faithfulness, even when it feels unnoticed or unrewarded, aligns us with God's greater purposes, often beyond what we can see or imagine.

Joseph's faithfulness didn't only impact his life; it had a profound effect on those around him. His integrity and dedication earned the trust of the prison warden, and he was entrusted with significant responsibilities. This faithfulness, even in the darkness of a prison cell, set the stage for Joseph's later rise to power in Egypt. His steadfast commitment to doing what was right, regardless of his circumstances, eventually positioned him to save not only his family but also countless others from famine. Joseph's story illustrates that faithfulness can have far-reaching effects, often beyond what we can see or imagine. It shows that our commitment to staying true to our principles, even when it seems unnoticed or unrewarded, can pave the way for greater purposes.

Joseph's unwavering commitment to his values, even in prison, is a testament to how faithfulness can become an act of worship. His consistent integrity, even when he was unseen and unappreciated, mirrored a life lived in worship to God. This reflects a broader principle: our faithfulness, in both small and great things, is a daily offering to God, demonstrating our trust and reliance on Him. But Joseph's story is not just about personal faithfulness. His commitment to doing what was right had ripple effects, impacting those around him and setting the stage for God's greater plan.

Faithfulness as a Form of Worship

Isaiah 40:31 beautifully captures the essence of resilience: *"But those who trust in the Lord will find new strength. They will soar high on wings like eagles. They will run and not grow weary. They will walk and not faint."* Trusting in God's promises provided the strength needed to navigate the toughest days in the camp. Each morning, as I rose from my bunk, I prayed for renewed strength and the courage to face whatever lay ahead.

In that prep room, I began to see my work as a form of worship. I reorganized the workflow, making the process more efficient, and my efforts did not go unnoticed by the correctional officers. But beyond the practical improvements, this time became a period of deep personal reflection and spiritual renewal. I would often sing hymns to encourage myself, and though tears of frustration sometimes accompanied those songs, they were also a reminder that my faithfulness to God was my true anchor in this storm. I saw that my faithfulness to God had to translate into faithfulness in executing my responsibilities—even when no one was present.

Returning to Regular Life and New Challenges

Eventually, the lockdown ended, and camp life returned to its regular rhythm. However, I still needed to secure a permanent job. The positions I had been advised to seek were all filled, so I was placed in the camp kitchen. (This was before finding my permenant job in the Power House.) This was not the ideal assignment; the environment was tough, with a lot of tension among the inmates. But I approached it with the same mindset of faithfulness, determined to do my job with integrity, regardless of the challenges.

Philippians 4:13 continued to be my guiding light: *"For I can do everything through Christ, who gives me strength."* This scripture encapsulated the essence of my journey in the camp. Each day was a testament to the strength and resilience that came from my relationship with Christ. It was through Him that I found the resilience to overcome challenges and maintain my convictions.

Faithfulness in the Face of Pressure

The kitchen was a tough environment, full of conflicts and power struggles. Each day brought new challenges, from navigating the intricate social dynamics among the inmates to dealing with the pressures of maintaining order and productivity in a chaotic setting. It wasn't just the physical work that was demanding; the psychological and emotional strains were equally taxing. There were moments when other inmates tried to pressure me into compromising my principles, particularly during times when we were asked to leave the area for questionable activities. Some inmates used these moments as opportunities to gain favors or simply avoid the responsibilities of the kitchen. The pressure to conform was strong, as leaving with the others would have been the easier route, avoiding conflict and maintaining a façade of camaraderie. But I stood

Chapter 3: Faithfulness Anchors Stability

firm, refusing to leave until my job was done. I knew that once I compromised my principles, even in seemingly small matters, it would become easier to justify larger compromises in the future.

This is a reason I distinguish between the camp and real prison because I knew the worst that would happen to me was that people would talk about me or try to ostracize me. Unlike in maximum-security facilities, where violence could be a constant threat, in the camp, the consequences were more social than physical. Still, the social pressure was intense. There is an inherent need in all of us to belong, to be part of a group. In the kitchen, choosing to stand apart meant becoming a target for gossip and isolation. My stance didn't win me any friends, and there were days when the loneliness felt like another form of punishment. But I knew that my faithfulness to my convictions was more important than fitting in.

I could not wait to get out of the kitchen, though. It was confusion every day—an environment where ethical lines were often blurred, and survival instincts ruled over moral considerations. Each day felt like a test, not just of my patience but of my commitment to my values. There were times when the chaos around me seemed overwhelming, when the easy choice would have been to give in, blend in, and avoid the constant tension. But I realized that it was in these very moments of confusion and conflict that my true character was being shaped. Faithfulness wasn't just about the big, life-defining decisions; it was about the everyday choices to uphold my integrity, even when no one else was watching.

Choosing faithfulness over mere survival is not easy. It often requires going against our natural instincts to take the path of least resistance or the socially acceptable route. The temptation to blend in, to become like everyone else, was always present. I saw it every day in the way others would bend the rules or cut corners to make their lives a bit easier. Yet, I knew that faithfulness to my values, even in these seemingly small choices, would shape my character and define my legacy. In a place where it was easy to lose oneself in the crowd, to become just another inmate defined by a number rather than a name, staying true to my principles was a way of holding onto my identity, my humanity, and my purpose. It was a reminder that my worth was not determined by my environment or by the opinions of others, but by my unwavering commitment to what I knew to be right. I have no illusions about how I would act in a real prison environment, and I'm grateful I never had to find out.

While personal faithfulness is crucial, it often flourishes best within the context of a supportive community. Just as iron sharpens iron, so too does the presence of fellow believers encourage and strengthen our resolve to remain faithful. In the prison camp, the shared commitment among Christian inmates was a source of mutual encouragement, highlighting that faithfulness is both a personal and collective journey. Faithfulness, while often a deeply personal commitment, is also greatly influenced by the communities we are part of. The support and encouragement from others who share our values can be a critical factor in our ability to remain steadfast.

The Role of Community in Cultivating Faithfulness

Even in the challenging environment of a prison camp, the presence of a supportive Christian community can play a vital role in nurturing and sustaining faithfulness. In such a setting, where external connections are limited, the bonds formed within the camp become crucial. Fellow inmates who share a commitment to faith create a unique and powerful support network. These relationships offer encouragement, accountability, and a shared sense of purpose, which are essential for maintaining faithfulness amidst adversity.

Gathering with other believers for prayer, Bible study, or informal conversations provides an anchor in the storm. These communal activities remind individuals that they are not alone in their struggles. Sharing experiences and insights fosters a sense of solidarity and belonging, which can be deeply comforting. The simple act of coming together to read scripture or to pray collectively can renew one's strength and resolve to remain faithful, even when faced with daily hardships.

In the camp, where temptations and pressures to compromise may be constant, having fellow believers nearby serves as a source of accountability. Knowing that others are witnessing your actions and that you, in turn, are an example to them, reinforces the commitment to live out one's faith authentically. This mutual accountability helps maintain integrity and encourages individuals to stay true to their principles, despite the challenges they may face.

The community also provides emotional and spiritual resilience. During times of isolation or despair, the presence of a supportive group can offer solace. Listening to each other's stories, offering words of encouragement, and praying for one another can lift spirits and bolster faith. These interactions can remind individuals that their struggles are shared and that, through faith, they can find strength to persevere. This shared journey helps individuals realize that faithfulness is not just a solitary pursuit but a collective one, where each person's commitment helps strengthen the group as a whole.

In a prison camp, where external support is limited, the internal Christian community becomes a lifeline. It offers a space where faithfulness can thrive, where individuals can grow spiritually, and where resilience is built through the support of others who understand the unique challenges of the environment.

Engaging with this community enables individuals to maintain their faithfulness, knowing that they are part of a larger body of believers who are all striving to live out their faith together.

Choosing faithfulness in environments that are hostile to integrity can be emotionally taxing. The isolation and loneliness that come with standing apart from the crowd can feel like a burden too heavy to bear. Yet, it is in these moments of solitude that we often find clarity and strength. To navigate these emotional challenges, it is crucial to seek solace in prayer, drawing on God's presence for comfort and guidance. Building relationships with those who share our values can provide much-needed encouragement and support. Finding small moments of joy—whether through a kind act, a shared laugh, or a personal hobby—can also lighten the emotional load and renew our spirit. By tending to our emotional well-being, we equip ourselves to remain faithful even when it feels like the world is against us.

Finding Refuge in the Power House

Finally, an opportunity came for me to transfer to the Power House, where all the heat and air conditioning for the entire facility was generated. This job was a blessing. It allowed me to work alone for several hours each day, away from the drama and tension of the main camp. It was in the Power House that I found a sanctuary. I spent my time there writing, praying, and worshiping God. Despite my earlier vow not to speak for God again, I found that I couldn't help but sing His praises, even in that strange and difficult place.

Joseph's faithfulness in prison mirrors what I experienced in the Power House. Though confined and far from the life he once knew, Joseph continued to live out his convictions, earning the trust and respect of those around him. His unwavering faithfulness brought stability to his life, even in the midst of unjust circumstances. This is a powerful reminder that faithfulness is not dependent on our external conditions but on our inner commitment to God and our principles.

The Power House became my refuge, a place where I could reconnect with God and find the strength to keep going. It was there that I realized the truth of Psalm 91:1-2: *"Those who live in the shelter of the Most High will find rest in the shadow of the Almighty. This I declare about the Lord: He alone is my refuge, my place of safety; he is my God, and I trust him."* In the stillness of the Power House, I found a peace that transcended my circumstances, a peace that came from knowing that God was with me, even in the midst of my trials.

Faithfulness transcends the confines of religious rituals and becomes an everyday act of worship. When we commit ourselves to doing our best, even in mundane tasks or challenging circumstances, we are offering our lives as a testament to God's faithfulness. Each act of integrity, each moment of perseverance, is a reflection of the character of God. In this way, our entire life becomes an offering, a continuous worship that honors God not just with our words but with our deeds. By aligning our actions with God's will, we not only strengthen our faith but also bear witness to the transformative power of a faithful life.

Faithfulness and True Happiness

> *"True happiness... is not attained through self-gratification, but through fidelity to a worthy purpose."* - HELEN KELLER

Helen Keller's insight into true happiness resonates deeply with the concept of faithfulness. It's a reminder that real fulfillment comes from being faithful to our convictions and purpose, even when it requires sacrifice. Her words underscore the importance of staying true to our values, even in the face of adversity.

Embracing Faithfulness in Daily Life

Faithfulness is essential for living a conviction-driven life. It is the quiet strength that enables us to recover from setbacks, stand firm in our beliefs, and trust in God's promises. By embracing faithfulness, we not only overcome our challenges but also inspire those around us to do the same. Faithfulness anchors us, providing stability in a world that is often unpredictable and chaotic. It is through faithfulness that we find the strength to endure, the courage to stand firm, and the peace to trust in God's plan for our lives. Please don't misunderstand me! I still had my resolve never to preach for God again but I would never leave God because I literally had no one or place left to go!

In today's fast-paced world, where change is constant and values often shift, faithfulness can sometimes seem outdated. Yet, it is precisely in this environment that faithfulness becomes even more crucial. In the workplace, for example, maintaining integrity and staying true to one's commitments can set you apart in a culture that often values short-term gains over long-term relationships. Similarly, in personal relationships, faithfulness provides a foundation of trust and stability that is essential for enduring love and companionship. Whether we are facing ethical dilemmas at work or challenges in our personal lives, faithfulness serves as a guiding principle, helping us navigate through life's uncertainties with confidence and grace.

As we have seen through these stories and reflections, faithfulness is not just a passive trait but an active commitment that requires daily practice. It is through faithfulness that we build trust, cultivate relationships, and achieve our goals. To help you integrate the principles of faithfulness into your daily life, the following strategies provide practical steps that you can take to strengthen your resolve and stay true to your commitments.

Faithfulness is not just a passive trait but an active choice that we must make every day. To cultivate this essential virtue in our lives, here are some practical strategies that can help us develop and strengthen our faithfulness.

Strategies for Cultivating Faithfulness

Faithfulness is a key virtue that impacts every aspect of our lives, from our relationships to our leadership. It involves steadfast commitment, loyalty, and consistency, even in the face of challenges. Here are some strategies to help you cultivate faithfulness:

1. **Commit to Small Acts of Faithfulness:** Faithfulness is often demonstrated in small, everyday actions that build a foundation of trust and reliability. Begin by being faithful in the little things—whether it's keeping your promises, being punctual, or consistently supporting others. These small acts accumulate over time, creating a larger pattern of faithfulness in your life.
2. **Prioritize Your Commitments:** Being faithful requires clarity about where your commitments lie. It's important to prioritize your responsibilities to avoid spreading yourself too thin. Evaluate your commitments regularly and ensure that you are dedicating the necessary time and energy to what truly matters. This helps you remain consistently faithful in the most important areas of your life.
3. **Stay Grounded in Your Values:** Faithfulness is deeply connected to your core values. When you stay grounded in your beliefs, it's easier to maintain your commitments, even

during challenging times. Regularly reflect on your values and let them guide your actions. In moments of doubt or difficulty, return to these values as a source of strength and motivation to stay faithful.

4. **Cultivate Patience and Perseverance:** Faithfulness often requires enduring through difficult seasons. Patience and perseverance are crucial for maintaining your commitments when results are not immediately visible. Develop resilience by setting long-term goals and breaking them down into manageable steps. Celebrate small victories along the way, reminding yourself that faithfulness is a marathon, not a sprint.

5. **Surround Yourself with Faithful People:** The company you keep can significantly influence your ability to remain faithful. Surround yourself with individuals who exemplify faithfulness—they will inspire and encourage you to stay the course. Building relationships with committed, reliable, and consistent people strengthens your own resolve to live a faithful life.

6. **Seek Strength in Prayer and Reflection:** A strong spiritual foundation sustains faithfulness. Regular prayer and reflection help you stay connected to your purpose and the divine support that undergirds your commitments. Make it a habit to seek guidance, renew your strength, and reaffirm your commitment through daily prayer or meditation.

7. **Be Faithful in the Face of Adversity:** True faithfulness is tested during times of adversity. Challenges often reveal the depth of our commitment and our ability to stay true to our word. When faced with difficulties, remind yourself of the long-term rewards of staying faithful. Let adversity be a refining fire that strengthens your commitment and resolve.

While personal faithfulness is crucial, it often flourishes best within the context of a supportive community. Just as iron sharpens iron, so too does the presence of fellow believers encourage and strengthen our resolve to remain faithful. In the prison camp, the shared commitment among Christian inmates was a source of mutual encouragement, highlighting that faithfulness is both a personal and collective journey.

Conviction Checkpoints

- **Self-Examination Question:** Reflect on a time you faced a significant setback. How did you recover, and what did you learn about the importance of faithfulness?
- **Actionable Step:** Identify an area in your life where you need to build resilience. Take one step this week to strengthen your faithfulness in that area.
- **Conviction Affirmation:** "My faithfulness to God anchors my life in stability, providing strength in times of trial and peace in times of uncertainty."
- **Prayer/Meditation Focus:** Spend time in prayer or meditation, asking for the strength to remain faithful in all situations. Seek God's guidance in areas where you feel challenged, and ask for the courage to stay true to your convictions.

Profile in Conviction

Daniel: Faithfulness in the Face of Lions

Daniel, one of the most prominent figures in the Bible, exemplifies unwavering faithfulness in the face of extreme adversity. As a young man, Daniel was taken captive from Jerusalem to Babylon, where he quickly rose to prominence because of his wisdom and unwavering commitment to God. Despite living in a foreign land, surrounded by people who did not share his beliefs, Daniel remained steadfast in his faith.

When King Darius issued a decree that no one was to pray to any god or man except the king for thirty days, Daniel's faithfulness was put to the ultimate test. Knowing the consequences, Daniel continued to pray to God three times a day, just as he had always done. His enemies, eager to see him fall, reported his actions to the king, and Daniel was thrown into the lions' den as punishment.

However, Daniel's faithfulness to God did not waver, even in the face of certain death. That night, God sent an angel to shut the mouths of the lions, and Daniel emerged from the den unharmed. His faithfulness not only saved his life but also led King Darius to issue a decree that all people in his kingdom should revere the God of Daniel.

Daniel's story is a powerful reminder that faithfulness, even in the most dangerous and challenging circumstances, brings divine protection and stability. His life stands as a testament to the strength that comes from unwavering commitment to God, no matter the cost.

Daniel's unwavering faithfulness in the face of persecution is a powerful example of what it means to remain steadfast in one's beliefs. Despite knowing the consequences, Daniel continued to pray to God, refusing to bow to the king's decree. His faithfulness was not just an act of obedience but a deep-seated commitment to his relationship with God. This story is not just an historical account; it is a living testimony of how faithfulness can carry us through the most daunting trials. In our own lives, we may not face lions, but the essence of these stories—trusting in God's plan and staying true to our faith—remains relevant.

Faithfulness extends beyond the monumental trials we face; it is built and nurtured in the everyday choices we make. Whether through small acts of integrity in our jobs, patience in our relationships, or consistency in our spiritual practices, each moment of faithfulness contributes to a life that is steady and rooted. Embracing this truth transforms our perspective, allowing us to see each day as an opportunity to grow stronger and more aligned with God's will.

Faithfulness is more than just a virtue; it is a way of life. It requires us to be consistent in our actions, steadfast in our beliefs, and unwavering in our commitments. Whether we are inspired by the stories of Daniel and Abraham, or by our own experiences, the call to live a faithful life is one that echoes throughout the ages. As we move forward, let us reflect on how we can be more faithful in our own lives, not just in the big moments, but in the small, everyday decisions that define who we are. By doing so, we not only honor our own values but also inspire those around us to live with the same level of commitment and integrity.

CHAPTER 4
PURPOSE POWERS PROGRESS

Purpose is a powerful driver of progress. Throughout history, individuals who have made significant impacts—whether in social reform, leadership, or personal transformation—often attribute their achievements to a clear sense of purpose. From Frederick Douglass to modern-day entrepreneurs, having a defined purpose has provided direction, motivation, and resilience in the face of adversity that helps us overcome obstacles and achieve our goals. During my time in the prison camp, the importance of having a clear purpose became evident. It was through this understanding that I navigated the most challenging period of my life and rediscovered my mission.

As you recall, when I first entered the prison camp, I was filled with anger and resentment. I had promised God that I would never speak for Him again. This promise was made in a moment of rage and disappointment, feeling betrayed by the very God to whom I had devoted my life. The initial days were filled with a profound sense of loss and purposelessness. I was a pastor who had lost his voice, a leader without direction, or followers.

Initial Struggles and Feeling Lost

When I first entered the prison camp, I was engulfed by a profound sense of anger and betrayal. My whole life had been devoted to serving God, leading a community, and being a voice for the divine. And yet, here I was, stripped of my freedom and everything I had built. I felt lost, like a ship with a broken compass, drifting aimlessly in a sea of confusion and despair. Each day seemed like an unending struggle to find meaning in a place where hope was scarce.

In those early days, the purpose seemed like a concept that belonged to a different time, a different version of me. I questioned everything. Was my life's work in vain? Had my faith been misplaced? The silence in my soul was deafening, and for the first time, I felt completely disconnected from the divine calling that had once been my guiding light. The routines of the camp were monotonous, and each task felt like a burden. Even the smallest chore reminded me of how far I had fallen, dragging me deeper into the abyss of purposelessness.

Moments of Clarity and Glimpses of Purpose

However, in the midst of this darkness, there were fleeting moments of clarity. Small acts of kindness began to pierce through the heavy fog of despair. I remember one particular day in the kitchen when a fellow inmate shared his struggles with me. Listening to him, offering words of encouragement, and seeing the glimmer of hope in his eyes reignited something within me. These seemingly insignificant interactions started to weave a fragile thread of purpose. They were like tiny beams of light breaking through a dense forest, showing me that perhaps my purpose hadn't disappeared—it had just taken on a different form.

The more I engaged with others, the more I realized that my purpose was not tied to a pulpit or a church building. It was about being present, offering hope, and showing compassion, even in a place that seemed devoid of these things. Each conversation, each moment of shared pain and understanding, was a reminder that my voice still had power, even if it was no longer amplified by a microphone.

Internal Conflicts and Redefining Purpose

Despite these moments, there were still days of intense internal conflict. Part of me resisted embracing this new understanding of purpose. I struggled with the idea that I could be of service in a place that had taken so much from me. The anger hadn't disappeared; it lingered, whispering that I had every right to withdraw, to keep my light hidden as a form of protest against the injustice I felt. I grappled with these conflicting emotions—anger versus compassion, despair versus hope, resignation versus resilience.

Over time, however, I began to see that my purpose was not a fixed destination but a journey, one that required constant reevaluation and adaptation. I realized that purpose was not about grand gestures or public recognition. It was about faithfulness in the small, everyday acts of service. It was about showing up, even when it was hard. It was about using whatever platform I had, however small, to make a difference. My understanding of purpose evolved from being something I did for God, to something God was doing through me, even in the most unlikely of places.

Finding Peace in Purpose

This shift in perspective brought a sense of peace I hadn't felt in a long time. Accepting that my purpose was still alive, though different from what I had envisioned, allowed me to find joy in the midst of hardship. It gave my days in the camp a sense of direction and meaning. I no longer saw myself as a victim of my circumstances but as someone who could still make an impact, one conversation at a time. This realization didn't erase the pain or the sense of injustice, but it provided a way to navigate through them. It was like discovering an inner compass that guided me through the darkest times, reminding me that I still had a role to play in God's greater plan.

The emptiness was all-consuming, a constant reminder that everything I had stood for seemed to be stripped away. Tasks that would normally be mundane became unbearable chores, each action feeling as though it were dragging me further into the abyss of despair. Without a sense of purpose, even the simplest routines felt like insurmountable burdens.

As the days turned into weeks, I struggled to find meaning in my new environment. The prison camp was harsh and unforgiving, with its own set of rules and dynamics. I felt like a ship adrift in a storm, with no anchor to hold me steady. The sense of isolation was overwhelming, and the question "Why me?" resurfaced with a vengeance. It was during these dark moments that I realized the importance of purpose in navigating adversity.

Ephesians 2:10 reminds us, *"For we are God's handiwork, created in Christ Jesus to do good works, which God prepared in advance for us to do."* This scripture had been a guiding light throughout my life, but it felt distant and irrelevant in the prison camp. However, the more I reflected on it, the more I realized that even in this place, I was still God's handiwork. My circumstances had changed, but my purpose had not.

Joseph's Journey of Purpose

The story of Joseph, found in the Book of Genesis, offers a profound example of how purpose can drive progress, even in the face of overwhelming adversity. Joseph's life was marked by a clear sense of purpose, which guided him through betrayal, slavery, and imprisonment. From the moment he shared his dreams with his brothers, Joseph was set on a path that, while filled with trials, was ultimately guided by God's purpose for his life.

Joseph's purpose became apparent early on when he had dreams that foretold his future position of power and leadership. However, sharing these dreams with his brothers led to jealousy and betrayal. They sold him into slavery, and Joseph found himself in Egypt, far from his home and family. Despite this, Joseph remained faithful to his purpose, working diligently in Potiphar's house.

Genesis 39:2-4 tells us, *"The Lord was with Joseph so that he prospered, and he lived in the house of his Egyptian master. When his master saw that the Lord was with him and that the Lord gave him success in everything he did, Joseph found favor in his eyes and became his attendant. Potiphar put him in charge of his household, and he entrusted to his care everything he owned."* Joseph's faithfulness and his commitment to his purpose led to his rise in Potiphar's house, where he managed all that Potiphar owned. Imagine Joseph's emotional landscape: the confusion and betrayal from his brothers, the desolation of being a slave in a foreign land, and the injustice of imprisonment despite his innocence. Yet, Joseph's faith in his God-given purpose kept him anchored. He might have felt abandoned, but he clung to the belief that his dreams were a glimpse of a larger plan, helping him endure the loneliness and despair that would have otherwise crushed his spirit.

Joseph's journey to discovering his purpose was fraught with emotional turmoil and mental struggle. Betrayed by his own brothers, sold into slavery, and later unjustly imprisoned, Joseph's life was a series of hardships that would have broken many. The sting of betrayal from those he once called family was a wound that ran deep. In the quiet, lonely nights of his prison cell, Joseph might have replayed the scene of his brothers selling him, questioning what he had done to deserve such cruelty. The isolation of prison only amplified these thoughts, making him feel forgotten and forsaken.

Yet, in the midst of this overwhelming sense of betrayal and isolation, Joseph held on to his faith. It wasn't easy. There were likely moments when doubt crept in, whispering that his dreams of greatness were merely illusions. Joseph might have questioned God's promises, wondering if he would ever be freed or if he was destined to spend his life behind bars. These were not just physical bars but the emotional and mental ones that stemmed from abandonment and injustice.

But Joseph's response to his circumstances reveals a deep well of resilience. Instead of succumbing to bitterness, he chose to focus on the tasks at hand, whether it was serving in Potiphar's house or managing the affairs of the prison. This dedication to his duties, even when he had every reason to give up, illustrates a powerful lesson about faithfulness and trust in God's plan. Joseph might have thought, I don't understand why this is happening, but I will remain faithful to the tasks before me, trusting that God sees and knows.

This choice to remain faithful amid trials allowed Joseph to find purpose even in the smallest of tasks. It was a testament to his unwavering faith and belief that God was still in control of his life, despite the injustices he faced. His integrity and commitment to doing what was right, regardless of his circumstances, became a beacon of hope, not only for himself but for others around him. Joseph's story reminds us that faithfulness in the face of adversity is not just about surviving but about allowing God to use our struggles for a greater purpose.

However, Joseph's journey was far from easy. His refusal to compromise his integrity when Potiphar's wife attempted to seduce him led to his unjust imprisonment. Yet, even in prison,

Joseph's sense of purpose did not waver. Joseph's faithfulness in the face of betrayal, slavery, and imprisonment helped me remember that purpose can sustain me through even the most challenging circumstances. Joseph's commitment to living out his God-given purpose, regardless of his circumstances, allowed him to move forward from being a slave to becoming the second most powerful man in Egypt. This revelation softened my heart towards living my purpose intentionally while I served my time in the prison camp.

Rediscovering Purpose in the Camp

In the camp, daily life was a monotonous routine of chores, meals, and mandatory counts. There was little to break the tedium, and the temptation to sink into despair was strong. Yet, amidst the bleakness, there were moments of clarity and insight. One particular moment stands out. I was assigned to work in the kitchen, a place that few wanted to be. The work was grueling, and the environment was hostile. However, it was here that I began to see glimmers of my purpose.

Each time I listened to a fellow inmate's story or offered a word of encouragement, I felt a spark reignite within me. These small acts, seemingly insignificant in the grand scheme, became building blocks for a larger sense of purpose. It was as if each conversation, each shared struggle, was chipping away at the walls I had built around my heart. Slowly, the anger and resentment were replaced with a quiet determination to serve, even if only in the smallest of ways.

Proverbs 19:21 provides further clarity: *"Many are the plans in a person's heart, but it is the Lord's purpose that prevails."* This verse became a mantra as I navigated the complexities of life in the camp. While I had many plans for my life outside, I realized that God's purpose for me was unfolding even in this unlikely place. This alignment provided a sense of peace and confidence that, despite the challenges, I was on the right path.

During my time in the camp, interactions with other inmates were crucial in shaping my understanding of purpose. These conversations, though often brief and informal, became moments of insight and reflection. I began to notice how my role in the camp went beyond just performing daily tasks; it extended into the realm of influence and support for those around me. Whether it was offering a listening ear to someone struggling with their circumstances or sharing words of encouragement to a fellow inmate who was losing hope, these moments had a profound impact on me.

I realized that discovering my purpose wasn't necessarily about monumental achievements or public recognition. Instead, it was about being present, attentive, and willing to show kindness and understanding. In the camp environment, where many felt forgotten and disconnected, these small acts of compassion created a ripple effect. My purpose became clearer each day as I saw how simple gestures could bring light to someone else's darkness.

Reflecting on these interactions, I understood that purpose often reveals itself through service to others. It became evident that purpose is not only something we search for but something that unfolds naturally when we commit to living out our values. By maintaining integrity and faithfulness in my conduct, I found that purpose was intertwined with every action, every choice I made to uplift those around me. This understanding brought a sense of fulfillment, even in an environment that was otherwise bleak.

Through this process, I learned that purpose is both individual and collective. It's about how we use our personal experiences and strengths to positively impact the lives of others. It's about finding meaning in the everyday, recognizing that each moment is an opportunity to reflect God's love and bring hope to those who need it most. This realization shifted my perspective, reminding me that even in the most challenging circumstances, we can discover and fulfill our purpose by being a source of light and encouragement to others.

Reflections on Faith and Prayer

Throughout my time in the camp, there were countless moments when doubt and despair seemed overwhelming. I remember one evening in particular when the weight of my situation felt unbearable. The noise of the camp quieted down, leaving only the distant murmurs of other inmates. I sat alone in my bunk, wrestling with thoughts of hopelessness. It was a night where everything seemed to press in on me—questions about my past decisions, thoughts about my future, and fears that maybe, just maybe, God had abandoned me.

In that moment of darkness, I turned to prayer, not out of obligation but out of sheer desperation. I poured my heart out to God, expressing my anger, confusion, and fear. I didn't hold back, as there was no one else to listen and nowhere else to turn. As I prayed, a sense of calm slowly began to wash over me. It wasn't an immediate solution or a miraculous change in my circumstances, but a quiet assurance that I was not alone. The presence of God felt nearer than ever, almost as if I could feel His hand on my shoulder, guiding me through the darkness.

This experience was not a one-time event. Many nights, I found solace in the simple act of bowing my head and speaking to God, laying my burdens before Him. Prayer became my anchor, a steady rock that I could cling to when the storms of doubt threatened to pull me under. It was in these moments of prayer that I rediscovered my sense of purpose. God was using this time, these challenges, to refine me, to teach me resilience, and to deepen my trust in Him.

Each time I felt that sense of peace and direction, I was reminded that faith is not just about the good times when everything is going well. True faith is about trusting God in the midst of trials, believing that He is at work even when we cannot see the outcome. I've come to believe that we don't need faith when all is well! We need faith when we face reversals and calamities. These moments of prayer didn't always provide the answers I was looking for, but they provided something even more valuable—a reassurance that God was with me, that He had a plan, and that my purpose was unfolding even in the darkest of times.

Even in the kitchen, where I hated being, God used me to speak for Him and share His kingdom with those who were lost. I even received expressions of gratitude from the guys with whom I spoke. Guys had real problems. Wives sent letters with divorce papers, families cut off the camper abruptly and wouldn't respond to emails. So many stories that I cannot even recount them. I just knew that guys were hurting and had no real outlet to share them or receive some modicum of hope. I couldn't resist helping even in my emotionally and spiritually broken state. New guys were placed in the kitchen so I believed God had appointed me to work an assignment that I didn't want so I could give hope to guys who were in despair. I even started to consider what it looked like to preach again.

At first, I remained resolute in my decision not to speak for God. Yet, the inmates saw something in me that I had almost forgotten—a calling, a purpose. They insisted that I hold a service, but I refused, directing them to the chaplain instead. But their persistence wore on me, especially when one inmate who had been there for almost a decade had a heart-to-heart with me. This brother was what is considered my "Rabbi". He had my back and advocated for me even when I wasn't around–because I was breaking all the rules! I sat in a chair that *be-*

Chapter 4: Purpose Powers Progress

longed to someone else in the TV room or sat in a seat in the dining hall that *belonged* to someone else. The irony in all this was that we were in prison and none of it belonged to us. The most intense disagreements happened over petty things like these. My Rabbi took to me and this was really the favor of God. He was one of the most senior guys in the camp and I could always talk with him. He saw something in me that I had momentarily lost sight of—my purpose.

He shared with me that most of the guys don't really respect preachers because they are fake. He recalled, that there were a couple preachers who had been in the camp over his tenure and they lived worse lives than those who didn't even know God. (He said, "Preachers and politicians were the worst!") One of them would have his wife visit on the first Saturday then his girlfriend came the following weekend. This continued until he was released months later and his wife was never the wiser. One thing for certain was that there were no secrets in the camp. Every conversation on the phone, every letter or package someone received was known throughout the camp. He just said, "Rev., you need to do it."

Finally, I relented. Organizing an inmate-led service was no small task, especially with the chaplain's initial resistance. However, with permission from the camp administrator and counselor, we held our first service on a Saturday. To my surprise, nearly the entire camp—around seventy men—showed up. The opening hymn was "Blessed Assurance," and the sound of the men singing together was powerful. Even the counselor and COs took notice, recognizing the significance of what was happening.

While we sang, in thunderous acclaim, *"This is my story. This is my song,"* the CO and counselor appeared at the door and just stood there. I thought, "Oh Man, what did I do now?" Then they walked away. After I had cleaned up the room, put the Bibles and hymnals away, I departed to go to the Unit. On my way out, I was called in to the office. I braced for a tongue lashing because they had really stuck their necks out for me but I couldn't understand what I could have done. He started, "I've been here since this facility opened and I can tell you that I've never seen anything like that! These guys need you and I've got your back." I thanked him and left. Stunned, I walked back to the Unit torn because my heart still wasn't really into preaching on a consistent basis.

In those days, before I worked in the Power House, I was in the unit on Saturday nights and guys came by to thank me. This began a wrestling match between God and me. "You want me to preach for you while in prison? I'm not sure." I'll commit to week by week but not long term.

Scripture says, "For I know the plans I have for you," declares the Lord, "plans to prosper you and not to harm you, plans to give you hope and a future." (Jeremiah 29:11) This scripture was a poignant reminder that, despite my resistance, there was a divine plan at work. It encouraged me to stay focused on my purpose and trust that the challenges I faced were part of a larger journey toward personal development and growth.

The service became a regular gathering, providing a sense of community and spiritual nourishment for the men each Saturday. It was a clear reminder that even in the most unexpected places, God's purpose for our lives remains steadfast. This experience reignited my sense of mission, reminding me that my voice, though silenced by circumstances, still had the power to uplift and inspire others. I was back in Christian community and it made a big difference!

Creating Community Through Services

Having the opportunity to create and lead worship services nurtured me on a deep level. These services became a cornerstone of our community, offering a space where inmates could gather, share, and find solace amid their struggles. Organizing these services wasn't always easy, but the effort was more than worthwhile. Various men offered their singing and musical ability which really made the services more full and enjoyable. I quickly realized that these moments of shared worship went far beyond religious observance; they were about building a sense of belonging and connection among men who often felt isolated and forgotten.

As we came together to sing, pray, and read scripture, a noticeable change began to take place. Inmates who rarely spoke or interacted with others started to open up. There was a sense of camaraderie that developed, a shared understanding that we were all in this together, regardless of our backgrounds or personal histories. The services provided a break from the daily grind of camp life, offering a moment of peace and reflection. It was a time when we could let our guards down and be vulnerable with one another.

I saw firsthand how these services impacted the attitudes and behaviors of those who attended. There was a marked difference in the way some of the men carried themselves. Conversations that once centered around complaints or frustrations shifted toward hope and encouragement. I noticed that some inmates, who were initially skeptical or dismissive, began to attend regularly and even participated. Over time, the atmosphere in our camp started to change subtly. There was less tension, and a greater sense of unity emerged. One of the greatest joys in the camp was when we had nacho night! Some guys knew how to take the commissary items and make a nacho bowl the likes of which I have not enjoyed since. These became bigger and more unified over time because in the beginning these nights were held based on race or TV room.

Leading these services also brought personal realizations for me. I saw that my purpose extended beyond merely surviving my sentence; it was about making a positive difference in the lives of others. Observing these transformations, however small, reinforced the importance of community and the role faith plays in building resilience. I came to understand that fostering a sense of belonging and shared purpose could lead to profound changes in individuals and the community as a whole. This realization deepened my own sense of purpose and commitment, motivating me to continue serving others, even when it was challenging.

Purpose as a Guiding Compass

Purpose acts as a compass, guiding us through the storms of life. It helps us stay focused and motivated, even when the path is fraught with difficulties. When we are clear about our purpose, we can navigate obstacles with confidence and resilience. This clarity not only benefits us personally but also has a profound impact on those around us.

In the prison camp, having a clear purpose provided a sense of direction and motivation. It helped me make decisions that were aligned with my values and mission, rather than being driven by despair or anger. This focus on purpose allowed me to turn a place of punishment into a place of ministry and growth.

Furthermore, a clear purpose fosters a sense of community and shared vision. It brings people together, creating a unified front that can tackle even the most daunting challenges. By consistently communicating and reinforcing our purpose, we were able to create a supportive and uplifting community within the camp. This collective effort was instrumental in overcoming the obstacles we faced and emerging stronger than before.

You may not be aware of this but, there is an active church in prison. On my first night in the camp, the members of the church brought me snacks, drinks, and sweats to wear. They informed me that the members of the church "tithed" from their weekly commissary to help those who came in with nothing. I gladly joined this community. But there were unspoken tensions once the services started because the "head" of the church usually led the Christian community; but, I was beginning to be seen as the leader (which didn't really matter to me at all). In prison, there are always power struggles. I believe it's because prison represents a removal of personal agency and dignity so inmates look for any opportunity to reclaim it. The Catholics, Protestants, Muslims all had their own leader and there were multiple people vying for dominance especially when the leader was released. I had no desire to lead anything and reluctantly held the services weekly— though some part of me enjoyed going through the hymnal to pick songs and returning to my discipline of preparing weekly messages. When I took the job in the Power House, it gave me the freedom to plan the services without distraction.

The services became a cornerstone for creating a sense of unity and belonging. They were more than just religious gatherings; they were a testament to the power of purpose in fostering community resilience. Men who had once felt isolated found a sense of family. Those struggling with despair found hope. In the shared commitment to these gatherings, we found strength in numbers, our collective purpose overshadowing individual fears and uncertainties.

Personal Reflection and Growth

The experience in the prison camp had a profound impact on my personal growth. It taught me the importance of staying true to my values and purpose, even when it would have been easier to give up. It reinforced the idea that true leadership is about serving others and working towards a greater good, rather than seeking personal gain.

I remember a particularly challenging period when I was confronted by an inmate who was hostile to the idea of faith. He questioned my motives and mocked my beliefs. It would have been easy to respond with anger or retreat into silence. However, I knew that my purpose was to be a beacon of hope and strength. I responded with kindness and compassion, and over time, this inmate began to open up and share his own struggles. This experience reinforced the power of purpose in transforming lives and breaking down barriers.

Throughout this journey, the scriptures provided guidance and strength. Ephesians 2:10, Proverbs 19:21, and Jeremiah 29:11 were not just verses to be read but promises to be lived out. They reminded me that our work had a divine purpose and that, by staying true to that purpose, we were fulfilling God's plan for us.

Strategies to Discover Purpose

Discovering one's purpose is a journey that requires introspection, patience, and a willingness to explore different paths. It's about aligning your life with what truly matters to you and what makes you feel fulfilled. Here are some strategies to help you uncover and embrace your purpose:

1. **Reflect on Your Passions and Interests**
   - One of the first steps in discovering your purpose is to reflect on the activities and interests that bring you joy and fulfillment. What are the things you naturally gravitate towards? What hobbies or tasks make you lose track of time? Identifying these passions can provide valuable clues to understanding your purpose.

- Consider journaling regularly to document your feelings about different activities. Over time, patterns may emerge, highlighting what truly resonates with your inner self.

2. **Examine Your Core Values**
   - Your values are fundamental beliefs that guide your behavior and decision-making. Reflecting on what matters most to you—such as integrity, compassion, family, or innovation—can help you define your purpose. Knowing your values allows you to set goals that are aligned with your authentic self.
   - Make a list of your top five values and consider how they align with your current life choices. Are you living in a way that honors these values?

3. **Listen to Your Inner Voice**
   - Purpose often comes from within. Take time to quiet external noise and listen to your inner voice. This might involve meditation, prayer, or simply spending time alone in nature. Tuning into your intuition can help you uncover insights about your true desires and calling.
   - Practice mindfulness or meditation to help silence the distractions and connect more deeply with your inner thoughts and feelings.

4. **Learn from Life Experiences**
   - Reflecting on past experiences—both positive and negative—can provide insights into your purpose. Challenges and successes alike shape who you are. Consider what you have learned from significant events in your life and how these lessons might point towards your purpose.
   - Identify three significant events in your life and ask yourself: What did I learn from each experience? How did these events shape my beliefs and goals?

5. **Seek Guidance from Mentors and Role Models**
   - Sometimes, the perspective of others can provide clarity on your purpose. Seek out mentors, role models, or trusted friends who know you well. Their observations and advice can help you see your strengths and passions more clearly.
   - Schedule regular conversations with a mentor or a trusted friend to discuss your thoughts and get feedback. Their insights might reveal aspects of yourself that you hadn't noticed.
6. **Engage in Service to Others**
   - Purpose is often found in serving others and contributing to the greater good. Volunteering or helping those in need can provide a sense of fulfillment and clarity about your life's mission. Acts of service can reveal what you are passionate about and where you can make a meaningful impact.
   - Find a cause or community service project that resonates with you and commit to volunteering regularly. Notice how these activities make you feel and what they reveal about your purpose.
7. **Set Clear Goals and Take Action**
   - Once you have a sense of your purpose, set clear, actionable goals to pursue it. Purpose is not just about knowing; it's about doing. Break down your goals into manageable steps and take action. As you make progress, you'll gain more insight and refine your purpose.
   - Create a vision board or a detailed action plan outlining your goals related to your purpose. Regularly review and adjust your plan as you gain more clarity and experience.

8. **Be Open to Change and Growth**
   - Your purpose might evolve over time as you grow and your circumstances change. Be open to new experiences and opportunities that may alter your understanding of your purpose. Flexibility is key to a purposeful life.
   - Periodically reassess your goals and purpose. Ask yourself if they still align with your current passions and values. Don't be afraid to make changes if needed.

Conviction Checkpoints

- **Self-Examination Question:** Reflect on a time when you faced significant challenges. How did having (or lacking) a clear sense of purpose affect your ability to navigate those challenges? Identify your personal purpose and consider how it has shaped your life and decisions.
- **Actionable Step:** Set specific goals that are aligned with your personal mission statement. Take concrete steps toward achieving these goals, ensuring that they reflect your values and purpose.
- **Conviction Affirmation:** "My purpose is a divine compass, guiding my steps and fueling my progress through every challenge."
- **Prayer/Meditation Focus:** Pray for alignment with God's purposes. Ask for clarity and strength to pursue the path that He has set for you, trusting that His plans are for your good and will lead to prosperity and growth.

Profile in Conviction

William Wilberforce—A Life Driven by Purpose

William Wilberforce, a British politician, and philanthropist, is a prime example of how purpose can drive monumental progress. Born in 1759, Wilberforce became a Member of Parliament at a young age. However, it was his Christian faith that ignited his passion for social reform, particularly the abolition of the slave trade.

Despite facing significant opposition and ridicule, Wilberforce was unwavering in his conviction that slavery was a moral evil that needed to be eradicated. He devoted his life to this cause, tirelessly campaigning for the abolition of the slave trade in the British Empire. His dedication to this purpose was evident in his persistence; year after year, he introduced bills in Parliament to end the trade, only to see them defeated.

Wilberforce faced not only political opposition but also personal doubts and health issues that nearly derailed his mission. Yet, each time he contemplated stepping back, his sense of divine purpose reignited his commitment. His unwavering faith and the clarity of his mission became his driving forces, enabling him to endure criticism, threats, and the exhaustion that came from years of relentless campaigning.

However, Wilberforce's resolve never wavered. His purpose-driven life led to the eventual passage of the Slave Trade Act of 1807, which abolished the British slave trade. His work did not stop there, as he continued to fight for the emancipation of all slaves in the British colonies, a goal that was realized with the Slavery Abolition Act of 1833, just three days before his death.

Wilberforce's life is a testament to the power of purpose in driving progress. His unwavering commitment to justice and equality, fueled by his faith, led to one of the most significant social reforms in history.

His story reminds us that when we align our lives with a higher purpose, we can achieve progress that impacts not only our lives but also the world around us.

Purpose is not just a lofty ideal; it is a practical compass that guides our daily actions and decisions. Whether you are facing adversity, navigating career paths, or building relationships, let your purpose be your guide. Reflect deeply on what drives you, align your actions with this calling, and watch as it transforms not only your life but the lives of those around you. As you pursue your purpose, remember that it is in the alignment of our actions with our deepest values that we find true fulfillment and make our most significant impact on the world.

Reflecting on my time in the prison camp, I now see how purpose acted as a guiding compass, steering me through some of the darkest and most challenging moments of my life. In the beginning, I felt like a ship lost at sea, with no sense of direction or hope. The isolation and monotony of the camp environment threatened to swallow me in despair. Yet, it was through embracing small acts of kindness, moments of shared humanity, and the willingness to serve others, that I began to rediscover a sense of purpose.

This renewed purpose didn't come all at once. It was a gradual realization that my life still had meaning, even if the context had changed. By engaging with others, listening to their stories, and offering a word of hope, I found that my purpose had not been stripped away; it had merely transformed. No longer tied to a pulpit or a congregation, my purpose was about being a light in the darkness, a source of encouragement and faith in a place where both were in short supply.

These experiences in the camp not only solidified my understanding of purpose but also reshaped my outlook on life. Purpose is not confined to the walls of a church or defined by the roles we assume in society. Instead, it is about how we live out our values and beliefs, regardless of where we find ourselves. My time in the camp taught me that purpose is not static; it adapts and grows with us, acting as a compass that points us toward actions that align with our deepest convictions.

Even today, the lessons I learned about purpose continue to shape my life. They remind me that every interaction, no matter how small, carries the potential to impact another person profoundly. They encourage me to live with intention, ensuring that my words and actions reflect the values I hold dear. Purpose is not just about achieving great things but about remaining faithful in the small, everyday tasks that God places before us. It is in these seemingly insignificant moments that our true purpose is often revealed.

As I move forward, I carry with me the understanding that purpose is the compass guiding my journey. It provides direction, strength, and resilience, allowing me to navigate life's challenges with confidence and grace. By staying true to this guiding compass, I know that I am not only fulfilling my God-given calling but also inspiring others to discover and embrace their own sense of purpose. In this way, we continue to progress, growing stronger in faith and more committed to living lives of meaning and impact.

CHAPTER 5

JOY IS A CHOICE NOT A CONDITION

Joy is a choice we make, regardless of our circumstances. It is a profound inner happiness that comes from a deep relationship with God, rather than from external conditions. During my time in the prison camp, I learned to find joy even in the most challenging situations.

The prison camp was a place designed to strip away joy and hope. The daily routine was monotonous, and the environment often unwelcoming. Yet, it was within this unlikely setting that I discovered the true essence of joy. It wasn't dependent on my surroundings but rather on my relationship with God and my perspective on life.

One of the first lessons I learned about joy came from an unexpected source. An older camper, who had been there for many years, seemed to carry a perpetual smile on his face. Despite the conditions, he found reasons to be joyful every day. One day, I asked him how he managed to stay so positive. He replied, "Joy does not simply happen to us. We have to choose joy and keep choosing it every day." This resonated deeply with me and became a guiding principle.

Initially, I found it incredibly difficult to accept the advice of choosing joy. It felt almost naïve, as if joy was a luxury that could only be afforded by those without real problems. I wrestled with this concept in the quiet moments of the day, when the weight of my situation would press down on me like a heavy blanket. There was a particular day that stands out in my memory when everything seemed bleak. The routine of the camp felt stifling, the air seemed colder, and hope felt like a distant, unreachable shore.

That day, I remember standing in the yard, my thoughts circling around the uncertainties of my future, my family, and the life I once had. As I stood there, a fellow inmate, someone I had hardly spoken to before, came up and made a joke about the worn-out condition of our prison uniforms. It was such a simple, seemingly insignificant comment, but it was enough to break through my dark thoughts. We both laughed, a genuine, hearty laugh that felt like the first deep breath after holding it in for too long.

In that brief moment, the cloud of despair lifted, and I felt a lightness I hadn't experienced in weeks. I realized then that joy wasn't about the absence of trouble; it was about finding moments of light in the midst of darkness. I began to understand that joy is not just a reaction to external circumstances but a deliberate choice. That laugh, shared with a stranger in a place where joy seemed impossible, taught me that I could choose to look for joy, even in the smallest of things.

Another instance that reinforced this choice was during a late afternoon when the sun was setting. I remember looking out at the horizon, the sky ablaze with hues of orange and pink, and feeling an overwhelming sense of peace. For a few moments, I allowed myself to simply be present, to appreciate the beauty of the sunset, and to feel gratitude for the gift of that day. It wasn't a grand event, just a sunset, but it reminded me that joy could be found in the simplicity of appreciating what was still good, even in a challenging environment.

These experiences gradually reshaped my understanding of joy. I began to see it as a quiet, resilient force—one that could be nurtured and grown, even in the harshest of conditions. It was like a plant growing in a crack of concrete, finding a way to flourish where it seemed impossible. The more I chose to acknowledge and embrace these small joys, the more they seemed to appear, transforming my perspective and lightening my spirit, even if only for a few moments at a time.

Though scripture had always guided me, it seemed distant and irrelevant within the prison camp's confines. Yet, the more I pondered it, the clearer it became that even in this place, I was still God's handiwork (Ephesians 2:10). My circumstances had changed, but my purpose had not.

Finding joy in the small things became my daily practice. Whether it was a simple sunrise over the camp, a kind word from a fellow camper, or the quiet moments of prayer and reflection, I learned to appreciate and find joy in these fleeting moments. It was in these small acts of grace that I felt the presence of God most profoundly.

One particular incident stands out. It was a cold winter morning, and we were all bundled up in our heavy coats, waiting for the Saturday breakfast to be completed. Winters in northeastern Pennsylvania were brutal. The sky was usually overcast, casting a dreary, gray pall over the camp. Nature rarely offered anything of note during this season, and the cold seemed to seep into our bones. As I stood there, I noticed a small bird perched on the roof. Despite the cold and the dreariness of the day, the bird began to sing. Its melody was clear and sweet, cutting through the cold air like a beacon of hope. In that moment, I felt an overwhelming sense of joy. It was a reminder that even in the bleakest of circumstances, beauty and joy could still be found. If this little bird could find something to sing about, why couldn't I?

As I continued to make the conscious decision to seek out joy, I noticed a profound emotional transformation taking place within me. Initially, choosing joy felt like a small act of defiance against the overwhelming negativity that seemed to pervade every corner of the camp. However, the more I chose joy, the more it became a powerful antidote to the despair that had once felt all-consuming.

I began to feel lighter, not in a way that made me forget my circumstances, but in a way that allowed me to carry them differently. The emotional burden of worry and uncertainty started to lift, replaced by a sense of resilience. I found that I could face each day with a newfound strength, bolstered by the joy I had decided to embrace. It was as if joy had become a shield, protecting my heart from the sharp edges of fear and doubt.

This shift was not just internal; it manifested in how I interacted with others. Where I once felt trapped, hemmed in by my own thoughts and the constraints of the camp, I began to experience moments of true freedom. The freedom came not from a change in my physical surroundings but from a change within myself. By choosing joy, I reclaimed a part of myself that had been lost to the darkness of my situation. I realized that while I couldn't control everything around me, I could control my response to it. This realization was liberating.

Interestingly, my choice to embrace joy had a ripple effect on those around me. In conversations with other campers, I found myself sharing words of encouragement, offering a listening ear, or simply bringing a lighter, more hopeful presence into the room. These actions, though small, started to change the atmosphere. I noticed that others, too, began to seek out moments of joy, whether it was through shared stories, reminiscing about better times, or engaging in friendly banter. The camp, a place known for its heavy mood and unhappy realities, occasionally echoed with laughter and shared smiles. It all started because someone found joy in their circumstance and shared it with me.

One particular instance stands out. During one of our group meetings, I shared the experience of finding joy in the simple act of watching the sunset. To my surprise, a few others mentioned that they had also started paying attention to the sunsets, finding a strange sense of peace in those moments. It was a small change, but significant. It showed me that joy was not just a personal endeavor but a communal experience. The camp became a haven for Canadian Geese! Although we were constantly told not to feed them, no one paid attention. Dozens of geese would gather, feasting on leftovers from the dining hall—especially the bread! But the real joy came in Spring, when they nested behind the unit and we could watch the baby geese trailing after their mothers. These small, simple moments brought unexpected joy and helped the time pass more easily. By choosing joy, we had opened a door for others to step through as well.

The impact of these communal activities extended far beyond the confines of each Bible study session or worship service. There were noticeable changes in the overall atmosphere of the prison camp, marked by a shift in how the inmates interacted with each other. Joy, as it turned out, was contagious. Its presence softened the rough edges that confinement and hardship had sharpened.

One particular instance stands out vividly in my memory. It was a humid summer evening, and tensions in the camp had been unusually high due to a recent altercation between two inmates over a trivial matter. The atmosphere was thick with frustration and anxiety. That evening, during our regular Bible study, one of the inmates—who had been a part of the conflict—shared a deeply personal testimony. He spoke about his struggles with anger and how his faith had helped him to find peace amidst turmoil. His honesty and vulnerability had a profound effect on everyone present.

As he spoke, the room grew quiet. The tension that had been so palpable earlier seemed to dissipate, replaced by a collective sense of empathy and understanding. When he finished, we prayed together, not just for him, but for peace and unity within our community. There was a palpable shift in the room. It was as if a burden had been lifted from all of us.

In the days following that Bible study session, I observed a noticeable difference in the camp. Conversations were more amicable, smiles more frequent, and the usual petty arguments seemed to lessen. I am not implying that the camp transformed into a utopia. However, it became more bearable and unified as we each moved past our personal frustrations and acknowledged that life was still worth living—and worth living well—despite being separated from our families. In many ways, we had no choice but to forge a sense of community if we were going to survive. It was a powerful reminder that joy and peace, when shared communally, could ripple outward, transforming not just individual hearts but the broader environment as well.

Another time, during a group prayer session, a sense of joy so profound filled the room that it left everyone visibly moved. Some campers who rarely spoke up shared spontaneous words of gratitude. One camper mentioned how the joy he felt in that moment made him feel free, even within the confines of the prison walls. These moments became a source of strength for us all, a reminder that even in the midst of hardship, joy could break through, providing light and hope. Gratitude, as it turns out, is a catalyst for joy. Whenever we focused on the things we were thankful for, the mood and atmosphere around us noticeably shifted.

These experiences reinforced my belief that collective joy is a powerful force for positive change. They demonstrated that the simple act of coming together in faith could create a supportive, uplifting environment that fostered healing and growth. It wasn't just about finding joy for ourselves; it was about building a community where joy could flourish, making our time in the camp not just bearable but meaningful. I wish I could tell you these were permanent changes but they were usually short-lived. However, I had determined to keep pursuing joy no matter what happened.

Through these communal experiences, I learned that joy thrives best when it is shared. Each Bible study, prayer meeting, or worship service became a catalyst for spreading joy, creating a sense of solidarity among us. In those moments, we weren't just inmates passing time; we were a community, united by faith and joy, experiencing a sense of freedom and purpose that transcended our circumstances.

This emotional transformation didn't mean that every day was easy or that I never faced moments of deep sadness. But it did mean that I had discovered a source of strength that could sustain me. Joy became a thread that wove through my days, connecting the moments and holding me together when life seemed to be falling apart. It wasn't just about feeling happy; it was about living in a way that honored the life God had given me, no matter the circumstances.

The book of James offers wisdom for moments like these: *"Consider it pure joy, my brothers and sisters, whenever you face trials of many kinds, because you know that the testing of your faith produces perseverance"* (James 1:2-3). This scripture became a reminder that my trials were opportunities to grow in faith and perseverance. The hardships of the camp were refining me, teaching me to rely more on God's strength and less on my own.

As the days turned into weeks and the weeks into months, I began to understand that joy was not just an emotion but a state of being. It was about finding contentment and peace in the present moment, regardless of the external circumstances. This understanding transformed my experience in the prison camp. I no longer saw it as a place of punishment (though it was) but as an opportunity to grow closer to God and to find joy in His presence.

The Apostle Paul, in his letter to the Philippians, writes, *"Rejoice in the Lord always. I will say it again: Rejoice!"* (Philippians 4:4). This command to rejoice always, regardless of circumstances, was a challenge. It reminded me that my joy was rooted in my relationship with God, which was unchanging and eternal, even when everything else seemed uncertain.

The sense of community that developed was a testament to the power of purpose in driving progress even in the most challenging circumstances.

Nehemiah, when addressing the people of Israel, reminded them, *"Do not grieve, for the joy of the Lord is your strength"* (Nehemiah 8:10). This verse became a lifeline during the toughest times. It reminded me that my strength came from the joy of the Lord, a joy that transcended my immediate situation. This divine joy was a wellspring of strength, enabling me to endure and even thrive in the face of adversity.

"The most wasted of all days is one without laughter," said E.E. Cummings.

Even during the most difficult days, signs of joy could be found. It was a reminder that joy is not a luxury but a necessity for our well-being.

Joseph Campbell once said, "Find a place inside where there's joy, and the joy will burn out the pain." His words captured the essence of how powerful joy can be. By turning inward and embracing joy, I found that it had the strength to diminish the weight of the pain and struggles I was facing.

As Henri Nouwen once reflected, "Joy does not simply happen to us. We have to choose joy and keep choosing it every day." His words became a guiding principle, emphasizing that joy isn't passive—it's an active, daily choice to seek out life's blessings.

Choosing Joy Intentionally

Choosing joy intentionally, especially in undesirable situations, is a deliberate act of faith and trust in God. It means looking beyond our immediate circumstances and finding reasons to be thankful. This perspective shift can be challenging, but it is crucial for maintaining our spiritual and emotional well-being.

In his letter to the Thessalonians, the apostle Paul encourages, *"Rejoice always, pray continually, give thanks in all circumstances; for this is God's will for you in Christ Jesus"* (1 Thessalonians 5:16-18). This passage beautifully weaves together joy, prayer, and gratitude, showing how these practices are deeply intertwined. When we commit to constant prayer and gratitude, we naturally cultivate a sense of joy, even when faced with challenging circumstances.

Gratitude plays a significant role in cultivating joy. When we focus on what we are thankful for, our perspective shifts from what we lack to what we have. This shift can transform our outlook and help us find joy in the midst of trials. Keeping a gratitude journal or simply taking a moment each day to list things you are thankful for can significantly impact your sense of joy.

As I continued to explore the power of joy in my life, I found it fascinating how modern psychological research aligns with ancient biblical wisdom. Psychological studies have increasingly highlighted the profound impact that practicing gratitude and joy can have on our mental and emotional well-being. Research indicates that regularly practicing gratitude can alter brain chemistry, enhancing neurotransmitter function and increasing levels of dopamine and serotonin, which are known to boost mood and overall mental health.

One study from the Greater Good Science Center at the University of California, Berkeley, found that individuals who kept a daily gratitude journal reported higher levels of optimism, better sleep, and fewer health problems compared to those who did not. Another study published in The Journal of Positive Psychology showed that people who consciously focused on moments of joy and gratitude experienced a significant increase in happiness and life satisfaction. These findings illustrate that joy and gratitude are not just abstract concepts; they are concrete practices that can bring about real, positive changes in our lives.

This scientific insight aligns profoundly with biblical wisdom. Psalm 16:11 reminds us, "You make known to me the path of life; in your presence there is fullness of joy; at your right hand are pleasures forevermore." This verse underscores that true joy is discovered in God's presence and reveals the strong link between our spiritual practices and emotional health. When we focus on gratitude and joy, we draw nearer to God's presence, finding a peace and fulfillment that transcends any situation we face.

Integrating these insights from psychology with my own spiritual journey reinforced the idea that joy is both a divine gift and a practical habit that can be cultivated. Understanding that choosing joy and practicing gratitude can have tangible benefits provided me with additional motivation to incorporate these practices into my daily routine. It became clear that the joy I experienced was not just an emotional lift but a holistic practice that engaged my spirit, mind, and body.

I began to see moments of joy not only as spiritual victories but as part of a comprehensive approach to well-being. This holistic view helped me to appreciate the interconnectedness of faith and science. It showed me that God's design for joy and gratitude is intricately woven into the very fabric of our being. By embracing joy, I was participating in a practice that had been validated both by my faith and by scientific inquiry. This dual validation made the pursuit of joy feel even more purposeful, encouraging me to seek out joy not just for its spiritual rewards but also for its practical, life-enhancing benefits.

In times when I struggled to find joy, these insights reminded me that joy was accessible. It wasn't dependent on changing my circumstances; it was about changing my perspective. By practicing gratitude, whether through prayer, reflection, or writing in a journal, I could tap into the joy that God had already made available to me. This understanding gave me a sense of agency and empowerment, knowing that joy was within my reach, regardless of where I found myself.

Paul and Silas Through Fresh Eyes

As I sought to embrace joy, one biblical story repeatedly surfaced, offering both comfort and inspiration: the account of Paul and Silas singing hymns in prison, found in Acts 16:25. Despite being unjustly imprisoned, beaten, and confined to the innermost cell with their feet shackled, these two men chose to lift their voices in praise. In the darkness of night, amidst the despair and filth of a Roman prison, Paul and Silas made the remarkable decision to worship God.

Reflecting on their story, I was struck by the audacity of their joy. They could have easily succumbed to despair, anger, or fear. Instead, they chose to lift their voices in praise, transforming a place of punishment into a sanctuary of worship. This act of defiant joy didn't just lift their spirits; it affected all those around them. The other prisoners listened, and eventually, an earthquake shook the foundations of the prison, leading to their miraculous release.

Paul and Silas's response became a model for me. Their story demonstrated that joy is not merely a response to good circumstances but a powerful act of worship that can be chosen even when circumstances are bleak. I often found myself thinking of them on the days when my own situation felt most unbearable. There was one particular day when everything seemed to go wrong. The weight of uncertainty about my future, the monotony of camp life, and the strain of being away from my family pressed heavily on me. I felt a deep sense of isolation, as if I were locked in a cell of my own making.

In that moment of despair, the image of Paul and Silas came to my mind. I remembered how their voices, raised in praise, had echoed through the darkness of their confinement. Inspired by their example, I made a decision to follow suit. I began to sing, softly at first, hymns that I had learned as a child, songs that had always brought me comfort. The words felt like a balm to my soul, soothing the wounds inflicted by fear and worry. As I sang, I felt the walls of my own prison begin to tremble—not physically, but emotionally. The chains of despair loosened, and a sense of peace settled over me.

That day, I learned firsthand the power of praise. By choosing to focus on God's goodness rather than my circumstances, I found a wellspring of joy that could not be diminished by my surroundings. Singing became a regular practice, a way to connect with God and lift my spirit, even when everything else seemed bleak. I realized that joy was not only a source of strength but also a declaration of faith. It was a way of saying, "I trust You, God, even in this."

Chapter 5: Joy Is a Choice Not a Condition

Seeing joy as a form of worship fundamentally transformed my spiritual life, deepening my relationship with God in ways I hadn't previously imagined. Instead of viewing joy as merely a fleeting emotion or a response to favorable circumstances, I began to understand it as a deliberate expression of faith and devotion. This shift in perspective allowed me to approach every day, no matter how mundane or challenging, as an opportunity to worship and honor God through my choices and attitude.

Seeing joy as a form of worship fundamentally transformed my spiritual life, deepening my relationship with God in ways I hadn't previously imagined. Instead of viewing joy as merely a fleeting emotion or a response to favorable circumstances, I began to understand it as a deliberate expression of faith and devotion. This shift in perspective allowed me to approach every day, no matter how mundane or challenging, as an opportunity to worship and honor God through my choices and attitude.

Connecting the Mundane with the Divine

This new perspective transformed how I viewed everyday activities. No longer did I see them as mere obligations or chores; instead, they became sacred opportunities to honor God. Whether it was cooking a meal, interacting with others, or even taking a walk outside, each action held the potential to be a joyful celebration of God's grace. This mindset made my day-to-day experiences richer and more meaningful, as I actively looked for God's hand in the smallest details of life. By finding joy in the ordinary, I was able to elevate those moments, turning them into offerings of praise.

Although I worked in the Power House, I often found myself drawn to a group of older campers who spent their time folding silverware and wrapping it in napkins. The discussions they had while working were lively and full of energy. A few times each week, I'd stop by to join in, eagerly diving into the topic of the day. Around that table, we experienced a full range of emotions—joy, frustration, and even moments of silence depending on the subject. Yet, most days, as the cleanup began, someone would inevitably toss in a lighthearted comment, bringing smiles and laughter to the room.

Peace and Fulfillment through Joy as Worship

Understanding joy as an act of worship brought a profound sense of peace and fulfillment regardless of my circumstances. It reminded me that my joy was rooted in God's unchanging character, not in the temporary situations of life. This realization allowed me to remain anchored even when external conditions were unstable or challenging. Choosing joy became a way to align my heart with God's promises, reinforcing my trust in His plan. In embracing joy as worship, I found that my life was not only more peaceful but also filled with a deeper sense of purpose. Every moment became an opportunity to reflect God's love and faithfulness to those around me.

This shift in understanding joy as worship not only enriched my own spiritual journey but also inspired others to seek a similar connection with God. By embodying joy in all situations, I became a living testimony of God's faithfulness, encouraging those around me to also find joy in their lives. This shared sense of joy fostered a community of faith that thrived on mutual encouragement and the shared goal of glorifying God through our everyday actions. I observed guys receive bad news, and yet, they forced themselves to find some measure of joy. These actions were not merely a coping mechanism—they were essential, because the alternative was sinking into despair, and there was already more than enough of that to go around. Finding joy became a conscious choice for survival.

Joy and Gratitude in Practice

In the prison camp, I practiced this intentional choice of joy and gratitude. Every day, I made it a point to find something to be thankful for, no matter how small. Some days, it was the warmth of the sun on my face; other days, it was a kind word from a fellow camper. By focusing on these moments of gratitude, I found it easier to maintain a sense of joy.

One particularly challenging period was during the winter when snow and wind limited our activities. We were often stuck inside the Unit, and the thought of going outside was unappealing. The days were long, and it was easy to feel trapped and hopeless. Yet, even in these conditions, I found ways to cultivate joy. I organized small gatherings where we would share stories, sing hymns, and encourage each other. These moments of fellowship were a light in the darkness, a reminder that joy could still be found even in the most trying times.

In life, every person needs to discover what spiritual disciplines draw them closer to God. I have known that singing old hymns and spirituals, as well as prayer, draw me close to God when I feel distant. When joy ebbs, this is the time to return to those spiritual disciplines that draw you close to God. The maintenance of joy in difficult situations is directly related to my closeness and connection with God. The more I feel distanced from God, the less joy I will have.

This is why I liked working in the Power House because I was by myself and could sing, pray, cry, and scream, and no one would know. In that Power House, and the irony of the name is not lost on me, I always left feeling stronger.

Personal Reflection and Growth

The journey of discovering joy in the prison camp was not just about finding moments of happiness. It was about a deeper, more profound sense of contentment and peace that came from trusting in God's plan. The scriptures provided guidance and strength during this time. James 1:2-3 reminded me that trials and challenges were opportunities for growth and perseverance. Philippians 4:4 encouraged me to rejoice always, regardless of the situation. Nehemiah 8:10 reinforced that the joy of the Lord was my strength, giving me the resilience to face each day with hope and positivity.

Reflecting on my time in the prison camp, I realize that the decision to choose joy, even in the darkest of circumstances, has fundamentally shaped my outlook on life. This choice wasn't merely about surviving each day; it was about transforming my perspective and my heart. The decision to find joy amidst adversity became a guiding principle that I've carried with me into life after the camp.

Since my release, I've faced numerous challenges—transitions back into everyday life, societal stigma, and personal setbacks. However, the lessons learned about joy in those constrained spaces have given me a resilience I never knew I had. Now, when faced with difficulties, I remind myself of those moments in the camp when joy was a conscious, deliberate choice. I recall how joy didn't necessarily change my situation, but it changed how I experienced it. This mindset has helped me to approach hardships with a sense of peace and hope that transcends my circumstances.

Choosing joy taught me that it is not just a fleeting emotion dependent on external conditions, but a state of mind and heart that we cultivate through faith and intention. This realization has been liberating. In my post-camp life, I've learned to see challenges as opportunities to practice joy, knowing that joy can coexist with pain and uncertainty. It has become a source of strength, helping me to remain hopeful and optimistic, even when life seems to be unraveling.

One of the most profound impacts of choosing joy has been the ability to inspire and uplift others. I've found that by embodying joy, I can influence the atmosphere around me, just as we did in the prison camp. Whether it's in my family, my ministry, or my community, I've seen how maintaining a joyful outlook encourages others to do the same. It opens doors for deeper connections and meaningful conversations, often leading to shared moments of joy that bring us closer together.

Moreover, choosing joy has deepened my spiritual walk. It's drawn me closer to God, reminding me of His presence in every situation. Joy has become a form of worship, a daily act of trust in God's plan and goodness. This perspective has transformed my prayers and my daily interactions, turning even the mundane into a testament of faith.

The decision to embrace joy during those difficult days in the camp has not only shaped how I handle adversity but has also enriched my understanding of what it means to live fully. It's given me a sense of purpose, knowing that my journey can serve as a beacon of hope for others. My experience has proven that joy is not only attainable but also sustainable, even in the most unlikely environments. It's a reminder that joy can thrive where we least expect it, as long as we are intentional in seeking it. This realization continues to motivate me to face life's inevitable challenges with a resilient and hopeful mindset, assured that joy is always within reach.

Strategies for Harnessing Joy

Harnessing joy, especially in challenging circumstances, is not a passive act but a deliberate choice. Here are practical strategies to cultivate joy in your daily life, regardless of the situation you find yourself in:

1. **Practice Gratitude Daily:** Gratitude is a powerful tool for cultivating joy. By focusing on what you are thankful for, you

shift your perspective from what is lacking to what is abundant. Start each day by listing three things you are grateful for, no matter how small they may seem. This practice trains your mind to look for the positives in every situation.

2. **Engage in Prayer and Meditation:** Regular prayer and meditation help center your mind and spirit, drawing you closer to God. These practices offer a space to reflect on God's goodness, seek His presence, and find peace amidst chaos. Set aside time each day to pray or meditate, focusing on scriptures that remind you of God's promises and the joy found in His presence.

3. **Find Joy in Small Moments:** Joy is often found in the simple, everyday moments—a sunrise, a kind word, or a favorite hymn. Train yourself to notice and savor these small joys. Take a moment to pause, breathe deeply, and appreciate these instances of grace. They are reminders of God's love and presence, even in difficult times.

4. **Build a Supportive Community:** Joy is contagious. Surround yourself with people who uplift and encourage you. Engage in activities that foster connection, such as group prayers, Bible studies, or fellowship gatherings. Sharing your joys and burdens with others creates a sense of belonging and support, making it easier to find joy even in adversity.

5. **Focus on Serving Others:** Acts of service can bring immense joy. Helping others shifts the focus away from your own problems and allows you to experience the fulfillment that comes from making a positive impact. Look for opportunities to serve, whether it's volunteering, offering a listening ear, or simply being kind to those around you.

6. **Cultivate a Mindset of Rejoicing:** Make rejoicing a habit, not just a reaction to good news. The Apostle Paul's exhortation to "rejoice in the Lord always" (Philippians 4:4) is a call to make joy a constant part of your spiritual prac-

tice. Regularly remind yourself of God's faithfulness and the blessings you have received. Rejoice not because everything is perfect, but because God is present.
7. **Embrace Hope and Trust in God's Plan:** Joy is rooted in hope. Trust that God has a plan for your life, even when circumstances are difficult. Remind yourself of His faithfulness in the past and His promises for the future. This hope will sustain you and keep your joy alive, regardless of what you face.
8. **Express Joy Through Creativity:** Whether it's singing, writing, painting, or any other form of creative expression, these activities can be powerful outlets for joy. Use your talents to express your gratitude and joy. These creative acts not only bring personal fulfillment but also inspire joy in others.

By incorporating these strategies into your daily life, you can cultivate a sense of joy that transcends circumstances. Joy, when harnessed, becomes a source of strength, resilience, and inspiration, allowing you to navigate life's challenges with grace and confidence. Remember, joy is a choice you make every day, a commitment to see the world through the lens of God's love and presence.

Conviction Checkpoints
- **Self-Examination Question:** Reflect on a time when you found joy in a challenging situation. How did this experience shape your perspective on joy? Identify ways you can choose joy in your daily life.
- **Actionable Step:** Make a list of small things that bring you joy. Incorporate these into your daily routine and take time to appreciate them, fostering a habit of choosing joy.

- **Conviction Affirmation:** I am convicted that joy is a choice, not a condition. I will find joy in the small moments and trust in God's presence, no matter my circumstances.
- **Prayer/Meditation Focus:** Pray for the ability to find joy in every situation. Ask God to help you see the blessings and beauty around you, even in difficult times.

Profile in Conviction

Dietrich Bonhoeffer

Dietrich Bonhoeffer was a German pastor and theologian who stood firm in his convictions during one of the darkest times in history—Nazi Germany. Bonhoeffer was an outspoken critic of Adolf Hitler and the Nazi regime, particularly its policies toward Jews and its efforts to control the German churches.

Bonhoeffer's conviction was rooted in his deep Christian faith and his belief that it was his duty to oppose evil in all its forms. Despite the immense pressure to conform, he helped found the Confessing Church, a movement that stood against the Nazi takeover of the Protestant churches. He also became involved in a plot to assassinate Hitler, believing that such an act was necessary to stop the greater evil.

Bonhoeffer's commitment to his convictions ultimately led to his imprisonment and execution. While in prison, he continued to write and minister to his fellow prisoners, offering spiritual support and maintaining his belief in God's justice and mercy. His book, *The Cost of Discipleship*, is a powerful reflection on what it means to follow Christ, especially in times of great moral crisis.

One of Bonhoeffer's most famous quotes is, "Silence in the face of evil is itself evil: God will not hold us guiltless. Not to speak is to speak. Not to act is to act." This statement encapsulates his belief that conviction must be accompanied by action, even at great personal cost.

Dietrich Bonhoeffer's life and death serve as a powerful reminder that conviction often requires courage, sacrifice, and an unwavering commitment to what is right, regardless of the consequences. His legacy continues to inspire those who face moral and ethical challenges, demonstrating the profound impact of standing firm in one's beliefs.

As I reflect on my journey, both during my time in the prison camp and in the life that has unfolded since, one truth has become abundantly clear: joy is not a mere byproduct of favorable circumstances. It is a powerful, intentional choice that we make every day. Joy transcends our external situations and touches the very core of our being, anchoring us in something greater than ourselves. It is a testament to our faith and resilience, a declaration that, no matter what happens, our spirit cannot be crushed.

The experiences and insights shared in this chapter illustrate that joy is not an abstract concept reserved for the spiritually elite. It is practical and accessible, available to anyone willing to embrace it. Whether through the beauty of simple moments, the strength of communal support, or the transformative power of gratitude, joy is a force that can reshape our lives and the lives of those around us. It is a light that shines brightest in the darkness, offering hope where there seems to be none.

CHAPTER 6
TRUSTING GOD IS ESSENTIAL

Trusting God is a fundamental aspect of faith, especially when faced with uncertainty and hardship. While incarcerated, learning to trust God became an essential part of my spiritual journey. It was a lesson that transformed my outlook on life and deepened my relationship with Him.

During my time in the prison camp, trusting God was not just a theological concept; it became a lifeline. This lifeline was essential during the countless nights when anxiety threatened to overwhelm me. I learned that trust isn't the absence of fear, but the choice to rely on God amidst the fear. This choice to trust led to unexpected peace, even in the harsh environment of the camp. By consciously making this decision each day, I found myself feeling more resilient and less burdened by the weight of my circumstances. I remember one particular day when fear and uncertainty threatened to overwhelm me. The weight of my situation felt unbearable. As I sat alone in my bunk, thoughts of despair circled my mind—doubts about my future, worries about my family, and the seemingly endless days stretched out before me. The isolation was suffocating, and the sense of being cut off from the outside world intensified my fear.

In those moments of deep anxiety, I turned to prayer, seeking solace and guidance. With my Bible in hand, I flipped to passages that spoke of God's faithfulness and unfailing love. Verses like Psalm 23, *"Even though I walk through the darkest valley, I will fear no evil, for you are with me,"* became a source of comfort. I clung to the promise that God was with me, even in that bleak and isolated place. As I meditated on these words, a sense of peace gradually began to wash over me. It wasn't an immediate change, but a gentle shift—like a small light piercing through the darkness.

There was also a time during my legal battles when the outcome was uncertain. The fear of losing everything I had worked for, the possibility of being separated from my loved ones, and the thought of enduring further hardship were all-consuming. I felt like I was standing on the edge of a precipice, with no clear path forward. Yet, in those moments, I made a conscious decision to surrender my fears to God. I chose to trust that His plan for me was greater than what I could see at that moment. This act of surrender didn't come easily; it required letting go of my desire for control and embracing faith over fear.

As I placed my trust in God, I felt a profound sense of relief. The heavy burden of anxiety lifted, replaced by a quiet assurance that no matter the outcome, I was not alone. God's presence reassured me, providing a sense of clarity and purpose that I couldn't find on my own. These experiences taught me that trust is not just a feeling but a deliberate choice to rely on God, even when circumstances seem insurmountable.

Choosing to Trust God

Through these challenging times, I realized that trusting God does not mean that fear and doubt disappear entirely. Instead, it means choosing to turn to God in those moments of weakness and allowing His peace to guard my heart and mind.

It's a trust that is built through daily, intentional acts of faith, through prayer, reflection, and the willingness to believe that God's love and plan for me are unchanging, even in the face of adversity.

The prison camp was a place filled with uncertainty. Although there were daily routines, plans could shift in an instant due to some larger responsibility, often a lockdown in the penitentiary. During those moments, it was easy to feel a sense of powerlessness. However, it was in this environment that I learned to surrender my fears and anxieties to God and trust in His plan.

Proverbs 3:5-6 offers timeless wisdom: *"Trust in the Lord with all your heart and lean not on your own understanding; in all your ways submit to Him, and He will make your paths straight."* This verse became my foundation, a constant reminder to place my trust in God, rather than relying solely on my own limited perspective.

My first night at the camp was a profound reminder of trusting in God's care. One of the guys casually remarked, "Hey man, we saw your wife pulled over on the side of the road for a long time. Give me her number, and when I call home tonight, I'll have my wife call her so she knows you're okay." I had no idea this had happened because I was busy being processed. Yet, these guys, who worked in the landscape department, were looking out for her well-being. I knew she had struggled to leave after I self-surrendered, but beyond that, I was in the dark. Even though we were apart, God was still watching over us, orchestrating care in ways I couldn't have anticipated.

"Never be afraid to trust an unknown future to a known God." - CORRIE TEN BOOM

While I might not know what the future held, I could trust the One who holds the future. It encouraged me to place my faith in God's sovereignty and goodness, even when I couldn't see the bigger picture.

As I began to trust God more deeply, I noticed a significant shift in my perspective. I had always been so self-reliant, and being in a place where I no longer had control left me feeling inadequate. But over time, rather than dwelling on the uncertainties and challenges, I started to recognize the opportunities for growth and transformation. Trusting God allowed me to let go of my need for control and embrace the possibility that even in difficult circumstances, there was room for something greater to emerge.

The Apostle Paul writes in Philippians: *"Do not be anxious about anything, but in every situation, by prayer and petition, with thanksgiving, present your requests to God. And the peace of God, which transcends all understanding, will guard your hearts and your minds in Christ Jesus"* (Philippians 4:6-7). By trusting God and presenting my concerns to Him, I could experience His peace, even in the midst of uncertainty.

Trusting God even when we don't understand what is happening can be one of the most challenging aspects of faith. There were many times in the camp when the reasons for certain events were beyond my comprehension. I had to learn to trust God in those moments, believing that He had a greater plan at work, even if it was not immediately clear to me. The prophet Isaiah reminds us: *"For my thoughts are not your thoughts, neither are your ways my ways,"* declares the Lord. *"As the heavens are higher than the earth, so are my ways higher than your ways and my thoughts than your thoughts"* (Isaiah 55:8-9). God's wisdom and understanding far surpasses mine, and I must trust His greater plan.

Chapter 6: Trusting God Is Essential

One particular incident stands out as a turning point in my journey of trust. Trust inside a confined area like a prison camp is nearly non-existent. Prison breeds distrust on every level. Even people with whom you have a relationship, you still don't know if they will truly have your back. Whenever inspection time came, you never knew if someone would use your space to hide contraband so they would not be charged with an additional offense. This happened to me. The guards did a sweep, and someone planted their phone in my bunk area.

Because of how I had conducted myself during my time at the camp, the guards knew right away that the phone couldn't possibly be mine. Rather than responding with the typical knee-jerk reaction of throwing me into the SHU (Special Housing Unit) for solitary confinement, they took the time to investigate. They opened the phone and discovered that the person responsible hadn't even bothered to erase its contents. This made it clear that the phone had been planted in my bunk area to frame me. At the time, though, I was completely unaware of what was going on behind the scenes. All I knew was that a phone had been found—a serious offense in the camp. Ironically, I spent that entire day thinking to myself, "I'm so relieved I don't have a phone. I'd be in some real trouble." Little did I know, I was the one being suspected all along.

This situation occurred during a time when I had a rare bunkmate on the top bunk—the only time I shared my space with someone else in the entire camp. After the investigation concluded and the individuals responsible were identified, I learned that the phone had been hidden among my belongings in an attempt to shift the blame onto me. From that point on, whenever the COs called for a "shake down," I made it a point to linger by my bunk until they arrived, ensuring I wouldn't be framed again.

God will protect you even when you don't even know the plots that are against you. This experience reinforced the importance of trusting God and reminded me that He is always in control, even when circumstances seem dire.

Trusting God is a Biblical Requirement

The Bible is rich with stories of individuals who demonstrated profound trust in God, often in the face of overwhelming odds. These stories have been a source of inspiration for me, reminding me that trust in God can lead to extraordinary outcomes, even when the path is unclear.

Take Abraham, for instance. In Genesis 12, God called Abraham to leave his homeland, his family, and everything he knew, to go to a land that God would show him. Abraham had no detailed map or clear destination; he only had God's promise. Despite the uncertainties, Abraham trusted God and set out on this journey. His faith was not in a roadmap but in God's guidance. Abraham's trust in God's promise was rewarded with the establishment of a great nation, a lineage that would bless all the families of the earth. Reflecting on Abraham's faith challenges me to trust God's plan for my life, even when the way forward seems uncertain. Abraham's journey was not without its moments of doubt. He faced famine, conflicts, and years of waiting for God's promise to be fulfilled. Yet, he continued to trust. His story resonates deeply with anyone who has ever felt the weight of waiting, reminding us that God's promises are worth holding onto, no matter how long it takes.

Shadrach, Meshach, and Abednego's story, found in Daniel 3, vividly demonstrates the power of unwavering faith. When these three Hebrew boys faced the fiery furnace, they boldly declared to King Nebuchadnezzar, *"The God we serve is able to deliver us from it... But even if he does not, we want you to know, Your Majesty, that we will not serve your gods or wor-*

ship the image of gold you have set up." This wasn't merely about seeking deliverance from the flames; it was about their deep-rooted loyalty to God, regardless of the outcome. Their refusal to bow—whether or not they were thrown into the furnace—revealed that their allegiance to God went beyond the threat of death. Their faith wasn't circumstantial; it was intrinsic to their identity and relationship with God.

Their statement, *"Even if he does not,"* wasn't a wavering doubt in God's power to save them, but rather a testament to the strength of their devotion. They were proclaiming that their obedience wasn't contingent on divine rescue. While they trusted fully in God's ability to deliver them, they recognized that His deliverance was not the basis of their loyalty. Their faith rested entirely on God's sovereignty and their commitment to serve Him regardless of the consequences. In the same way, their courage teaches us that real faith persists even when the outcomes are uncertain. It's a faith that trusts God's plan, even when that plan is beyond our understanding.

Similarly, Peter's experience walking on water (Matthew 14:22-33) underscores this lesson. When Peter saw Jesus approaching on the water, he said, *"Lord, if it's you, tell me to come to you on the water."* At Jesus' invitation, Peter stepped out of the boat into the raging sea. As long as he kept his eyes fixed on Jesus, Peter did the impossible—he walked on water. But the moment he focused on the wind and the crashing waves, fear took over, and he began to sink. Jesus, with compassion, reached out to save him, gently asking, "Why did you doubt?"

This story illustrates a profound truth about trust and faith: when we keep our focus on God, we can navigate even the stormiest of circumstances. Peter's steps on the water weren't about his ability, but about his trust in Jesus. The moment his attention shifted to the surrounding chaos, doubt crept in. Yet, even when he faltered, Jesus was right there to lift him up. This reminds me that faith isn't about never facing fear or doubt—it's about choosing to step out in trust anyway. And when we falter, God is always there, ready to catch us, showing that His faithfulness is steadfast, even when our own faith wavers.

These biblical stories are not just ancient tales; they are powerful lessons that speak directly to our everyday lives. They show that trust in God often involves stepping into the unknown, standing firm in our convictions despite the consequences, and keeping our eyes on God amid life's storms. For me, these examples serve as reminders that God's faithfulness is not dependent on our circumstances. They inspire me to trust that God is working, even when I cannot see the full picture.

Reflecting on my journey, I see parallels with these timeless accounts. Just as Abraham, the Hebrew boys, and Peter had to trust God in unimaginable circumstances, so too did I in my own trials. These stories provided not only comfort but, a model for enduring faith. These biblical accounts provide a framework for understanding that the same God who guided Abraham, delivered the Hebrew boys, and caught Peter will also guide, deliver, and support us when we place our trust in Him.

One of the ministries I adopted while inside was the "ministry of hope." In addition to my own spiritual journey, I witnessed other remarkable acts of faith among my fellow campers. Each story was a testament to the sustaining power of trust in God, providing a sense of solidarity in our shared experiences. It seemed like the camp went from no news to bad news regularly. It was a dry spell, then something bad happened. It was a rollercoaster. When campers received the inevitable bad news from the phone calls or in letters, they would make their way to me. In all honesty, I was not always in the mood to give hope as I was receiving bad news about my legal situation. Every appeal I had filed was swiftly denied, even though to this day I know there were valid issues. (But that is a topic for another book on the criminal justice system.) Guys were served divorce papers, notifications of a loved one's death, financial challenges, etc. In all of these situations, the camper found their way to me for solace and encouragement. It is true that hope is an enduring value—especially in prison.

Viktor Frankl, a Holocaust survivor, said, "Everything can be taken from a man but one thing: the last of the human freedoms—to choose one's attitude in any given set of circumstances, to choose one's own way."

Another significant lesson in trust emerged from my interactions with fellow campers. Many of them faced bleak prospects—long sentences with little hope of early release. Yet, even in the face of these realities, I witnessed extraordinary demonstrations of trust and faith in God. One camper, in particular, stood out. His trust in God's plan for his life was unshakable, and despite his circumstances, he radiated a sense of peace and joy that was almost contagious. His favorite scripture, which he quoted often, was Jeremiah 29:11: *"For I know the plans I have for you,"* declares the Lord, *"plans to prosper you and not to harm you, plans to give you hope and a future."* He repeated this passage so often—ad nauseum, some might say—but he lived it out with such conviction that it became a cornerstone of his resilience. Remarkably, his trust was rewarded. His sentence, once thought unchangeable, was reduced, and he went home much earlier than anyone had anticipated. It was a powerful reminder that trusting in God's timing, even when it seems improbable, can lead to outcomes beyond what we can imagine.

Personal Reflection and Growth

The journey of trusting God in the prison camp was transformative. It taught me that trust is not just a passive acceptance of circumstances but an active choice to rely on God's promises and character. By trusting God, I found peace and strength to face each day with hope and confidence.

Psalm 56:3-4 says, *"When I am afraid, I put my trust in you. In God, whose word I praise— in God I trust and am not afraid. What can mere mortals do to me?"* This scripture became a constant reminder that my trust in God could overcome any fear or uncertainty.

There are countless profound examples of how God "showed Himself strong" on behalf of people who, in their desperation, cried out to Him. What struck me most was witnessing individuals who weren't necessarily "sold out" Christians decide to "try God" in their most dire circumstances, and time after time, I saw Him come through in ways that were nothing short of miraculous. I personally witnessed broken relationships being healed, severe punishments being averted, sentences being reduced, and even last-minute transfers being canceled. These were undeniable moments of divine intervention that left many in awe, myself included. It was a reminder that God's power isn't confined to those who have fully surrendered to Him but is available to anyone who reaches out in faith, even in their darkest moments.

Overcoming Obstacles to Trusting God

Trusting God is a profound act of faith, but it's not always easy. Many people, including myself, have faced struggles when it comes to placing full trust in God. One of the most significant barriers to trusting God is the fear of the unknown. Life is filled with uncertainties, and it's natural to want a clear plan and tangible security. We often find comfort in knowing what's ahead, and when God asks us to step into unknown territory, it can be terrifying. This fear can paralyze us, keeping us from moving forward in faith. I remember feeling this fear acutely during my time in the prison camp. The uncertainty of my future weighed heavily on me. Would I ever get out? What would happen to my family, my ministry, and my life outside these walls? The unknown loomed large, and trusting God in those moments required a conscious effort to place my fear in His hands.

Another challenge that makes trusting God difficult is dealing with past disappointments and unanswered prayers. When we've experienced pain, betrayal, or loss, it can be hard to believe that God has good plans for us. Unanswered prayers can lead to feelings of abandonment or doubts about God's presence. These feelings can create a wall of skepticism, making it difficult to trust that God is still working for our good. I've had my share of disappointments and unanswered prayers, both during my time in prison and in other aspects of life. There were moments when I questioned God's intentions, wondering why He hadn't intervened in the ways I had hoped. It was during these times that I had to remind myself that God's ways are higher than my ways, and His thoughts are higher than my thoughts (Isaiah 55:8-9). Trusting God doesn't mean we won't face disappointment; it means believing that He is still good and that His plan is perfect, even when we can't see it.

Our natural desire for control is another significant obstacle to trusting God. We like to be in control of our lives, our circumstances, and our future. Trusting God often requires us to let go of our need to control outcomes and to surrender our plans to His will. This surrender can be incredibly challenging, especially for those of us who are used to managing every detail of our lives. I struggled with this in my own life, especially when faced with legal battles and imprisonment. I wanted to take control of the situation, to find a way out on my own terms. Yet, I learned that true trust requires surrender—releasing control and allowing God to lead, even when it feels like we're letting go of our grip on security.

Acknowledging these struggles is the first step toward overcoming them. It's okay to feel fear, doubt, or a desire for control. These are natural human emotions. However, we must not let these feelings dictate our relationship with God. Overcoming these obstacles involves constantly turning to God in prayer, which helps us build our trust. When fear and doubt arise, prayer provides a direct line to God's comfort and reassurance. By bringing our concerns to Him, we invite His peace into our hearts, which transcends our understanding (Philippians 4:6-7).

Surrounding ourselves with a community of believers can also provide the encouragement we need. Sharing our struggles with trusted friends, mentors, or faith leaders allows us to receive counsel and reminders of God's faithfulness. Being part of a supportive community offers accountability and comfort, showing us that we are not alone in our journey of trust.

Reflecting on past instances of God's faithfulness can bolster our trust as well. By remembering how God has worked in our lives and the lives of others, we reinforce the belief that He will continue to be faithful. Keeping a journal of answered prayers, personal testimonies, and scriptural promises can serve as a tangible reminder of God's trustworthiness.

Building trust in God is a lifelong process. It involves daily choices to surrender our fears, disappointments, and desire for control to Him. By acknowledging these common struggles and actively seeking ways to overcome them, we grow in our faith and deepen our trust in God's unfailing love and plan. For many, trusting God becomes difficult after experiencing betrayal or unanswered prayers. I, too, wrestled with these feelings, wondering why certain prayers went unanswered. Yet, over time, I learned that God's silence doesn't equate to absence. Instead, it often signifies His deeper work within us, preparing us for greater things to come.

A Testament to Faith: One Man's Journey of Trust in God

In the midst of the challenging environment of the prison camp, there was one individual whose story of unwavering trust in God stood out as a beacon of hope for everyone around him. This man had faced a daunting journey. Originally sentenced under the harsh regulations of the 1994 crime bill, he had already spent more than 13 years in prison. He had worked his way down from a medium-security facility to the camp where we met, a testament to his good behavior and determination to keep faith even in the bleakest of circumstances.

His story was not just about enduring a long sentence; it was about the faith that carried him through those years. Despite the seemingly insurmountable odds against him, he never lost his faith. He was known in the camp for his devotion to God, a faith that shone brightly even in the darkest moments. His life was a living example of trust in God's greater plan, a trust that never wavered, not even when the future seemed uncertain. And, he could "throw hands" and "cuss like a sailor". He was an eclectic mix of holy and profane at the same time.

Each day in the camp, he dedicated himself to serving others. He organized Bible studies, led prayer meetings, and always had a word of encouragement for anyone who needed it. His presence was a source of encouragement, his faithfulness a reminder that God was present even in a place where hope often seemed lost. What was remarkable about him was not just his leadership but his unwavering belief that God would see him through, even when he was facing what seemed to be an endless sentence.

There were times when his situation seemed hopeless. His sentence stretched far into the future, with many more years to serve before he would be eligible for release. The system that had placed him there seemed unyielding, a monolithic structure that offered little chance for mercy or reconsideration. But his faith was not tied to the system; it was anchored in something far greater. He believed with all his heart that God had a plan for him, that he was not forgotten, and that his faith would be rewarded.

His belief in God's faithfulness never faltered. He spent hours in prayer, not just for himself but for others in the camp. His faith was active, a force that not only sustained him but also uplifted those around him. He often spoke of his trust in God's timing, encouraging others to hold onto their faith no matter how bleak their circumstances appeared. His faith was infectious, his hope contagious. He was a living testimony to the power of trusting God, even when everything else seemed lost.

As the years passed, his hope did not diminish. Instead, it grew stronger. He believed deeply that God would intervene on his behalf, that a way would be made where there seemed to be no way. His optimism was not based on wishful thinking but on a profound trust in God's sovereignty and goodness. His faith was tested many times, but each time, he emerged stronger, his belief unshaken.

One day, he received news that would change his life forever. His appeal had been accepted, and a judge had agreed to reduce his sentence. This decision meant that he would go home around five years earlier than originally planned. The joy that filled the camp that day was indescribable. It was not just his victory; it was a victory for everyone who had watched his journey, who had seen his faith in action, and who had been inspired by his unwavering trust in God.

His release was a powerful reminder to all of us that God is faithful, even when the circumstances seem impossible. His story was more than just a legal victory; it was a testament to the power of faith and the reality of God's presence in our lives. His unwavering trust had not only brought him through his darkest days but had also paved the way for his freedom.

As he prepared to leave the camp, he shared his story one more time with the group. He spoke of the years of waiting, of the times when doubt had tried to creep in, and of the countless prayers he had lifted to God. He spoke of the peace he had found in trusting God, even when the answer seemed delayed. His parting message was simple yet profound: "Never lose faith. God is always working, even when we can't see it. Trust Him with everything, and He will make a way."

His journey of faith did not end with his release; it continued to inspire those of us who remained. His story was a vivid illustration that trusting God is not just about expecting miraculous changes but about living faithfully each day, believing that God's plan is at work in every situation. His life in the camp, his unwavering trust, and his ultimate release were all powerful examples of what it means to live a life of faith. His story showed us that trusting God is a shared human experience, one that resonates across different people, situations, and challenges.

Witnessing such profound trust in action, I began to reflect on the broader implications of trusting God, not only as a personal belief but as a force that could impact mental, emotional, and relational well-being.

Benefits of Trusting God

Trusting God is not only a spiritual act; it also has profound emotional and psychological benefits. When we place our trust in God, we often experience a significant reduction in anxiety and stress. The act of surrendering our worries to a higher power provides a sense of relief, allowing us to let go of the constant need to control every aspect of our lives. This sense of trust fosters inner peace, creating a stable foundation upon which we can build our emotional resilience.

Studies have shown that spirituality and faith can have a positive impact on mental health. Research from institutions like Harvard Medical School and the Mayo Clinic highlights that individuals with strong faith or spiritual beliefs often report lower levels of anxiety, depression, and stress. One study found that people who regularly engage in spiritual practices, such as prayer or meditation, experience lower blood pressure and enhanced coping mechanisms in the face of life's difficulties. This suggests that the practice of trusting in a higher power contributes to a calm and centered state of mind, enabling individuals to approach challenges with a sense of equanimity.

Research highlights the tangible benefits of trust and faith, including reduced stress and improved mental health. Studies have shown that individuals who engage regularly in prayer and spiritual practices exhibit lower levels of anxiety and depression. These findings affirm what the Bible teaches—trusting in God brings peace that surpasses understanding.

Faith also provides a sense of purpose and meaning, which is crucial for psychological well-being. When we trust that our lives are part of a greater divine plan, we find it easier to navigate the uncertainties and trials we face. This trust instills a hope that is not dependent on current circumstances, providing a steady anchor in the storms of life. By believing that there is a purpose to our struggles, we are able to reframe negative experiences, seeing them as opportunities for growth rather than insurmountable obstacles. This perspective shift is known to boost mental health, as it helps prevent feelings of hopelessness and despair.

Psychologically, trust in God can enhance one's sense of self-efficacy and personal strength. When we believe that God is guiding and supporting us, we feel more capable of facing difficult situations. This belief fosters resilience, encouraging us to take proactive steps in challenging circumstances rather than becoming paralyzed by fear or uncertainty. The knowledge that we are not alone, that there is a divine presence walking with us, can be a powerful motivator to persevere and push forward, even when the path ahead seems daunting.

Moreover, trusting God can lead to improved relationships and social well-being. People who trust in God are often more inclined to exhibit patience, kindness, and empathy toward others, reflecting the divine qualities they aspire to embody. This not only enhances personal relationships but also contributes to a supportive and nurturing community. Being part of a faith community provides a network of encouragement and accountability, which is crucial for sustaining mental and emotional health. The shared experiences and collective faith within these communities can create a sense of belonging and reduce feelings of isolation.

Trusting in God can also transform how we handle failures and setbacks. Instead of viewing these moments as personal defeats, we can see them as part of God's broader plan for our lives. This shift in perspective allows us to approach setbacks with a learning mindset, focusing on what God might be teaching us through these experiences. This approach fosters a resilient attitude, where failure is seen not as an endpoint but as a stepping stone toward greater wisdom and spiritual maturity.

By embracing trust in God, we engage in a holistic form of well-being that nurtures our spirit, mind, and emotions. This integrated approach to health acknowledges that our spiritual lives are deeply interconnected with our mental and emotional states. When we trust in God, we align our lives with a higher purpose, find peace amidst chaos, and build a resilient mindset that carries us through life's inevitable challenges. This trust ultimately leads to a more fulfilling and balanced life, one that is marked by peace, purpose, and a profound sense of joy.

This shift from self-reliance to God-reliance represents a significant transformation in a believer's life. It's a journey that moves us from depending on our limited abilities to embracing the boundless wisdom and support of God. It's about understanding that strength is found not in controlling every detail but in trusting that God's hand is in every aspect of our lives.

Moving from Self-Reliance to God-Reliance

One of the most profound transformations in the journey of faith is the shift from relying solely on our own strength and understanding to depending on God. This transition marks a significant turning point in our spiritual development, one that fosters growth in both faith and humility. Moving from self-reliance to God-reliance is not an overnight change but a gradual process that involves rethinking how we approach life, make decisions, and interact with others.

The Illusion of Control

For much of our lives, we are taught to be self-sufficient, to rely on our own abilities, intellect, and resources to navigate the world. This mindset is often reinforced by societal values that prize independence, achievement, and personal success. While there is value in being capable and taking responsibility for our actions, an overemphasis on self-reliance can lead us to believe that we are in control of everything. We may feel that it is entirely up to us to solve our problems, secure our future, and manage every aspect of our lives.

This illusion of control can be comforting at times, but it also carries a heavy burden. When things go wrong, when our plans fail, or when we face situations beyond our control, the weight of responsibility can become overwhelming. Fear, anxiety, and stress are often byproducts of trying to maintain control over every aspect of our lives. This is where the shift from self-reliance to God-reliance offers profound relief and transformation.

Recognizing the Limits of Self-Reliance

The first step in moving toward God-reliance is recognizing the limitations of self-reliance. This realization often comes through personal experiences of failure, hardship, or moments when our strength and wisdom are simply not enough. It is in these times of vulnerability that we are reminded of our human limitations and the need for divine guidance and support.

In my own life, there were numerous occasions when my best efforts fell short, and I found myself at the end of my own resources. Whether it was during moments of personal crisis, challenging decisions, or overwhelming responsibilities, the realization that I could not do it all on my own opened the door to a deeper reliance on God. Admitting our limitations is not a sign of weakness; rather, it is a recognition of our humanity and an invitation to let God's strength be made perfect in our weakness.

The Growth of Faith and Humility

Shifting from self-reliance to God-reliance is a humbling process. It requires acknowledging that we do not have all the answers and that our understanding is limited. This humility is the fertile ground in which faith grows. As we let go of the need to control every outcome, we begin to trust more fully in God's wisdom, timing, and plans for our lives.

This shift fosters a deeper sense of peace because it alleviates the pressure to always have everything figured out. Instead of trying to predict and control every detail, we learn to rest in the assurance that God is in control, and His plans for us are good. This trust does not eliminate difficulties or challenges, but it changes how we respond to them. Instead of reacting with fear or anxiety, we approach life's uncertainties with confidence in God's sovereignty.

Transforming Decision-Making

Relying on God instead of solely on ourselves changes how we make decisions. Rather than relying only on our own understanding or conventional wisdom, we seek God's guidance through prayer, reflection, and consultation with others who share our faith. This approach allows us to make decisions that align with God's will, even when they may seem counterintuitive or go against societal norms.

For example, there might be times when logic suggests pursuing a particular career path, investment, or relationship, but through prayer and discernment, we sense God leading us in a different direction. Choosing to follow God's lead, even when it defies conventional wisdom, is an act of faith that often yields unexpected blessings and growth. This shift in decision-making from a self-centered to a God-centered approach allows us to live lives that are more aligned with our true purpose and calling.

Impact on Relationships

Moving from self-reliance to God-reliance also transforms our relationships. When we rely solely on our own strength, we may become overly critical, controlling, or anxious in our interactions with others. We may struggle with trusting people, fearing that they will let us down, or we might find ourselves constantly trying to fix or manage the lives of those around us.

However, as we learn to rely on God, we become more gracious, understanding, and patient with others. Trusting God means believing that He is at work in the lives of those around us, just as He is in ours. It frees us from the need to control or fix others, allowing us to love them as they are, encouraging their own journeys of faith. This reliance on God fosters healthier, more authentic relationships built on mutual respect and trust.

Finding Freedom in God-Reliance

Ultimately, the shift from self-reliance to God-reliance leads to freedom. It frees us from the illusion that we must have all the answers and bear all burdens alone. It liberates us from the constant pressure to succeed by our own merits. Instead, we find joy and peace in knowing that we are supported by a loving God who is infinitely wise and powerful.

Living a life of God-reliance does not mean passivity or inaction; rather, it means actively seeking God's guidance, trusting His plans, and resting in His promises. It is a dynamic relationship that involves listening, responding, and growing in faith. As we continue to lean on God, we discover that His grace is sufficient, His guidance is trustworthy, and His love is unfailing.

This transformation from self-reliance to God-reliance enriches every aspect of our lives. It deepens our faith, strengthens our relationships, and gives us a clearer sense of purpose. It equips us to face life's challenges with courage and grace, knowing that we do not walk alone. By placing our trust in God, we experience the fullness of life that He intends for us, marked by peace, joy, and a confident hope in His unfailing love.

Integrating Trust in God into Everyday Life

Trusting God is often thought of as something we turn to during crises or significant life events. However, trust in God is equally essential in our daily routines and minor decisions. Integrating trust into everyday life allows us to experience peace, wisdom, and guidance consistently, rather than only in moments of severe challenge or despair. Trusting God should be a daily practice, woven into the fabric of our lives, influencing how we handle everyday stressors, make career decisions, and interact with others.

Handling Daily Stressors with Trust

Everyday stressors—like traffic jams, tight deadlines, unexpected expenses, or last-minute changes—can easily unsettle our peace of mind, triggering anxiety and frustration. Without a strong foundation of trust, these moments can lead to feelings of helplessness or anger. In the camp, we constantly dealt with what I called the "hurry up and wait" syndrome. We were rushed to be somewhere or complete a task, only to find ourselves standing idly by, waiting indefinitely for the next step. It was maddening at times. However, trusting in God gave me a more balanced and peaceful perspective, allowing me to navigate these moments with calm assurance. Trusting God reminds us that He is ultimately in control, and we don't have to shoulder the burdens of life's pressures alone.

For instance, consider a day when everything seems to go wrong—your car breaks down, you're late for a crucial meeting, and an urgent deadline looms. In such moments, a person who trusts in God might start by pausing to pray, asking for patience, wisdom, and strength to handle the day's challenges.

This simple act of reaching out to God can immediately shift our mindset, allowing us to see beyond the immediate chaos and focus on what truly matters. Trusting God helps us to view obstacles not as insurmountable problems but as opportunities to grow in patience, resilience, and reliance on God's grace.

Moreover, trusting God in everyday stressors encourages us to take a step back and find perspective. It reminds us that these momentary troubles are temporary and that God's purpose for us extends beyond our immediate circumstances. By keeping a focus on God's larger plan, we can navigate stress with a sense of peace, knowing that every challenge is an opportunity to learn and trust Him more deeply.

Interacting with Others through the Lens of Trust

Trusting God also influences how we interact with others, fostering relationships based on love, respect, and understanding. When we trust that God is working in and through the people around us, we are more likely to approach others with patience, empathy, and an open heart. This trust helps us see beyond surface-level conflicts or misunderstandings, encouraging us to seek reconciliation and peace.

For example, during a heated discussion with a coworker or family member, trusting God allows us to stay calm and composed, rather than reacting out of frustration or defensiveness. This discipline is crucial, particularly in tense environments like the camp, where frustration often felt like it was only a hair trigger away. By leaning on God's guidance in those moments, we learned to respond with grace instead of anger, fostering peace where conflict might otherwise have erupted.

We can remind ourselves that God is present in every interaction, guiding us to respond in ways that reflect His love. Trusting God allows us to be patient, to listen more deeply, and to respond with kindness, even when others are difficult.

It helps us remember that our identity and worth are rooted in God, not in the approval or opinions of others. This perspective transforms our relationships, making them more harmonious and grounded in mutual respect.

Trusting God in our relationships also involves praying for the people in our lives, asking God to bless them, guide them, and work through our interactions. It means being willing to forgive, to extend grace, and to love unconditionally, knowing that God's love for us is the model for how we should love others. By trusting God, we create an environment where relationships can flourish, and where we can be agents of God's peace and reconciliation.

Integrating Trust into Routine Activities

Trusting God can be integrated into the most routine activities of our daily lives. This integration makes every moment an opportunity for spiritual growth and connection with God. For example, as we plan our day, we can trust God by inviting His guidance in setting our priorities. This might mean starting the day with a prayer for wisdom and clarity, asking God to help us focus on what truly matters.

Trusting God in routine activities might also involve pausing throughout the day to acknowledge His presence. Whether cooking dinner, commuting to work, or engaging in a workout, we can use these moments to thank God for His provision, reflect on His faithfulness, and seek His guidance. This ongoing dialogue with God turns routine moments into opportunities for connection, making our lives a continuous act of worship and trust.

In our work and service, trusting God can mean doing our best, not just for personal gain but as an offering to God. It involves working with integrity, treating colleagues with respect, and handling challenges with grace. When we trust that God is in control, we are free to give our best without anxiety about outcomes, knowing that God will use our efforts for His purpose.

By consciously choosing to trust God in everyday decisions, we cultivate a habit of reliance on Him that becomes second nature. This trust is not passive; it requires us to actively seek God's presence, listen for His guidance, and align our actions with His will. Over time, this practice transforms our daily lives, filling them with a sense of peace, purpose, and divine alignment. It helps us navigate both the small and significant moments with a steady heart, knowing that we are never alone and that our trust in God is a source of strength and wisdom.

To cultivate this deep-rooted trust, one must actively engage in practices that reinforce faith. The following strategies are practical steps that can help us build and sustain our trust in God, making it an integral part of our daily lives.

Strategies for Building Trust in God

1. **Immerse yourself in scripture**

    Regularly reading and meditating on the Bible helps ground your trust in God's promises. Scriptures like Proverbs 3:5-6 and Philippians 4:6-7 remind us to rely on God's wisdom rather than our own understanding. Consistent engagement with God's word provides reassurance during challenging times and anchors your faith in His reliability and goodness.

2. **Cultivate a habit of prayer**

    Make prayer a central part of your daily routine. Through prayer, you share your fears, doubts, and gratitude with God, inviting His guidance and peace into your life. Prayer builds a personal connection with God, making it easier to trust His plan, even when you cannot see the path ahead.

3. **Reflect on past faithfulness**
Take time to remember moments when God has come through for you in the past. Reflecting on these instances strengthens your faith for current and future challenges. Keeping a journal of these experiences can serve as a reminder of God's faithfulness, encouraging you to trust Him more deeply.

4. **Surround yourself with a faith community**
Engage with others who share your faith through church, study groups, or supportive friendships. Being part of a community provides encouragement and accountability. It allows you to share your struggles and gain strength from others' testimonies, reinforcing your trust in God's plan.

5. **Practice gratitude**
Focusing on gratitude helps shift your perspective from what is lacking to what is already present. Regularly expressing thanks for both big and small blessings cultivates a mindset of trust. Gratitude reminds you of God's goodness and builds a resilient spirit that is able to trust God in all circumstances.

6. **Lean on God during uncertainty**
Trusting God means surrendering control and acknowledging His sovereignty, especially when life is unpredictable. Embrace the peace that comes from knowing that God's understanding surpasses our own. When faced with uncertainty, choose to rely on God's wisdom and timing, believing that He is working for your good.

7. **Find strength in hope**
Trusting God involves maintaining hope, even in the direst situations. This hope is not based on circumstances but on the character and promises of God. Remembering that

God has a plan for your life, as stated in Jeremiah 29:11, helps sustain your trust and gives you a sense of purpose even in difficult times.

Conviction Checkpoints

- **Self-Examination Question:** Reflect on a time when you faced uncertainty and how you chose to trust God. How did this experience shape your faith? Identify areas in your life where you need to trust God more.
- **Actionable Step:** Make a list of scriptures and quotes that encourage trust in God. Keep them in a place where you can see them daily and meditate on them, especially during challenging times.
- **Conviction Affirmation:** I am convicted that trusting God is essential for finding peace and strength in uncertain times. I will rely on His promises and character to guide me through life's challenges.
- **Prayer/Meditation Focus:** Pray for the strength to trust God in every situation. Ask Him to help you surrender your fears and anxieties to Him and to fill you with His peace.

Profile in Conviction

George Müller

George Müller was a Christian evangelist and the founder of several orphanages in England in the 19th century. What makes Müller's life extraordinary is his radical faith in God's provision. Without asking for donations or financial support from anyone, Müller believed that God would provide for all the needs of the orphans under his care—and time and time again, God did just that. His unwavering trust in God is an incredible testament to the power of faith in action.

Müller's conviction wasn't theoretical; it was tested daily. At the height of his work, Müller was responsible for the care of over 10,000 orphans. Every day, they needed food, clothing, and shelter, and Müller never faltered in his belief that God would provide. His method was simple yet profound—he prayed. And through those prayers, provisions would come, often at the very last minute. Müller documented these miracles in his journals, revealing a life lived in complete trust in God's goodness and faithfulness.

One of the most famous stories about Müller's faith comes from a time when the orphanage had no food for breakfast. Instead of panicking, Müller gathered the children together and prayed, thanking God for the meal He was going to provide. Within minutes, there was a knock at the door. A local baker stood there with fresh bread, saying he had felt led to give it to the orphanage. Moments later, a milkman's cart broke down in front of the orphanage, and he offered them milk before it spoiled. This was just one of many instances where Müller's faith was rewarded with God's provision.

Müller's life serves as a powerful example of what it means to trust God completely. His reliance on prayer and his refusal to waver in faith, even when circumstances looked dire, demonstrate the deep conviction that God is always in control and will meet the needs of those who trust in Him. Through his unwavering faith, Müller cared for thousands of orphans and left a legacy of faith that continues to inspire believers today.

Müller's story challenges us to ask: Do we truly trust God to provide in our lives, or do we rely more on our own efforts? His life shows that when we place our faith fully in God, even the most impossible situations can be transformed by His provision and grace.

Trusting God is not just a comforting concept, but a way of life that sustains us through uncertainty and hardship. My journey, particularly during my time in the prison camp, revealed that trust is an active choice to surrender control and rely on God's promises, even when the future is unclear. Trust doesn't eliminate challenges, but it empowers us to face them with the confidence that God is working for our good, even when we can't see the full picture.

Life is filled with moments that test our faith, but trusting God offers peace amidst chaos and hope in the unknown. Proverbs 3:5-6 reminds us to trust in the Lord and lean not on our own understanding—this is a daily commitment to place our fears, plans, and anxieties in God's hands. In doing so, we find not only strength for the journey but also the assurance that we are never walking alone, and that His plans for us are greater than we can imagine.

CHAPTER 7

COMMUNITY IS CRUCIAL

The significance of community emerges clearly in the restrictive environment of a prison camp. Community offers not only a support system and a sense of belonging but also a crucial reminder that we are not alone in our struggles. Throughout my time in the prison camp, I realized that building and maintaining a strong community was not just important for survival but also essential for personal growth.

The words from Hebrews 10:24-25 provided a strong reminder of the power of community: *"And let us consider how we may spur one another on toward love and good deeds, not giving up meeting together... but encouraging one another."* This passage highlighted the vital role of mutual support and connection, reinforcing how important it is to lift each other up, especially during life's most difficult moments. It reminded me that community is not just a comfort but a source of strength that helps us persevere.

The Vital Role of Community Support

Community support is more than just a comforting thought; it is a vital lifeline, especially during the most challenging times. When individuals face hardships—whether they are personal, professional, or spiritual—being part of a community provides a safety net that helps prevent them from feeling isolated or overwhelmed. The emotional and psychological support that comes from community members is crucial because it offers different perspectives, helping individuals see beyond their immediate struggles. When we are caught up in our own problems, it's easy to feel like there is no way out. However, when others share their experiences and insights, it broadens our understanding and reminds us that we are not alone in our difficulties.

The role of community extends far beyond emotional comfort; it is also essential for spiritual growth. In times of doubt or spiritual dryness, being part of a faith-based community can reignite one's passion for God and His word. Members of a community encourage one another to stay rooted in their faith, provide accountability in living out spiritual values, and offer prayer support during times of need. This spiritual camaraderie builds resilience, helping each member of the community to grow stronger in their faith.

Moreover, community acts as a mirror, reflecting back to us the values and principles that we strive to uphold. Through interactions with others who share our faith, we are reminded of the importance of walking the path of righteousness. Community members often challenge one another to be better, to act with more love, more patience, and more grace. They serve as accountability partners, ensuring that each person is not straying from their spiritual journey.

In essence, being part of a community means never having to face life's battles alone. It provides a support system that lifts you up when you're down, guides you when you're lost, and celebrates with you when you achieve victory. The collective strength and wisdom found in community is an invaluable resource for anyone seeking to lead a life of purpose, faith, and integrity.

Understanding the deep and multifaceted role that community plays in our lives, it becomes clear why nurturing these connections is not just beneficial but necessary. With this awareness, we can begin to explore how to actively recognize and engage with our communities, finding and building the support networks that God intends for us.

Biblical Foundations of Community Support

The concept of community is deeply rooted in biblical teachings, showing us that faith is not meant to be lived out in isolation. Throughout Scripture, we find numerous examples where community played a vital role in spiritual growth, resilience, and the spread of the Gospel.

One of the most striking examples is found in the early church as described in the Book of Acts. In Acts 2:42-47, we read about the believers coming together, not just for worship, but for fellowship, shared meals, and mutual support. *"They devoted themselves to the apostles' teaching and to fellowship, to the breaking of bread and to prayer"* (Acts 2:42). This passage paints a vivid picture of a community that was bound together by a common purpose and love for one another. Their sense of community was so strong that they were willing to sell their possessions and distribute to anyone in need, demonstrating that their faith went beyond personal devotion to include practical acts of love and care for each other.

The early church thrived because of this strong sense of community. It provided a foundation for spiritual growth, as believers encouraged one another, learned together, and held each other accountable. It also offered a source of strength and resilience, helping them to withstand persecution and hardship. The unity and love displayed by this community not only deepened their faith but also served as a powerful witness to others, leading to the spread of Christianity.

Even Jesus, the Son of God, understood the importance of community. Throughout His ministry, He surrounded Himself with the twelve disciples. These weren't just followers; they were friends, confidants, and co-laborers in the mission. Jesus used His time with the disciples to teach them, to share meals, to rest, and to pray. In doing so, He demonstrated that community was a critical component of His ministry. By investing in these relationships, Jesus showed us that spiritual growth is a collective journey, not a solitary one. His interactions with the disciples illustrate that even the strongest among us need the support and companionship of others.

In addition to the twelve, Jesus also engaged with broader communities. He visited towns and villages, preached to large crowds, and took time to engage with individuals. These interactions were not just about imparting wisdom; they were about building connections, fostering understanding, and demonstrating love and compassion.

The Bible makes it clear that community is not just an option but an essential part of a healthy spiritual life. Whether through the close-knit bonds of the early church or the intentional relationships Jesus built with His disciples, these biblical examples remind us that we are called to live in fellowship with others. Community provides a space for us to learn, to grow, to be challenged, and to find strength in the collective support of like-minded individuals.

Recognizing the significance of community, as seen through the early church and the life of Jesus, it's evident that building and maintaining connections is crucial. These biblical examples encourage us to seek out and nurture our own communities, understanding that through them, we find not only support but also the opportunity to grow and thrive in our faith.

Overcoming Barriers to Building Community

While the value of community is undeniable, many people face significant barriers that make it challenging to connect with others. These obstacles can stem from past experiences, personal insecurities, or even misconceptions about what it means to be part of a community. Addressing these barriers is essential to fully embracing the support and growth that comes from being part of a faith-based community.

One of the most common barriers is the fear of rejection. Many individuals worry about not being accepted or valued within a group. This fear can be especially pronounced in environments like a prison camp, where trust is hard to come by, and vulnerability can feel risky. To overcome this fear, it's important to start by acknowledging it. Recognizing that many people share this concern can help normalize the feeling. In these environments, seeking out smaller, more intimate groups, such as a small groups or prayer circles, can provide a safer space to build trust. Finding people with whom you share common ground—be it faith, background, or experiences—can also create a foundation for meaningful connections.

Past hurts and betrayals can also be significant barriers to building community, particularly in a prison camp where past traumas are common. Experiences of betrayal or disappointment often leave emotional scars, making it difficult to trust others again. Overcoming this barrier involves a process of healing, which may include prayer, reflection, or simply allowing oneself time to process these experiences. While this healing can be challenging in a camp environment, it's important to remember that not everyone is the same and that past experiences do not dictate future ones. Taking small steps towards new connections, like joining in group activities or engaging in casual conversations during communal time, can gradually rebuild trust.

Feelings of unworthiness are another obstacle many face when trying to connect with others. In settings like a prison camp, where guilt and regret may weigh heavily, individuals might struggle with believing they don't deserve to be part of a supportive community. These feelings can stem from internalized messages about one's value or past mistakes. It's crucial to understand that community is not about perfection but about connection and support. Everyone has value, and everyone deserves to be part of a community that uplifts and encourages them. Practicing small acts of kindness, engaging in conversations, or participating in group prayer can help foster a sense of belonging and worth.

For those outside a camp setting, similar feelings of unworthiness or fear of judgment might prevent them from seeking community support. These individuals can benefit from finding groups that align with personal interests or values, such as hobby clubs, volunteer teams, or church groups. It's helpful to remember that everyone has their own insecurities and fears, and many are looking for the same sense of belonging. Taking small steps, like attending a local church service or a support group meeting, can open the door to new connections.

In any environment, the first steps toward building community can feel daunting. If joining a large group feels overwhelming, look for smaller, more intimate settings where interaction is easier. This might be a small Bible study, a support group for shared experiences, or simply reaching out to one or two people for deeper conversations. Being patient with oneself is important; building trust and connections takes time. Allowing oneself to move at a comfortable pace can make the process of finding and engaging with community more manageable. Practicing vulnerability, even in small ways, can foster trust and encourage others to open up as well.

Chapter 7: Community is Crucial

By acknowledging and addressing these barriers, whether in a prison camp or in broader society, individuals take significant steps toward finding and nurturing communities that will support their personal and spiritual growth. Moving past these obstacles opens the door to meaningful connections that provide strength, encouragement, and a sense of belonging. As individuals engage with others and share their stories, they build a network of support that reflects the true spirit of community, helping each other to grow, thrive, and find peace.

By acknowledging and addressing these barriers, we take important steps toward finding and nurturing the communities that will support our faith journeys. Moving past these obstacles opens the door to meaningful connections that can provide strength, encouragement, and a sense of belonging. However, useful it is to overcome these obstacles, I still had apprehensions to joining the community in the prison camp.

Overcoming Apprehensions in Finding Community

Reflecting on my journey, there were times when the idea of finding and becoming part of a community was daunting. I vividly remember moments of hesitation and apprehension, wondering if I would truly fit in or if opening up to others would be worth the risk. The fear of vulnerability and the possibility of being misunderstood often made me want to retreat into solitude, convincing myself that I could handle things on my own. In a cloistered environment like prison, you need a people-connection or you are doomed. Everyone needs to belong.

When I first arrived at the camp, I was hesitant to join the daily prayer gatherings. To be honest, the drama surrounding the camp's "church" community was off-putting. While I was warmly greeted, each person seemed more interested in criticizing others and "warning" me about their fellow believers than fostering genuine fellowship. It didn't take long for me to decide that I wanted no part of it. I declined the invitations politely, offering a reasonable excuse. As I observed the camp's dynamics, it became clear that the small group attending daily prayer wasn't particularly well-liked or respected, and I wasn't eager to align myself with what seemed like a group of spiritual misfits. Despite needing a tribe, I found myself reluctant to join the very group I was naturally closest to in belief.

Eventually, though, I decided to attend sporadically, keeping myself on the fringes. It wasn't a terrible experience, but I couldn't ignore the disheartening behavior I witnessed. After sharing prayer, these same men would talk behind each other's backs with astonishing regularity. It was insufferable. One day, as the usual back-channel chatter began, I finally spoke up. I asked one brother why he felt it was acceptable to criticize another believer when we were so few in number. I couldn't understand how we, the Christian group, could be more divided than any other group in the camp. The Muslims, for example, had loud, heated disagreements, but they did so openly. There was no underhandedness or subterfuge.

A series of conversations followed, and I noticed a shift—not just in them, but in me as well. If I was being honest, I had also participated in the unproductive gossip. I wanted the Christian community to be a true example to others, but we were far from it. One major source of division involved how "tithes" were managed. There was suspicion that the head of the church used excess commissary for himself, leaving nothing for newcomers. On top of that, when men left, they often donated their clothes and other items to ease the transition for others, but the distribution was rarely clear. After some difficult conversations, we established greater accountability for church donations. This marked a turning point. Transparency built trust, and slowly, suspicion gave way to unity.

From that moment, my understanding of community shifted. What once seemed like a risky, uncomfortable venture became an essential part of both my spiritual growth and personal connection. Through accountability and truth, we began to reflect the values we professed, and our fractured group became a genuine source of support and strength.

Recognizing the profound impact that community can have, it's important to move beyond initial apprehensions and take practical steps to find and nurture these connections. By understanding and overcoming our hesitations, we can open ourselves up to the blessings that come from being part of a supportive and faith-filled community.

Finding Community Beyond Your Base

While faith-based communities provide vital spiritual support and growth, it's essential to recognize that community is not confined to the walls of a church or prayer circle. In a prison camp setting, where opportunities to interact with others outside of organized religious groups are limited, finding community in broader contexts can be incredibly valuable. This approach not only broadens one's perspective but also allows for personal growth in unexpected ways.

Community can be found in various environments where people gather, offering support, encouragement, and companionship. In the camp, I discovered that community wasn't just about those who shared my faith but also about those who shared my day-to-day experiences. Engaging in conversations with fellow inmates, even those who didn't share my religious beliefs, provided a sense of camaraderie and mutual understanding. We found common ground in shared struggles and aspirations, which fostered a sense of unity. These interactions reminded me that community is about connection, understanding, and shared humanity, not just shared beliefs.

I'm a debater by nature—there wasn't a verbal duel I would walk away from willingly, at least not during my time at the camp. After the Sunday morning meal, before football season kicked in, we'd dive into deep theological discussions. The camp was a melting pot of belief systems—Hebrew Israelites, Moors, Five Percenters, Black Muslims, and Sunni Muslims. Everyone seemed to target Jesus and Christianity. Initially, I sat back and observed, but I couldn't resist joining in. For hours, we would argue about religious traditions, each defending our own perspective. I had always believed in Christian apologetics, but I'd never encountered such a concentrated environment for it. I'd argue my case passionately, winning many debates, although I doubt I changed any minds. The discussions got so intense that I started requesting books from Amazon to strengthen my arguments. It became a highlight of the week—someone would bring up a topic, and we'd go at it for hours. But it was all in good fun, a mutual exchange of ideas, and I found myself part of a new tribe: the spiritually curious.

Of course, there were also the racial divisions, and each person had to align with their own group in the TV room. Navigating that space was a whole other challenge. I got into more trouble in the TV room than I care to admit—sitting in the wrong seat, not following the schedule for shows, and other unspoken rules. Eventually, I had to start watching TV after 11 p.m. when I got off work, just to avoid conflict. You had to earn your place, even for something as simple as picking a show or claiming a seat. Thankfully, my "Rabbi" had my back. He'd sneak in a show I liked on the schedule, knowing it'd save me a headache. It really does matter who's in your corner in prison. After many fits and starts, I finally found authentic community both inside and outside of the Christian circle. It took time to navigate the complexities of camp life, but eventually, I built meaningful connections that transcended religious affiliations and broke through the barriers of mistrust and division.

Work Communities as Sources of Connection

In the camp, everyone had a job, which naturally fostered a sense of community. Whether it was in the kitchen, maintenance, landscape, or other work assignments, these settings created opportunities to build relationships through shared responsibilities. Working alongside others towards a common goal allowed us to see each other's strengths and vulnerabilities, creating a sense of respect and solidarity. Simple gestures like lending a hand, sharing a meal, or engaging in light-hearted banter became the foundation for deeper relationships. These everyday moments were opportunities to support each other, lift spirits, and create a sense of belonging, even in a place as unlikely as a prison camp.

In my own experience, the kitchen became a space where community was formed despite the challenges and conflicts. The shared task of preparing meals for everyone not only required teamwork but also provided a chance for connection. Conversations during breaks, mutual assistance during busy times, and shared laughter over a joke or a story helped us bond. Even when tensions ran high, the act of working together towards a shared goal forged a sense of unity. These work-related interactions highlighted that community could be built on the foundation of shared effort and mutual respect, transcending differences in background or belief.

Expanding the Concept of Community

The lessons learned in the camp extend to life beyond its walls. Community is wherever people come together to support, encourage, and uplift one another. In work environments, whether in a prison camp or in more traditional settings, these relationships can be a vital source of emotional and psychological support. They provide opportunities for learning, growth, and mutual encouragement. Building relationships with colleagues not only enhances the work experience but also provides emotional support and a sense of belonging.

Finding community in different contexts, such as work settings, emphasizes that community is about connection and shared humanity. By recognizing that every interaction has the potential to build a sense of community, we open ourselves to forming meaningful relationships in various aspects of life. These relationships, grounded in mutual respect and understanding, provide a network of support that is crucial for personal growth and resilience.

Finding Community in the Everyday

Engaging with others in different settings not only strengthens faith but also enriches our understanding of the world and our place in it. Each interaction, each relationship, becomes a testament to the power of community to uplift, inspire, and transform. Recognizing that community can be found in multiple forms opens up new opportunities to connect with others and build a network of support. It allows us to see the value in every interaction, understanding that community is not limited to those who share our beliefs but includes anyone who contributes to our growth, well-being, and understanding.

Building Relationships

It is no small feat to build relationships with those who so easily lie and deceive. In the camp, forging authentic connections was often a complex and delicate process, requiring discernment, patience, and a willingness to see beyond the Façades that many wore as a means of survival. Trust is a fragile thing, especially in an environment where betrayal and deceit can feel like daily realities. Building relationships in such a setting was not an exact science; it demanded intuition and a profound understanding of human nature. It required navigating the unspoken rules of prison camp life, discerning who to trust and who to keep at a distance.

Nurturing Trust Through Shared Experiences

One of the most impactful aspects of community in the camp was the development of genuine relationships, which were built on mutual respect and a shared understanding of the hardships we all faced. These connections were not instantaneous; they were nurtured over time through shared experiences, conversations, and the simple acts of being present for one another. Despite the difficult environment, these relationships provided a sense of normalcy and support. They offered a glimpse of what life could be beyond the barbed wires and guarded perimeters, a life where genuine human connection could still flourish.

The Hidden Strength of Vulnerability

In an environment where vulnerability was often perceived as a weakness, showing one's true self was a significant risk. Prison camps are places where displays of honesty and openness could easily be misunderstood as signs of fragility or a lack of resilience. In such a setting, every individual carefully curated their external persona to avoid showing any chinks in their armor. Despite this pervasive need to protect oneself, it was precisely through these rare moments of vulnerability that the strongest and most genuine bonds were formed.

Opening up about one's fears, doubts, or personal struggles required a level of courage that was not easy to muster.

Yet, those who dared to be vulnerable discovered that it often paved the way for deeper connections. Trusting another person with your inner fears was a significant act of bravery, creating a foundation of mutual respect and understanding. It was through these shared confessions that relationships were strengthened. Having someone listen without judgment, especially in a place where judgment was often passed so freely, created a safe space amidst the harsh reality of camp life. These moments of sharing not only lightened the emotional burden but also wove the inmates into a closer-knit community, knitting them together in a tapestry of shared humanity.

However, the openness that vulnerability requires was not easily displayed. The reality of camp life meant that every inmate was walking a fine line between showing their true feelings and keeping a strong exterior. More often than not, you would see people pulling away to be by themselves. They would walk the perimeter track in silence, their thoughts racing as they tried to make sense of their circumstances. Others sought solace in the gym, pounding out their frustrations in physical exertion, finding a temporary release from the emotional strain that weighed heavily on their shoulders.

Rarely would someone openly share their struggles without some gentle nudging from those who had managed to earn their trust. Even when vulnerability was shown, it was often shrouded behind metaphorical concrete walls, carefully guarded so that no sign of weakness could be easily seen. This guardedness was part of the survival instinct that the camp environment instilled in everyone. It was understood that showing too much of your true self could lead to ridicule, manipulation, or even betrayal. Thus, vulnerability was approached with caution, like handling a double-edged sword that could either defend or harm.

The Façade of Indifference

What you noticed in this environment was a common attempt to save face, to appear unfazed and invulnerable. This façade of indifference was a protective mechanism against the perceived dangers of vulnerability. Bad news was met with a mask of stoicism. If someone received divorce papers, their reaction was a nonchalant, "No big deal!" If an appeal failed, the response was, "So what?" New charges filed? "It happens to everyone." These phrases of deflection became a part of the everyday language, a way to shield oneself from the emotional impact of the harsh realities of life in the camp.

This stoicism was not because the inmates were emotionless, but because maintaining an outward appearance of strength was vital for survival. Admitting to pain, loss, or disappointment was seen as giving others ammunition to use against you. And so, vulnerability, when it was shown, had to be earned, reserved only for those rare connections that had proven themselves to be trustworthy. It was through these connections that inmates found the strength to navigate the complexities of camp life, knowing that there was at least one person who truly understood their struggles.

Navigating Vulnerability with Discernment

In this environment, displaying vulnerability was not about being weak but rather about having the discernment to know when and with whom to share. It required a delicate balance—being strong enough to handle the daily challenges on your own while also recognizing when you needed the support of others. This discernment in showing vulnerability was crucial. It meant understanding that while not everyone in the camp could be trusted, there were still those with whom you could build meaningful relationships.

In retrospect, it was these moments of vulnerability, hidden behind a strong exterior, that truly defined the sense of community in the camp. It taught us that vulnerability is not the absence of strength but the presence of trust. It is not about being defenseless; it is about recognizing that true strength lies in the ability to show your authentic self to those who will cherish and guard that honesty.

The ability to be vulnerable, even in a place that discouraged it, was a quiet rebellion against the isolating effects of incarceration. It was a way of reclaiming one's humanity, of saying, "Despite the circumstances, I still choose to connect, to feel, and to trust." It was through these rare but meaningful connections that the fabric of the community was strengthened, making life in the camp a little more bearable and the challenges a little less overwhelming.

The Inner Circle: A Lifeline of Strength and Resilience

Amidst the daily uncertainty and constant challenges of camp life, finding genuine connection was not just a luxury—it was a necessity for survival. Over time, I became close to a select group of campers who shared my values, my goals, and, most importantly, my commitment to maintaining integrity even in such a difficult environment. This group became my inner circle, a tightly knit network of mutual trust and support that stood as a bulwark against the trials and tribulations we faced daily.

Intuitive Support: Reading Between the Lines

One of the remarkable aspects of our inner circle was the intuitive understanding we developed. Over time, we became attuned to each other's moods and unspoken signals. We could sense when someone was struggling, even if they didn't say a word. It was often in these moments that a simple suggestion would be made: "Why don't we take a walk?" or "Let's hit the gym for a bit." These casual invitations were more than just opportunities for physical exercise; they were lifelines. They provided a chance to step away from the eyes and ears of others, to find a quiet corner of the camp where deeper conversations could unfold.

These walks around the camp's perimeter or workouts in the gym became our sanctuaries, places where the veneer of toughness could be stripped away. As we walked or worked out side by side, the rhythm of our steps or the repetition of our movements seemed to create a cadence that made it easier to talk about the things that weighed on our minds. It was in these moments that the true power of community was felt—not in grand gestures, but in the quiet presence of a friend who knew you well enough to recognize when you needed to talk, even if you hadn't admitted it to yourself.

The Power of Silent Solidarity

Sometimes, it wasn't about talking at all. There were days when words fell short, when the emotional weight was too heavy to be lifted through conversation alone. On these days, just the presence of a trusted friend was enough. Walking in silence, feeling the camaraderie and understanding that didn't require words, was its own form of healing. This silent solidarity spoke volumes, reminding us that we were not alone in our struggles. It was a powerful reminder that community is as much about being there for others as it is about allowing others to be there for you.

Breaking Down the Walls

The strength of our inner circle lay in its ability to break down the walls that camp life often forced us to build around ourselves. In the harsh environment of a prison camp, vulnerability was rarely shown and trust was not freely given. Yet, within the bounds of our group, these walls could be lowered. There was a mutual understanding that we were each other's safety net. If one of us stumbled, the others were there to help lift him back up. This unwavering support fostered a sense of belonging that transcended the confines of the camp, giving us a sense of normalcy and human connection that was vital to our mental and emotional well-being.

A Brotherhood Forged in Adversity

Through shared experiences and mutual reliance, our inner circle became a brotherhood forged in the fires of adversity. We celebrated each other's small victories, mourned each other's losses, and provided a sounding board for the dilemmas that arose. This network of support was not just about survival—it was about thriving in a place designed to strip away one's identity and spirit. In supporting each other, we found a renewed sense of purpose and a reason to keep going. Our bonds provided a lifeline, reminding us that even in the bleakest of circumstances, the human spirit could find light through connection, understanding, and the unspoken promise that we were in this together.

In the end, it was these relationships that defined my experience in the camp. They were a testament to the power of community and the strength found in solidarity. It was through this inner circle that I realized that no matter how isolated or hopeless one might feel, there is always strength to be found in the company of those who care. This realization not only helped me navigate the daily challenges of camp life but also became a cornerstone of my understanding of the importance of community in any walk of life.

Navigating Trust and Betrayal

Trust was not given lightly; it was earned through consistent behavior and proven character. In an environment where many were skilled at deception, discerning genuine intentions was a daily challenge. There were times when trust was broken, and the pain of betrayal cut deep. However, these experiences also taught valuable lessons about resilience and forgiveness. They highlighted the importance of discerning the difference between those who genuinely sought connection and those who viewed relationships as a means to an end. Despite the risks, the reward of finding true, loyal friends made the effort worthwhile.

A Compelling Story of Snitching and Its Consequences

In the camp, rumors about informants and snitches were a constant undercurrent, whispers carried on hushed breaths and sidelong glances. Most knew the rules—unwritten but universally understood. You didn't snitch. It was a line you didn't cross because once crossed, it could never be undone. Snitching wasn't just seen as a betrayal of trust; it was a betrayal of the unspoken code that all of us abided by. It was this code that kept a semblance of order in a place where chaos always loomed close. But there was always someone willing to cross that line, driven by fear, desperation, or the promise of personal gain.

I remember one inmate in particular, whom I'll call "John" to protect his identity. John had been in the camp for about a year. He was a quiet man, kept mostly to himself, and avoided any unnecessary trouble. Like everyone else, he had a family waiting for him on the outside, and his biggest goal was to get out and stay out. He was serving time for a non-violent offense and was known to be a decent guy who played by the rules. In a place like that, where one's reputation was as much a survival tool as anything else, John's reputation was solid. He wasn't looking for trouble, and people generally left him alone.

Then came the rumor of a contraband sweep. The word spread quickly, as it always did. Whispered warnings flew through the camp like wildfire: "There's going to be a shakedown." Everyone knew what that meant. The guards would come through, flip bunks, tear apart personal belongings, and anyone caught with something they shouldn't have would face consequences. It was standard procedure, but that didn't make it any less nerve-wracking. Everyone was on edge, but most hoped it would blow over like usual.

However, this time, things went differently. The guards zeroed in on one bunk in particular—John's bunk. They found contraband hidden inside, items he would never be foolish enough to have. The whole camp buzzed with speculation. How could John, the rule-follower, have slipped up like that? The answer came soon enough: snitching. Someone had tipped off the guards, using John as a scapegoat to divert attention from their own misdeeds.

What happened next was swift and merciless. John was pulled aside, interrogated, and held in solitary confinement while the investigation unfolded. It didn't take long for the real story to come out. Another inmate, fearing repercussions from his own contraband stash, had planted the items in John's bunk and then tipped off the guards to look there. This inmate, desperate to cut a deal and avoid his own punishment, had sacrificed John to save himself. He had whispered in the ears of the guards, spinning a tale that painted John as the mastermind behind the contraband circulation.

John's innocence didn't matter anymore. Once labeled, once accused, the damage was done. The administration decided that John represented a security risk. His entire demeanor had changed; he was no longer the compliant, rule-abiding inmate they had come to expect. He was seen now as someone with the potential to disrupt the order of the camp. Without much warning, John was transferred to a higher security facility. The rumor mill buzzed with the news, spreading like an infection through the camp. "John got moved up," people whispered. "Higher security, more time added." The supposed infraction meant his early release was now off the table. The time he would serve stretched further into the future, a future that now seemed bleak and devoid of hope.

The betrayal hit the camp community hard. It wasn't just John who suffered; it was everyone. Trust, already a scarce commodity, became even rarer. Conversations grew quieter, more guarded. Friendships that once provided comfort and camaraderie turned cautious, each inmate wondering if the next person to fall would be him. The camp, which had a fragile semblance of order, now felt colder, more isolated. We all felt the chill of distrust, knowing that it could have been any one of us.

John's story became a cautionary tale, a reminder that even in a place where everyone was supposed to be on the same side, betrayal could still find a way in. For those of us who had built relationships and found solace in each other's company, it was a wake-up call to the harsh realities of life in the camp. Trust, we realized, was a double-edged sword—necessary for survival, but dangerous if misplaced. It was a commodity that could not be freely given; it had to be earned and continually reinforced.

In the end, John's unjust transfer was a stark reminder of the fragile nature of trust in the camp and the profound consequences of betrayal. But it also highlighted the resilience of the human spirit, the ability to rebuild and move forward even when the foundations are shaken. Trust was fragile, yes, but it was not entirely shattered. It took more time, more caution, but slowly, the bonds of community began to heal, reinforced by the shared understanding of the high stakes involved in each relationship.

Even in an environment designed to strip away hope, we found ways to trust again, knowing that without it, survival was merely a hollow existence. Trust became not just a strategy for getting by, but a means of finding purpose and meaning, even in the darkest of places.

The Impact of Genuine Connection

The friendships formed in the camp extended beyond mere survival; they became a source of personal growth and transformation. Through these relationships, we learned valuable lessons about trust, loyalty, and the power of community. They challenged us to be better, to support one another, and to find joy in the little moments. These connections, forged in the crucible of adversity, were not easily broken. They left an indelible mark on our lives, shaping how we viewed ourselves and our place in the world. In many ways, these relationships were a reminder that even in the most controlled and oppressive environments, the human desire for connection and community could not be extinguished.

Acts of kindness played a significant role in building a sense of community. Simple gestures, like sharing a meal or offering a listening ear, went a long way in fostering connections and providing emotional support. These acts of kindness were not just about helping others; they also helped me stay grounded and reminded me of the importance of giving and receiving support.

One camper, who had been there for nearly a decade, became a mentor and friend. He often shared his wisdom and insights about surviving camp life and maintaining a positive outlook. His guidance was invaluable, and his friendship was a testament to the power of community.

Navigating Community Challenges

Community is essential, but it is also complex. Not everyone in your community will stand by you during challenging times. Some people, even those you expect to support you, may leave when you need them most. This can be a painful reality, but it is important to understand that community is made up of more than just those who stand with you. It includes everyone, even those who leave or fail you.

During my ordeal, I experienced this firsthand. Those who I expected to be with me weren't, and those who were unlikely to stand by me were the ones who did. Even those whom my wife and I had made serious sacrifices for left us and did so noisily as a way to advance themselves on our seeming demise. This was a hard lesson, but it also brought a certain amount of comfort. Knowing that those who left me at a crucial time did so because they were not "fit for the fight" helped me to focus on the support that remained and to appreciate the strength of those who stood by me.

The Pain of Abandonment

As a pastor, you invest in people's lives, often going above and beyond to help them through their struggles, offering your time, resources, and emotional support. You walk with them through their darkest valleys, providing counsel, comfort, and hope. Yet, when trouble comes your way, you may find that some of these very people are the first to distance themselves. They act as if they do not know you, as if your proven character and years of sacrifice no longer matter. This sense of abandonment can be deeply wounding. It is natural to feel betrayed, to question why those you helped are now turning away. But it's crucial to remember that not everyone is equipped to handle the trials you face. Everyone is not fit for the fight, and that's okay. This reality does not diminish the good you've done or the genuine care you've shown. It simply reflects the varied capacities of individuals to stand firm under pressure.

Finding Strength in Those Who Remain

While some may walk away, others will surprise you with their unwavering loyalty. These are the people God has placed in your life for the long haul, the ones who will endure the storm with you. They are the friends who offer a listening ear, who pray with you in the darkest hours, who remind you of your worth when you doubt yourself. These individuals are invaluable. Their support is a testament to the power of genuine relationships and the strength that comes from standing together. The presence of these faithful companions reassures you that you are not alone and that your community, though smaller than expected, is richer and more profound because of the quality of those who remain.

Letting Go Without Resentment

It's important not to harbor anger or resentment towards those who leave. While the initial sting of their departure may hurt, carrying bitterness will only weigh you down. Instead, practice forgiveness and understanding. Acknowledge that everyone has their limitations and that some may not have the emotional or spiritual capacity to walk with you through every trial. Release them with grace, knowing that their departure makes space for those who are truly meant to be by your side. By letting go of resentment, you free yourself from unnecessary burdens, allowing you to focus on nurturing the relationships that truly matter.

Embracing God's Plan for Your Support System

The challenges of community also reveal a deeper truth about God's providence. Those who stick with you are the ones God has chosen to be part of your journey. Their loyalty is a reflection of God's faithfulness, providing you with the support you need to face your trials. Trusting in God's plan means accepting that some people are only meant to be in your life for a season, while others are placed there for a lifetime. This understanding brings peace and comfort, reminding you that your true strength comes not from the number of people who stand with you but from the quality of those relationships and the presence of God in your life.

Turning Pain into Purpose

The pain of abandonment can also serve a higher purpose. It deepens your empathy and compassion for others who feel isolated and betrayed. Your own experience of being left behind equips you to minister to others who are going through similar struggles. It enables you to offer genuine comfort and understanding, assuring them that they are not alone. By transforming your pain into purpose, you find healing and a renewed sense of mission. You recognize that every challenge, every betrayal, is an opportunity to grow closer to God and to strengthen the bonds with those who are truly committed to walking alongside you.

The Gift of Discernment

These experiences sharpen your ability to discern true character. They teach you to look beyond words and promises to observe actions and consistency. You become more aware of the qualities that define genuine friendship and support. This discernment becomes a valuable tool in building a community that is strong, resilient, and authentic. It helps you invest your time and energy into relationships that are mutually beneficial, where trust and loyalty are cultivated and cherished. This careful selection of who to trust ensures that your inner circle remains a safe haven, a source of strength and encouragement.

Appreciating the Hidden Blessings

In the midst of feeling hurt by those who left, it's easy to overlook the hidden blessings that arise from such experiences. The absence of certain people can lead to the presence of others who bring new perspectives, deeper relationships, and greater joy. Sometimes, those who leave make way for new individuals who offer the support you didn't even realize you needed. These unexpected blessings are reminders that God's plan is always at work, even in moments of pain and confusion. They affirm that community is not static but ever-evolving, shaped by the ebb and flow of relationships and the guiding hand of God.

In summary, navigating community challenges is an integral part of any journey. It requires resilience, forgiveness, and trust in God's greater plan. By focusing on the strength of those who remain, releasing resentment towards those who leave, and appreciating the hidden blessings, you find the peace and purpose needed to continue forward. The journey may not be easy, but with the right people by your side, it becomes a path filled with grace, love, and unwavering support.

"Fit for the Fight"

The notion of being "fit for the fight" is crucial in understanding why some people stand by you while others leave. The reality is that not everyone has the emotional or spiritual fortitude to endure tough times.

"Courage is rightly esteemed the first of human qualities because it is the quality which guarantees all others." - WINSTON CHURCHILL

Those who lacked the courage to stand with me during my most challenging times revealed their true character. It wasn't a reflection of my worth but of their capacity to handle adversity.

Another quote that resonated during this time is by Mother Teresa:

"I have found the paradox, that if you love until it hurts, there can be no more hurt, only more love."

This quote underscores the importance of recognizing that true community is forged in the fires of difficulty. Those who remained by my side were those who were truly "fit for the fight," and their presence provided a deep sense of support and validation.

1 John 2:19 says, "They went out from us, but they did not really belong to us. For if they had belonged to us, they would have remained with us; but their going showed that none of them belonged to us." This scripture reinforced the idea that those who leave us were never truly with us. Understanding this helped me focus on those who remained and who were genuinely committed to our shared journey.

Embracing the value of community is essential for our emotional and spiritual well-being. It allows us to support one another, share our burdens, and find strength in our collective faith. By building and maintaining strong relationships, we can navigate life's challenges with greater resilience and hope, knowing that we are not alone.

Strategies for Connecting with Your Community

1. **Identify Your Core Values**

    Before finding your community, it's essential to understand your own core values and beliefs. Reflect on what is most important to you—faith, integrity, compassion, resilience—and seek out those who share these same values. This shared foundation will make your relationships more meaningful and supportive.

2. **Engage in Regular Activities**

    Participate in activities that align with your interests and values, such as Bible study groups, fitness activities, or community service projects. Regular engagement in these activities helps build connections with like-minded individuals and fosters a sense of belonging.

3. **Be Open and Vulnerable**

    Building a genuine community requires openness and vulnerability. Be willing to share your struggles, challenges, and joys with others. This transparency creates deeper, more authentic connections, and allows others to feel comfortable doing the same.

4. **Practice Active Listening**

    Listening is a crucial component of building strong relationships. When you listen actively, you show respect and understanding, which fosters trust and mutual support within your community. Pay attention to what others say, and offer empathy and encouragement.

5. **Offer Support and Encouragement**

    Be proactive in offering support to those around you. Small acts of kindness, like offering a listening ear, a word of encouragement, or a helping hand, can strengthen bonds and reinforce the sense of community.

6. **Seek Diversity in Your Relationships**
   While it's natural to gravitate towards people similar to yourself, seeking diversity enriches your community experience. Engage with people from different backgrounds, cultures, and perspectives. This diversity will broaden your understanding and offer a more comprehensive support network.
7. **Stay Committed to Your Community**
   Building a strong community takes time and effort. Be committed to nurturing these relationships, even when it's inconvenient or challenging. Consistent presence and participation help solidify the sense of belonging and mutual support.

Conviction Checkpoints

- **Journal Prompt:** Reflect on a time when being part of a community helped you through a difficult situation. How did the support of others make a difference in your experience? Identify ways you can contribute to building a stronger community in your current environment.
- **Prayer Guide:** Pray for the strength and wisdom to build and maintain strong, supportive relationships. Ask God to help you be an encouragement to others and to recognize the value of community in your life.
- **Action Step:** Reach out to someone in your community who may be struggling and offer your support and encouragement. Look for opportunities to build connections and foster a sense of belonging among those around you.

Profile in Conviction

Corrie ten Boom – The Power of Forgiveness and Community

Corrie ten Boom, a Dutch Christian watchmaker, is renowned for her work in hiding Jews during World War II. She and her family were eventually arrested by the Nazis and sent to a concentration camp, where her sister died. Despite the unimaginable hardships she faced, Corrie emerged with an unshakable faith in God and a profound understanding of the power of forgiveness and community.

Corrie's life was a testament to the strength that comes from standing with others in times of need. After the war, she traveled the world sharing her story of survival and forgiveness, often speaking of the importance of community and the role it played in her life. Her experiences in the concentration camp, where she formed deep bonds with other prisoners, reinforced her belief in the necessity of supporting one another through adversity.

One of her most famous quotes captures the essence of her belief in the power of forgiveness:

"Forgiveness is an act of the will, and the will can function regardless of the temperature of the heart."

Like Corrie ten Boom, our lives often present us with challenges that test the strength of our convictions and the depth of our faith. Corrie's example teaches us that even in the face of betrayal and adversity, the choice to stand firm in our faith and support one another is a powerful act of resistance against despair. Her story is a powerful reminder that the presence of community, grounded in trust and love, can provide the strength needed to face even the harshest trials.

In the camp, I learned that community is both fragile and resilient, built on the delicate balance of trust, shared values, and the willingness to be vulnerable. The relationships formed within those barbed wire fences were more than mere friendships; they were lifelines that provided strength in the face of adversity. These bonds were forged not through convenience but through the trials of daily life, where each of us bore the weight of our circumstances together. It was in this crucible that I discovered the true power of community—a force that could uplift and sustain, even when the world outside seemed determined to tear us down.

Navigating trust and betrayal taught me invaluable lessons about human nature and the complexities of the heart. Not everyone was meant to stay; some would leave when their own fears and insecurities took over. Yet, it was through these departures that I realized the profound truth: those who remain by your side, despite the challenges, are the ones ordained to walk with you on your journey. Their loyalty is not born out of obligation, but out of a shared faith and mutual respect that surpasses mere circumstance.

The community I found in the camp was not perfect, nor did it always provide the answers I sought. But it offered something far more valuable—presence. The presence of others who understood the silent battles we each fought, the presence of listening ears that turned moments of despair into testimonies of hope, and the presence of hearts that beat with the same desire to find purpose and meaning in the midst of chaos.

As I look back, I realize that the strength of community lies not in its ability to solve all problems, but in its power to transform isolation into connection, and fear into courage. It is a reminder that no matter how dire the situation, we are never truly alone. God places people in our lives to walk with us, to share our burdens, and to celebrate our victories. Community, then, is not just a choice—it is a calling. A divine invitation to step out of the shadows of solitude and into the light of shared humanity.

In choosing to embrace community, we choose to embrace life in all its fullness, with all its joys and sorrows. We acknowledge that our journey is not a solitary one, but a path that intersects with others, creating a tapestry of experiences that shape who we are. As we move forward, may we always seek to build and nurture the communities around us, knowing that in doing so, we honor the very essence of what it means to be human. To love, to trust, and to stand together, even when the world tries to pull us apart.

CHAPTER 8
GRACE TRIUMPHS OVER INJUSTICE

Grace is more than just a religious concept; it is a profound and transformative force that can bring healing, redemption, and peace even in the most unjust circumstances. At its core, grace is an unmerited favor or kindness extended to others without expecting anything in return. It is the act of showing compassion and forgiveness, even when it seems undeserved. Grace breaks the cycle of bitterness and retaliation, offering a path towards reconciliation and understanding. Whether we recognize it through a spiritual lens or as a universal moral principle, grace has the power to touch hearts, soften hardened attitudes, and restore broken relationships.

During my time in the prison camp, my understanding of justice was constantly challenged, and my faith was put to the test. I encountered situations that were not just unfair but deeply unjust. Yet, amid these experiences, I discovered the profound power of grace. Both giving and receiving grace became essential tools in finding inner peace and bringing a sense of hope to others. Grace acted as a balm, soothing the wounds of injustice and providing a way to rise above the pain and anger that such situations often provoke.

The scripture from Ephesians 2:8-9 says, *"For it is by grace you have been saved, through faith—and this is not from yourselves, it is the gift of God—not by works, so that no one can boast."* This verse serves as a powerful reminder that grace is not something we can earn or achieve on our own; it is a divine gift, freely given by God. It illuminates the truth that grace can pierce through the darkest circumstances, offering hope when all other options seem closed. Unrestricted by human limitations, grace transcends our shortcomings and failures, presenting us with the opportunity for renewal and transformation.

The Journey to Understanding Grace

Understanding grace was not a revelation that came to me overnight; it was a journey marked by deep personal struggles and transformative encounters. In my early years, I was filled with anger and resentment, often feeling slighted by life's injustices and the harsh treatment I received from others. Growing up without my father left a void that was quickly filled with bitterness, and I became acutely aware of how cruel people—sometimes even those closest to me—could be. I was constantly on guard, ready to retaliate against anyone who mistreated or embarrassed me. Revenge became my defense mechanism, a way to reclaim power and control in a world that often felt hostile and unforgiving. I found satisfaction in seeing those who wronged me face difficulties, feeling vindicated by their misfortunes. It was a cycle of immaturity and self-destruction, and though I knew this path was damaging, I wasn't yet ready to change.

However, life has a way of confronting us with our deepest flaws, often when we least expect it. For me, this moment of reckoning came during a profound encounter with God. In a moment of raw honesty, I felt God's voice speak directly to my heart: "I can't use you with the condition of your heart." Those words hit me like a sledgehammer, piercing through the layers of anger and resentment I had built up over the years. I didn't want to admit it, but I knew deep down that God was right. My heart was hardened, filled with hatred and an ever-growing list of people I wanted to see suffer as payback for the pain they caused me. I had meticulously plotted my revenge, waiting for the perfect moment to strike back.

But in that divine confrontation, all my plans of retribution crumbled. I realized that holding onto such anger was not only poisoning my spirit but was also preventing me from fulfilling the greater purpose that God had for my life. The moment was both humbling and liberating. God began to birth in my heart a supernatural love for people, even for those who had hurt me. This transformation didn't happen instantly, nor did it come without struggle. Anger, after all, is a familiar comfort, and there were times when those old feelings would resurface, urging me to return to my former ways. But with God's help, I learned to manage my anger, to channel it into something constructive rather than destructive.

This journey to understanding grace has been crucial, especially during seasons of profound injustice. Without the inner work God had done in me, the anger and bitterness could have consumed me entirely, turning me against the world and everyone in it. Instead, the grace that had been extended to me became the grace I sought to extend to others. I learned that grace is not just a lofty spiritual concept but a practical, everyday decision. It's choosing to forgive when it's easier to hold a grudge, to love when hatred comes naturally, and to let go of the need for revenge in favor of a peace that surpasses understanding.

Had I not embraced grace earlier in life, this season of adversity and injustice would have destroyed not only my own peace of mind but also the well-being of those around me. Grace became my anchor, grounding me in the midst of chaos and providing a solid foundation on which to rebuild my life. It taught me that true strength is not in retaliation but in restraint, not in seeking revenge but in offering forgiveness. This revelation didn't just change my life; it saved it. It allowed me to transform moments of potential destruction into opportunities for growth and healing. Through grace, I found a way to rise above the pain, to be better rather than bitter, and to see the divine potential even in life's most challenging moments.

Initially, my heart was filled with bitterness and a desire for revenge. I struggled to let go of the sense of betrayal and injustice. But as I immersed myself in prayer and scripture, slowly, a shift began. I started to understand that harboring anger was only imprisoning me further. By embracing grace, I found a release—a freedom that allowed me to heal and move forward.

Understanding Injustice: A Deeper Reflection

Injustice is not just a word; it's a profound and often painful reality that many encounter unexpectedly, without rhyme or reason. It is the sudden disruption of one's life, the denial of rights and dignity, and the imposition of suffering that feels both unnecessary and deeply unfair. During my time in the camp, I faced numerous instances where injustice was not just a concept but a lived experience. It came in many forms—through the legal system's failures, the arbitrary and sometimes cruel actions of correctional officers, and even the betrayals or self-serving behavior of fellow campers. Each of these moments etched a deeper understanding of injustice into my heart, forcing me to confront the raw and unfiltered nature of a world where fairness is not guaranteed.

One of the most poignant examples of injustice I witnessed involved a fellow camper, a man known for his integrity and quiet demeanor. This individual was wrongfully accused of a serious violation that threatened not only his safety but also his freedom. Despite overwhelming evidence proving his innocence—testimonies from multiple witnesses, clear documentation that exonerated him—the system failed him. Instead of justice, he received a harsh punishment, a stark reminder of the arbitrary nature of power and authority within the walls of the camp.

Witnessing this egregious miscarriage of justice stirred something deep within me. It wasn't just anger; it was a mix of helplessness, outrage, and a profound sense of disillusionment. Here was a man who, like so many others, had come to the camp hoping for a semblance of justice, a chance to serve his time with dignity and perhaps find redemption. Instead, he was met with a system that seemed more interested in maintaining control and exercising power than in upholding truth or fairness.

This incident was a turning point for me. It opened my eyes to the harsh realities faced by those who are wrongfully accused and convicted, not just in the camp but in society at large. It challenged my understanding of justice, forcing me to question what justice truly means when it is stripped of compassion and fairness. It also made me reflect on my own circumstances, on the countless ways I had taken justice for granted, believing it to be an inherent right rather than something that must be continually fought for and defended.

In those moments, I grappled with my faith, wrestling with questions that had no easy answers. How could a just God allow such blatant injustice to occur? What was the purpose of suffering for those who had done no wrong? These questions haunted me, echoing in my mind as I watched my fellow camper endure his undeserved punishment. Yet, amidst the turmoil, I found a glimmer of clarity. I realized that injustice, painful as it is, can serve as a catalyst for change. It can awaken us to the realities of the world we live in, pushing us to act with greater empathy and resolve.

The experience also deepened my understanding of grace. In the face of injustice, grace becomes even more powerful. It is the force that enables us to respond with compassion rather than hatred, to seek restoration rather than retribution. Grace allowed me to extend kindness to those who were unjust, to forgive even when forgiveness seemed undeserved. It was a lesson in humility and strength, teaching me that true justice is not about punishment but about healing and reconciliation.

Injustice, I came to learn, is a test of character. It reveals who we are at our core and what we stand for. It demands a response, whether that be anger, resignation, or a commitment to seek justice in all its forms. For me, the choice was clear. I could not stand by and do nothing. I had to speak out, to advocate for those who had no voice, to use whatever influence I had to shine a light on the injustices that too often go unnoticed.

This understanding of injustice did not come easily, nor did it come without cost. It required me to confront my own biases and privileges, to acknowledge the ways in which I had benefited from systems that were unfair to others. It required me to step into uncomfortable spaces, to listen to stories that were difficult to hear, and to stand in solidarity with those who were suffering.

But through it all, I found a sense of purpose. I found that even in the midst of injustice, there is hope. There is the possibility of change, the potential for healing, and the power of grace to transform hearts and minds. Injustice may be a harsh reality, but it is not the end of the story. With grace and perseverance, we can work toward a world where justice is not a privilege for the few but a right for all. Many of us have faced moments where we felt wronged, betrayed, or unfairly treated. Whether it's in our personal lives, workplaces, or even in encounters with strangers, the sense of injustice can be overwhelming. However, choosing to respond with grace not only alleviates our own pain but also opens the door for healing and reconciliation.

A Reflection Inspired by Albert

Albert Einstein once said, "In matters of truth and justice, there is no difference between large and small problems, for issues concerning the treatment of people are all the same." This quote struck a deep chord with me during my time in the prison camp, highlighting a fundamental truth: that injustice, no matter its scale, requires our attention and response. Whether it stems from a personal slight or a systemic failure, every act of injustice has the power to dehumanize, diminish, and leave lasting wounds. Einstein's words served as a powerful reminder that any form of injustice—whether seemingly insignificant or monumental—carries a weight that can profoundly affect both individuals and communities, unsettling the very fabric of our humanity.

Understanding this concept profoundly reshaped my view of grace. In the harsh realities of the camp, where fairness seemed elusive, it was tempting to respond to injustice with bitterness, resentment, or a desire for retribution. It's easy to fall into the belief that grace should be reserved for those who deserve it, or that it can only be extended once justice is served. However, true grace transcends the need for revenge. It is a conscious decision to uphold one's integrity, to rise above the urge for retaliation, and to respond in a way that elevates both the giver and the receiver. I came to realize that grace isn't about turning a blind eye to injustice—it's about confronting it from a place of moral strength and choosing to act with compassion rather than vengeance.

The Choice to Extend Grace

In the face of profound injustice, the decision to extend grace can seem not only counterintuitive but also a form of weakness. Yet, it is precisely in these moments that grace holds the most transformative power. Choosing grace is not about condoning wrongdoing or allowing injustice to continue unchallenged. Rather, it is about ensuring that our response does not perpetuate the cycle of anger and hate. It is about holding onto our humanity and using our pain as a catalyst for compassion and understanding. This realization became a guiding principle for me, especially as I navigated the complex and often ambiguous realities of camp life.

For the camper who endured false accusations despite clear evidence of his innocence, the system seemed intent on making an example of him. Witnessing this blatant injustice was deeply unsettling, and every fiber of my being demanded retribution—craving to see wrongs corrected and justice served. Yet, in that moment, I recalled Einstein's words and the transformative power of grace. Instead of allowing the bitterness to consume me, I made a deliberate choice to respond differently—to rise above the desire for revenge and extend grace in the face of injustice.

I chose to reach out to this camper. I offered a listening ear, words of comfort, and a promise of solidarity. I shared moments of my own struggles with him, creating a bond of empathy and mutual support. This act of grace did not alter his circumstances; it did not change the unjust decisions that had been made. However, it did something perhaps even more significant—it provided him with a sense of dignity and reminded both of us of our shared humanity. In those conversations, the walls of the camp seemed to fall away, replaced by an invisible but unbreakable bond of trust and compassion.

Booker T. Washington's Wisdom on Grace and Dignity

Booker T. Washington once said, "I shall allow no man to belittle my soul by making me hate him." These words powerfully reminded me of the dignity that comes from upholding grace, even in the face of severe injustice. Washington's wisdom helped shape my own determination—to respond with love rather than hate, and to confront the harshness of my circumstances with a spirit that refused to be crushed or embittered.

Holding onto grace, especially in the face of injustice, is undoubtedly a difficult journey. It requires immense strength and constant self-reflection. The path demands that we frequently examine our emotions, recognizing that hate only serves to diminish us, while grace has the power to uplift. This became my daily practice in the camp. Each time I felt anger or resentment bubbling up, I returned to Washington's words. I reminded myself that preserving the integrity of my soul was far more valuable than the fleeting satisfaction of hate or retaliation.

By choosing grace, I found that I was not only preserving my own sense of self-worth but also creating a ripple effect. My acts of kindness, however small, began to inspire others around me. In a place where hope was often in short supply, grace became a beacon, a way to maintain our dignity and humanity despite the oppressive circumstances. Even in the darkest of times, the light of grace shone through, reminding us that while we might not be able to control our external circumstances, we could control how we responded to them.

Grace as a Response to Injustice

Embracing grace is not a passive act. It is a powerful, active choice that involves standing firm in one's values and beliefs, even when everything around you encourages you to do otherwise. Grace involves seeking justice, but not out of a desire for revenge; it seeks justice to restore, heal, and bring about true reconciliation. It is about refusing to allow injustice to harden your heart or to define your character. Grace is about maintaining the ability to see the humanity in others, to forgive even when it's undeserved, and to love even in the face of hate.

The power of grace lies in its ability to transform not only individuals but entire communities. By choosing grace, we create environments where people feel seen, heard, and valued. We build relationships based on trust and mutual respect, paving the way for healing and growth. The choice to extend grace, even in the midst of injustice, sets a powerful example that can inspire others to do the same. It is a choice that reflects strength, courage, and a commitment to a higher standard of living.

In the end, grace is about recognizing that everyone is fighting their own battles, often hidden from view. It is about acknowledging our shared humanity and choosing to respond with compassion, understanding, and love. By embracing grace, we not only transform our own lives but also contribute to a world that is more just, more loving, and more reflective of the values we hold dear.

Personal Encounters with Injustice: A Journey Through Grace

My own encounters with injustice have been deeply personal and painfully egregious. From the onset of my legal battles, I felt the crushing weight of a system more concerned with punishment than seeking truth or fostering rehabilitation.

The circumstances that led to my incarceration were riddled with legal and procedural missteps, blatant misjudgments, and an overwhelming series of obstacles that underscored the profound unfairness of it all. Each step along the way served as a painful reminder that justice is not always blind; at times, it turns a cold, indifferent gaze away from the truth.

During my time in the camp, I encountered yet another layer of injustice. There were times when I was singled out or mistreated, not for anything I had done, but because of who I was and what I represented. Whether it was my previous role as a pastor or my refusal to participate in unethical practices, the prejudice I faced was undeniable and often overwhelming. The camp became a microcosm of broader societal issues, exposing deep-seated biases and the human tendency to judge others based on preconceived notions rather than their true character.

Drawing Strength from the Greatest Example

In the midst of these injustices, I found myself searching for a way to cope that would not corrupt my soul. The temptation to retaliate, to harbor resentment, or to lose hope was ever-present. It was in these moments of profound struggle that I turned to the example of Jesus, who faced the ultimate injustice with unmatched grace and forgiveness.

One passage that continually resonated with me was from Luke 23:34, where Jesus, as He was being crucified, uttered the words: *"Father, forgive them, for they do not know what they are doing."* These words were not just a plea for forgiveness; they were a powerful declaration of grace in its purest form. Despite the pain, despite the betrayal, despite the mockery, Jesus chose forgiveness over vengeance, love over hatred, grace over retribution. This moment became a guiding light for me, a benchmark against which I measured my own reactions to the injustices I faced.

Every time I felt the sting of unfair treatment, I reminded myself of Jesus' response. His grace was not a sign of weakness but a profound strength that transcended human understanding. In choosing to emulate His example, I found a reservoir of strength I never knew existed. Grace became my shield, not to protect me from pain but to protect my heart from becoming hardened by it.

The Ripple Effect: Grace as a Catalyst for Change

Grace, I learned, is not just a personal refuge; it has a ripple effect that can touch the lives of many. Even in the harsh, often dehumanizing environment of the prison camp, acts of grace had the power to inspire, to heal, and to change the hearts of those around me. When I chose to respond to injustice with grace, it set a precedent. It showed others that there was another way to live, even in the midst of adversity.

In federal prisons, collective punishment—where a group of inmates is disciplined for the actions of one or a few—is supposed to be prohibited by regulations. However, there were times when, despite this rule, the entire camp was punished for the actions of one individual. One such instance involved a violation committed by a single camper, yet we were all subjected to the same disciplinary measures. The injustice of it was palpable, and anger simmered beneath the surface. None of us had done anything wrong, yet we all bore the consequences.

I had every reason to be frustrated, to protest the punishment, and to demand justice in a system that often seemed indifferent to fairness. But instead of reacting with anger or defiance, I chose to reflect on the example of Jesus, who, despite being wrongfully accused, maintained His grace and composure. I made the decision to accept the punishment without complaint, treating those in authority with respect, and refraining from speaking ill of them or the system.

While my response didn't change the rules or the outcome of the punishment, it did something else. It allowed me to navigate the situation with a sense of peace and integrity. Fellow campers, who had initially been angry and frustrated, began to notice how I handled the injustice without lashing out or fueling the tension. Some quietly acknowledged the difficulty of maintaining composure in such an unfair situation, and over time, a few even came to me to talk through their own frustrations.

It wasn't as though my response transformed how I was treated by the correctional officers, nor did it completely alter the dynamics of the camp, but it allowed me to set an example of grace under pressure. And in small, subtle ways, it opened up conversations about how to handle unfairness without letting it strip away one's dignity. Though we remained in a tough environment, the practice of responding with grace, rather than aggression, created a more personal sense of peace, even if it didn't immediately change the external circumstances.

This shift in behavior had a ripple effect. While the rules of the camp remained the same, the atmosphere within it began to change. People started to treat one another with a bit more respect, a bit more kindness. (This was the pattern after group punishment; then accusatory looks began.) In a place where isolation and resentment were the norms, grace found a way to break through. The environment didn't transform overnight, but my decision to act with integrity and grace in the face of collective punishment opened the door for a new kind of community, one built on understanding rather than bitterness.

The Power of Grace to Transform Hearts

Grace has a remarkable ability to soften hearts, including those hardened by years of injustice and suffering. It reaches into the deepest parts of our being, challenging our notions of right and wrong, strength and weakness. By extending grace, we not only maintain our own integrity but also create opportunities for healing and reconciliation.

Throughout my time in the camp, I witnessed grace do what force, argument, and anger could not. It brought peace in the midst of conflict. It turned enemies into allies. It opened doors to conversations that would otherwise never happen. Grace, I realized, was not a passive response but a powerful, active force for good. It had the power to change the trajectory of lives, mine included.

In reflecting on these experiences, I came to see grace not merely as a virtue but as a necessity. It is the balm that heals wounds, the bridge that connects hearts, and the light that shines in the darkest places. Grace, when embraced fully, has the potential to transform not just individuals, but entire communities. It is a gift from God that, when shared, multiplies and returns tenfold.

By choosing grace, I discovered a freedom that no physical bars could confine. It freed me from the shackles of bitterness and opened my heart to love and forgiveness. It showed me that while we may not be able to control the injustices we face, we can control how we respond to them. And in that response, we find our true strength.

The Consequences of Withholding Grace: A Path to Bitterness or Redemption

When grace does not rise to meet injustice, the outcome is often a descent into frustration, anger, and a perpetual cycle of mistreatment. These negative emotions do not serve to rectify the wrongs; instead, they can perpetuate a cycle of bitterness and retaliation, deepening the wounds rather than healing them. When we respond to injustice with hostility, we allow the darkness of the situation to overshadow our ability to see clearly, to love fully, and to live freely. We become captives not just of our circumstances, but of our own emotional reactions.

In an environment where tension and conflict are everyday realities, such as the prison camp, the absence of grace can create a breeding ground for resentment. Hostility begets hostility, anger fuels anger, and the prospect of reconciliation and healing is pushed further out of reach. Without grace, we close ourselves off to the transformative power of forgiveness. We miss the opportunity to break the cycle of negativity that binds us to our past hurts and grievances.

Grace, however, opens the door to a different outcome. By choosing grace, we invite the possibility of God's intervention. We create space for His presence to work in ways that we might not expect or even understand. As Paul writes in Romans 12:19, "Do not take revenge, my dear friends, but leave room for God's wrath, for it is written: 'It is mine to avenge; I will repay,' says the Lord." Choosing grace is an act of profound trust. It acknowledges that while we may not be able to rectify every wrong, we can leave room for God to work, trusting that His justice will ultimately prevail. In this way, grace becomes not just a response, but a powerful catalyst for divine intervention and transformation.

Life's Unfairness and the Subtle Blame on God

One of the greatest temptations in the face of injustice is to conclude that life is inherently unfair and, by extension, to subtly lay the blame on God. This perception can become a lens through which we interpret our experiences, leading to feelings of victimhood and helplessness. When we dwell on the unfairness of our circumstances, we imply that God is either indifferent to our suffering or incapable of doing anything about it. This mindset can corrode our faith, distancing us from the very source of comfort and strength that we need to endure our trials.

It is important to recognize that while life often appears unjust, God's grace is always sufficient to meet and overcome any injustice. This doesn't mean that we will always understand why certain things happen or why wrongs are sometimes left unaddressed for long periods. What it does mean is that God's perspective is infinitely greater than ours. As we are reminded in Isaiah 55:8-9, *"'For my thoughts are not your thoughts, neither are your ways my ways,' declares the Lord. 'As the heavens are higher than the earth, so are my ways higher than your ways and my thoughts than your thoughts.'"* This scripture calls us to trust in God's overarching plan, even when the immediate circumstances seem incomprehensible.

Choosing Grace Over Resentment

Choosing grace is not a denial of pain or injustice; rather, it is a decision to rise above these circumstances and trust in God's greater plan. It requires a deliberate effort to release our grip on resentment and open our hearts to forgiveness. This is not an easy task; it challenges our natural inclinations to fight back or withdraw. But grace has a unique power—it heals both the giver and the receiver. By extending grace, we are not just alleviating our own burdens; we are creating a ripple effect that can lead to healing in others.

When we choose grace, we are actively participating in God's redemptive work. We align ourselves with His purpose, which is to bring about reconciliation and restoration. Grace allows us to see beyond the immediate pain and recognize the potential for growth, healing, and even transformation. It's a testament to our faith, a demonstration that we believe God's way—though often different from ours—is ultimately better.

The Power of Grace to Transform Injustice

Grace does not ignore injustice; it confronts it with a power that is far greater. It's an acknowledgment that while we live in a broken world where wrongs are often committed, we serve a God who is able to bring good out of even the worst situations. Grace transforms our perspective, shifting our focus from the pain of what was done to us, to the possibility of what God can do through us. It takes the sting of injustice and turns it into an opportunity for spiritual growth, a deeper relationship with God, and a witness to His love and mercy.

The choice to extend grace in the face of injustice is one of the most powerful testimonies a person can give. It speaks volumes about the strength of our faith, the depth of our love, and the integrity of our character. It shows that we trust God's justice more than our own, that we value His approval over the approval of others, and that we are willing to lay down our right to be right in order to follow the example of Christ.

Embracing God's Grace in All Circumstances

In every trial and injustice, God's grace is available to us. It is not a one-time gift, but a continual outpouring that meets us at our point of need. When we embrace this grace, we find that it not only sustains us through difficult times but also empowers us to be agents of grace to others. It frees us from the chains of bitterness, opens our hearts to compassion, and allows us to live in a state of peace regardless of our circumstances.

By choosing grace, we align ourselves with God's character. We reflect His love and mercy to a world that is often harsh and unforgiving. We become living testimonies of His power to transform hearts and minds, to bring healing where there was once hurt, and to turn the tides of injustice with the steady, unyielding force of grace.

Embracing Grace to Overcome Injustice: A Deliberate Choice

Embracing grace is a deliberate and often difficult decision, especially in the face of injustice. It requires us to look beyond our immediate pain and frustration, and to respond not out of anger or desire for retaliation, but from a place of kindness, forgiveness, and understanding. Choosing grace does not mean we ignore the injustices we face. Instead, it means confronting them with a heart that is aligned with God's will, trusting in His sovereignty, and reflecting His love even when we are wronged. This act of grace is transformative, not only for ourselves but also for those around us. It elevates our character, preserving our integrity and dignity, and enables us to act with the compassion and mercy that are hallmarks of the Christian faith.

Grace empowers us to be like Christ, who in His greatest moment of injustice—His crucifixion—prayed for His persecutors forgiveness. By choosing to extend grace, we find inner peace and become conduits of God's grace, inspiring others to seek the same path. In doing so, we offer a powerful testimony of faith, demonstrating that grace is not a sign of weakness but a profound strength. It allows us to confront injustice without becoming consumed by it, showing that there is a higher way to live.

The Active Nature of Grace

Elie Wiesel's words ring true in this context: "There may be times when we are powerless to prevent injustice, but there must never be a time when we fail to protest." This statement reminds us that grace is not about passivity or silence in the face of injustice. Rather, it calls us to respond with a heart committed to healing and reconciliation, not revenge or destruction. We must still stand against wrongs, but grace allows us to do so with a spirit that reflects Christ's love and forgiveness. It seeks to build bridges rather than deepen divides, offering forgiveness where bitterness might grow and love where hatred could take root. Through grace, we trust in God's justice, even when human systems fall short.

The Role of Faith in Extending Grace

Faith is the cornerstone of the ability to extend grace. It provides the strength needed to choose grace over bitterness, peace over conflict, and love over hatred. Throughout my time in the prison camp, faith played a critical role in my journey of grace. It was through prayer, the comfort of scripture, and a deep-seated trust in God's overarching plan that I found the strength to offer grace, even in the most trying of circumstances. This faith in God's providence and justice enabled me to confront injustices without losing hope or becoming hardened by anger.

Reflections on the U.S. Justice System

Throughout my trial and time in the camp, it became painfully clear that the U.S. justice system has significant flaws, particularly in how it favors the prosecution. The pressure on defendants to plead guilty rather than go to trial is immense. Only about 2% of federal criminal defendants exercise their constitutional right to a trial. This astonishingly low number is a testament to the overwhelming power held by federal prosecutors, who boast a conviction rate close to 97%. These statistics reveal a system that is designed not to seek truth and justice impartially but rather to secure convictions, often at any cost.

The challenges defense attorneys face in this environment are substantial, with the odds heavily stacked against them from the outset. The imbalance of power can leave defendants feeling as though they are on the ropes from the very beginning, coerced into plea deals due to the fear of much harsher sentences if they dare to go to trial.

Beyond my own experiences, I heard stories from fellow inmates that highlighted even more layers of injustice. One inmate, who had managed to work his way down from medium security to our camp, shared a troubling account of how the system had failed him. He started as a low-level, recreational marijuana user and eventually became a small-time dealer (to financially support his habit). However, things escalated when an undercover federal agent, posing as a customer, not only bought from him but also actively encouraged him to expand his business. This undercover agent provided support, connections, and resources that inflated his operation to a scale that, once the authorities decided to intervene, allowed them to claim a major drug bust. The agents involved received promotions for dismantling the business they had essentially helped to build (with government resources), while the inmate was sentenced to over 20 years in prison. During his time behind bars, he saw his parents pass away, unable to be by their side due to the lengthy sentence imposed on him. Despite the clear entrapment tactics and manipulation by the federal agents, there was no accountability for their actions. This lack of accountability is not only a miscarriage of justice but also a betrayal of the trust that society places in law enforcement.

I remember a brother in the camp who proudly called himself a marijuana broker, never hiding his satisfaction with the quality of his product or the loyalty of his clientele. One of his customers was caught in a federal sting, and in a desperate attempt to cut a deal, the client handed over his marijuana dealer. When the feds combed through their text messages, they found only references to marijuana. But that wasn't enough for them. They twisted the narrative, claiming that the texts were coded messages for heroin and cocaine transactions. Despite his open admission that he dealt only marijuana—and nothing more—he was hauled into court. Boldly, he took the stand, declaring himself a proud "pot dealer," having never touched or sold hard drugs. Yet, in a shocking turn of events, the jury convicted him anyway.

These stories highlight the urgent need for reform within our justice system. While this doesn't negate the reality that there are true criminals who belong in prison, it does expose a troubling culture where securing convictions often takes precedence over ethical standards. The problem extends beyond individual cases—it's indicative of a system that prioritizes victories over justice. Restoring balance is crucial, ensuring that the pursuit of justice isn't overshadowed by the desire for prosecution wins. These systemic failures deserve a more thorough examination, which I plan to explore in a future book, *I Still Believe in America*. Despite these flaws, it's vital to hold on to hope and continue striving for change that reflects our nation's core values of fairness, justice, and equality for all.

As we navigate the complexities of injustice, extending grace becomes not just a reaction but a deliberate practice that transforms both ourselves and those around us. Embracing grace requires intentionality, commitment, and practical steps that help us live out this powerful virtue in our everyday lives. The following strategies offer guidance on how to cultivate and maintain a heart of grace, even when faced with life's greatest challenges.

Strategies for Embracing Grace

1. **Open Your Heart to God's Presence**
   To receive grace, one must first acknowledge the presence of God in their life. Spend time in prayer and meditation, inviting God's grace to fill your heart. Reflect on moments in scripture where God's grace was evident, allowing these stories to shape your understanding and acceptance of grace.

2. **Practice Forgiveness**
   Grace and forgiveness are intrinsically linked. Let go of grudges and bitterness towards others, as holding onto anger only blocks the flow of grace. Practice forgiving those who have wronged you, not for their sake, but for your own spiritual freedom.

3. **Embrace Humility**
   Recognize that none of us are perfect. A humble heart is more open to receiving grace. Accept your own shortcomings and limitations, understanding that grace is not about being perfect, but about being willing to grow and change.

4. **Seek Community Support**
   Sometimes, grace comes through the encouragement and support of others. Surround yourself with people who understand the importance of grace and can help you grow in it. Engage in group discussions or Bible studies focused on grace to learn from others' experiences.

5. **Reflect on God's Promises**
   Regularly revisit scriptures that emphasize God's grace. Verses like Ephesians 2:8-9 remind us that grace is a gift from God, not something we earn. Let these truths resonate in your heart, reinforcing your faith and trust in God's unconditional love.

Conviction Checkpoints

- **Self-Examination Question:** Reflect on a time when you faced injustice. How did you respond? How might extending grace in that situation have changed the outcome or your perspective?
- **Actionable Step:** Identify someone in your life who is facing injustice. Reach out to them with a gesture of grace, whether through a kind word, a listening ear, or an act of support.
- **Conviction Affirmation:** "I choose to extend grace, trusting that God's love will bring justice and healing in His time."
- **Prayer/Meditation Focus:** Pray for the strength to extend grace in the face of injustice. Ask God to help you see others through His eyes and to respond with compassion and understanding.

Profile in Conviction

Aung San Suu Kyi

Aung San Suu Kyi, the Burmese political leader and Nobel Peace Prize laureate, is an emblematic figure of grace in the face of injustice. Born in 1945, Suu Kyi spent much of her life advocating for democracy and human rights in Myanmar (formerly Burma), a country long dominated by military rule.

Despite winning a landslide victory in the 1990 general elections, the military junta refused to recognize the results and placed her under house arrest. Over the next two decades, Suu Kyi spent nearly 15 years under house arrest, separated from her family and subjected to isolation. Throughout her ordeal, she maintained a steadfast commitment to nonviolence and reconciliation, embodying grace under pressure.

Her response to her unjust imprisonment was rooted in her belief in nonviolent resistance and her deep sense of responsibility to the Burmese people. Suu Kyi's grace in the face of systemic injustice has inspired millions worldwide and earned her the Nobel Peace Prize in 1991. Her story is a powerful testament to the strength that comes from embracing grace, even when faced with overwhelming adversity.

Aung San Suu Kyi's unwavering commitment to nonviolent resistance, even while under house arrest, serves as a testament to the power of grace in the face of injustice. Her grace-filled approach did not only preserve her integrity but inspired a nation and the world. Her example reinforces that grace is a choice—a powerful one that can defy oppression and bring light to even the darkest circumstances.

Embracing grace is not about condoning wrongdoing or ignoring injustice. It's about choosing to respond with love and forgiveness, even when the world would justify anger and retaliation. Grace has the power to transform hearts, heal wounds, and inspire change. As we navigate the injustices of life, may we always choose grace, trusting that God's light will shine through us, making a difference in our lives and the lives of those around us. As we navigate the complexities of life, let us choose grace as our response to injustice. Let us be the vessels through which God's grace flows, bringing light into dark situations and hope where there is despair. By embracing grace, we not only find peace for ourselves but also contribute to a more just and compassionate world.

CHAPTER 9
EVERY LOSS TEACHES A LESSON

Loss is an inevitable part of life, touching each of us in different ways—whether it's the loss of freedom, relationships, dreams, or opportunities. In the unforgiving atmosphere of the prison camp, the weight of loss was an ever-present reality. The deprivation of autonomy, the inability to make even the simplest decisions, and the aching distance from loved ones were relentless reminders of my confinement. Yet, as time passed, I began to see that within each loss lay the potential for growth. These hardships, though deeply painful, became transformative lessons, shaping my character and strengthening my faith in ways I could never have foreseen.

In the beginning, the pain of loss felt overwhelming, like an ocean with no shore in sight. There was a sense of helplessness that came with the realization that the life I once knew was no longer accessible. The loss of freedom was particularly jarring. The daily routines that most people take for granted—waking up in one's own home, choosing what to eat, deciding where to go—were replaced with a rigid schedule controlled by others. This absence of control was not only a practical loss but an emotional and psychological one, stripping away layers of my identity. However, amid this stripping away, I began to understand that loss, as devastating as it can be, also provides space for something new to grow. It's like the pruning of a tree; though it seems harsh, it is necessary for new, healthier growth.

Understanding Loss Through Faith

James 1:4 provides a powerful lens through which to view the purpose of loss: "Let perseverance finish its work so that you may be mature and complete, not lacking anything." During my time in the camp, this verse transformed from mere scripture into a lifeline. It reminded me that the trials and losses I endured were not random hardships but opportunities—chances for personal growth, refinement, and a deeper connection to God's grace and faithfulness. Each challenge became a stepping stone toward becoming the person God intended me to be.

Loss often feels like a thief, taking away what we hold dear and leaving us with emptiness and despair. But when viewed through the lens of faith, loss is more accurately seen as a refiner's fire. It burns away the superficial and reveals what is truly valuable. It was in the depth of my losses that I discovered an unexpected clarity about what truly mattered. The material things, the accolades, the external validations—they all faded in significance. What remained was my relationship with God, my faith, and the character being forged in the fire of adversity.

The Transformation of Perceived Loss

One of the most profound realizations I had was that not all losses are what they seem. What we often perceive as a loss can, in God's grand design, be a setup for something far greater. The apparent setbacks were, in many ways, setups for a comeback that only God could orchestrate. In my own life, what initially appeared as the greatest losses became the fertile ground for a deeper, more resilient faith. The stripping away of freedom and status created a space where God could work more profoundly, teaching me dependence on Him in ways I had never known.

The Role of Gratitude in Loss

Finding gratitude amidst loss may seem counterintuitive, yet it is one of the most powerful catalysts for transformation. Gratitude shifts our focus from what has been lost to what remains and what can still be gained. In the camp, I made a deliberate effort to practice gratitude, starting with the smallest things—a kind word, a shared smile, the beauty of a sunrise. This practice didn't erase the pain of loss, but it reshaped how I experienced it. Gratitude opened my eyes to God's unwavering provision, revealing His presence even in the bleakest moments.

Loss as a Catalyst for Community

Interestingly, loss also became a catalyst for community. Shared adversity has a way of bringing people together. The camaraderie among fellow campers, many of whom were experiencing similar losses, provided a unique bond. We found strength in each other's stories, in our shared struggles and victories. This communal experience reinforced the idea that while loss can isolate, it can also connect us more deeply to others, fostering empathy and understanding. In the prison camp, the sense of shared loss often led to unexpected acts of kindness and solidarity that lightened the burden for everyone.

God's Sovereignty Over Loss

Ultimately, embracing the reality of loss requires a deep trust in God's sovereignty. It calls for the belief that God is not only aware of our struggles but is actively working through them for our good and His greater glory. Romans 8:28 affirms this, reminding us: "And we know that in all things God works for the good of those who love him, who have been called according to his purpose." This assurance enables us to confront loss not with despair, but with hope, knowing that God's purpose far exceeds our limited understanding.

Understanding the Nature of Loss

Loss manifests in countless forms, each carrying its own weight and requiring a unique kind of resilience to navigate. In the prison camp, the loss of freedom was the most glaring and immediate—an ever-present reminder of the constraints on my physical existence. However, other less tangible losses were equally impactful. The loss of privacy meant every moment was shared, every action observed, stripping away the sense of autonomy and personal space that most people take for granted. The loss of personal belongings, no matter how trivial they might have seemed in the outside world, represented a severing from the past and an erosion of personal identity. Most profoundly, there was the loss of dignity, a subtle yet powerful erosion of self-worth brought about by the constant surveillance, control, and dehumanizing aspects of incarceration.

One of the most insidious losses I faced was the loss of time. In the camp, days bled into each other, and the future felt like a distant mirage. The ticking away of time, marked not by meaningful milestones but by a monotonous routine, became a daily source of pain. Each day represented a missed opportunity—a day not spent with loved ones and a life event that passed by unnoticed. This loss of time carried a weight that was almost physical, pressing down on me with the realization that life was continuing outside these walls while I remained stagnant, caught in a loop of waiting.

Albert Camus once wrote, "In the midst of winter, I found there was, within me, an invincible summer." This profound sentiment resonated deeply with me during my time in the camp. Even in the darkest moments of loss, when everything familiar and comforting was stripped away, I discovered an inner strength—a resilience that remained untouchable by the harshness of my surroundings. That resilience became my own "invincible summer," a wellspring of hope and endurance that enabled me to find meaning, purpose, and growth, even in the most desolate of circumstances.

The Emotional Impact of Loss

The emotional toll of loss is profound and multifaceted, manifesting in waves of sadness, anger, frustration, and despair. Within the oppressive environment of the prison camp, these emotions were amplified, creating a constant undercurrent of turmoil that often felt inescapable. The initial response to loss was frequently one of shock and disbelief, a numbing sensation that made it difficult to fully grasp the reality of the situation. Over time, as the shock subsided, it gave way to a deep and pervasive grief, not unlike the mourning that follows a death.

Sadness became a constant companion, especially when reflecting on the loved ones from whom I was separated. The inability to participate in their joys, sorrows, and daily lives created an aching void that seemed impossible to fill. It wasn't just the physical separation that cut deep but the emotional distance—the missed birthdays, family gatherings, graduations, and the ordinary moments that had slipped through my fingers and could never be regained. This sadness often morphed into helplessness, a haunting sense that life was moving forward without me, beyond my control.

Anger and frustration were also frequent visitors. The perceived injustice of my situation, combined with the daily indignities and arbitrary treatment within the camp, stoked a deep-seated rage. This anger was directed at the system, at those responsible for my incarceration, and sometimes even at myself. Finding a healthy outlet for these emotions proved challenging. The camp environment often felt like a pressure cooker, and without an effective means of release, it seemed inevitable that the pressure would eventually boil over.

But perhaps the most dangerous emotion of all was despair. The creeping sense that there was no way out, no chance for redemption or change, hung over me like a dark cloud. Despair threatened to rob me of hope, leading me to believe that the fight was futile, that there was no longer a reason to keep pushing forward. Overcoming this despair required daily reminders of my faith, and a resolute belief that God had a purpose for me, even in the midst of these darkest trials.

Learning from Losses

Every loss carried a lesson, but these lessons were often hidden beneath layers of pain and needed intentional reflection and prayer to uncover. One of the most valuable lessons I learned was the importance of resilience. True resilience is not just about enduring physical hardship or maintaining a façade of strength. It is about cultivating emotional and spiritual fortitude, the ability to bounce back not only in body but in mind and spirit.

The loss of freedom, for instance, taught me about the power of inner freedom. While my body was confined, my mind and spirit could remain unbound. This realization led me to invest in my inner life through prayer, meditation, and a deepening relationship with God. By focusing on my inner spiritual health, I found a peace that was not dependent on my external circumstances. I learned that true freedom is found in the mind and soul, not in the physical ability to come and go.

> *"Success is to be measured not so much by the position that one has reached in life as by the obstacles which he has overcome while trying to succeed."* - BOOKER T. WASHINGTON

True success, I realized, is not about external achievements or status. It is about the character forged in the fire of adversity, the strength that comes from facing loss head-on and finding a way to grow from it.

The Role of Faith in Understanding Loss

Faith was the anchor that kept me grounded, helping me navigate the turbulent waters of loss and transform seemingly insurmountable pain into opportunities for growth and renewal. Scripture played a vital role in this journey, offering constant reassurance and guidance. One verse that deeply resonated with me during this time was Isaiah 41:10: "So do not fear, for I am with you; do not be dismayed, for I am your God. I will strengthen you and help you; I will uphold you with my righteous right hand." This passage reminded me that I was not alone, that God's presence and strength were there to support me, even when everything around me seemed to crumble. It wasn't about dismissing the pain but about trusting that God was using it to shape something greater, weaving my suffering into His larger, redemptive plan.

Another profound lesson was the necessity of letting go. Holding onto anger, resentment, or the desire for revenge can chain us to our losses, compounding the hurt. Ephesians 4:31-32 advises, "Get rid of all bitterness, rage and anger, brawling and slander, along with every form of malice. Be kind and compassionate to one another, forgiving each other, just as in Christ God forgave you." By surrendering these emotions and placing my trust in God's justice and mercy, I found a release that allowed me to heal. Letting go didn't mean the injustice was acceptable; it meant that I was no longer allowing it to dominate my life. This surrender was not a sign of weakness but a pathway to peace, an act of faith that God's justice would prevail in His timing.

Loss Is Not Permanent

One of the profound insights I gained during my journey was that loss does not always mark an ending—it can be the doorway to something greater. In times of hardship, I found strength in 2 Corinthians 4:17, which says, "For our light and momentary troubles are achieving for us an eternal glory that far outweighs them all." This verse reminded me that enduring trials is not in vain; they are shaping us for something far beyond our current understanding. Persevering through loss not only fosters personal growth but also aligns us with a deeper, eternal purpose.

In the camp, this concept became a reality. When I was assigned to work in the kitchen, my initial reaction was to view this as a loss of dignity and freedom. It seemed like a menial task that didn't utilize my skills or experience. Yet over time, this job became a surprising blessing. It allowed me to connect with others on a deeper level, foster relationships, and find small moments of joy and purpose in serving my fellow campers. What initially seemed like a loss transformed into a source of strength, demonstrating that God's plans often unfold in ways that defy our understanding.

The Perception of Loss

Our perception shapes our reality. Sometimes what we interpret as loss may actually be a redirection toward something more meaningful. By adopting a mindset of gratitude and seeking the hidden opportunities in every situation, we can reframe perceived losses into gains. Philippians 4:8 encourages this positive perspective: "Finally, brothers and sisters, whatever is true, whatever is noble, whatever is right, whatever is pure, whatever is lovely, whatever is admirable—if anything is excellent or praiseworthy—think about such things."

For example, during my time of incarceration, losing contact with certain people initially felt like a profound loss. It created a sense of isolation and abandonment. However, this solitude also provided the space I needed to deepen my relationship with God. It offered me the opportunity to focus on personal growth, reflection, and prayer. What I had perceived as a devastating loss of human connection actually became a divine opportunity to cultivate a deeper spiritual connection and to build resilience. Looking back, the relationships that faded made room for new, more meaningful connections that aligned with my renewed sense of purpose and faith.

God as the Redeemer of Loss

Loss, as painful as it is, provides a canvas for God to work His miracles of redemption. The beauty of the divine lies in His ability to take what seems irretrievably lost and breathe new life into it, transforming ashes into beauty and despair into hope. This belief served as my anchor, reminding me that no loss, however devastating, is beyond God's capacity to redeem. The promise of resurrection, whether literal or metaphorical, instilled hope that every setback could be a setup for a greater comeback.

Isaiah 61:3 encapsulates this hope beautifully, where God promises "to bestow on them a crown of beauty instead of ashes, the oil of joy instead of mourning, and a garment of praise instead of a spirit of despair." These words became a lifeline, a reassurance that God could and would transform the seeming finality of loss into an opportunity for renewal and rebirth. They remind us that God's ultimate purpose is to restore and heal, turning every painful experience into a testimony of His grace.

In moments of loss, I would turn to this scripture, holding onto the belief that God was not finished yet. Every day, even when the evidence of redemption was not immediately visible, I trusted that God's redemptive power was at work, rearranging and realigning my circumstances for a future that I could not yet see. This divine assurance infused my days with a quiet strength, enabling me to endure hardships with the hope of eventual restoration.

Personal Stories of Loss and Learning

The prison camp was a microcosm of life's challenges, bringing with it daily reminders of what we had lost. Yet it was also a place where the power of God's redemption shone through personal stories of resilience and transformation. One story that stands out is of a fellow camper who experienced the heart-wrenching loss of communication with his family. For him, the silence from the outside world was more painful than the physical constraints of the camp. This loss left him feeling isolated and abandoned, struggling to find purpose in a life that suddenly felt devoid of meaning.

Over time, however, this very loss became the catalyst for a new beginning. Instead of succumbing to despair, he made the courageous choice to reach out to those around him, forming bonds with fellow campers. What began as simple conversations grew into deep relationships that provided him with the community and support he so desperately needed. This experience taught him—and those of us who witnessed it—that sometimes God removes certain relationships to make space for new ones that are more aligned with His plans for our growth and well-being.

Another poignant story involved the common camp occurrence of theft. Personal belongings held immense value, not just materially but as reminders of the outside world and personal identity. When a cherished item that I received in the mail was stolen from my desk, my initial reaction was anger and frustration. The loss felt personal and unjust, stirring a sense of vulnerability in an environment where control over one's circumstances was already minimal. But as the days passed, I realized that holding onto anger over a lost item was counterproductive. It only served to deepen my sense of loss and injustice.

Through prayer and reflection, I began to see this incident differently. Instead of focusing on what I had lost, I turned my attention to the relationships and experiences that truly mattered. I chose to let go of my attachment to the item, freeing myself from the grip of negative emotions. This shift in perspective was liberating. It taught me the profound value of focusing on the intangible aspects of life—relationships, faith, and personal growth—that no one could steal or diminish.

The Impact of Loss on Personal Growth

Loss cultivates resilience—a quality essential for enduring life's inevitable challenges. Facing and overcoming loss develops an inner fortitude, a capacity to rise above adversity with grace. Each loss teaches us to adapt, to find new ways to cope, and to discover alternative paths toward fulfillment and peace. In the camp, witnessing the resilience of fellow inmates who continued to find hope despite their losses was inspiring. Their strength in the face of adversity served as a powerful reminder that our spirit can endure more than we often realize.

Fostering Empathy, Compassion, and Understanding

Beyond personal resilience, loss also has the capacity to foster greater empathy, compassion, and understanding toward others. Shared experiences of hardship often lead to a sense of solidarity, breaking down barriers and creating connections based on mutual struggles. In the camp, loss became a common denominator that united individuals from different backgrounds. This shared experience of suffering helped cultivate empathy—an understanding that while our circumstances might differ, our feelings of pain and loss were universal.

This empathy extended beyond the walls of the camp, influencing how we interacted with one another. Acts of kindness, no matter how small, carried significant weight, offering comfort and reminding us of our shared humanity. When a fellow inmate lost contact with his family, others would come together to offer support, proving that even in an environment characterized by loss, there could be moments of profound connection and care. These acts of empathy and compassion demonstrated that loss, rather than isolating us, can become a bridge that connects hearts.

The Humbling Power of Loss

One of the most transformative aspects of loss is its ability to humble us. In the face of loss, we are reminded of our limitations, our fallibility, and our need for reliance on something greater than ourselves. This humbling is not about diminishing our self-worth but about recognizing our dependence on God and His grace. It teaches us that no matter how strong or capable we think we are, there are moments when our strength alone is insufficient.

In the camp, this sense of humility became a pathway to spiritual growth. Losing the familiar comforts and privileges that I had once taken for granted forced me to reflect on my dependence on God. It was a humbling realization that my well-being was not solely in my hands; rather, I had to trust in God's provision and timing. This humility led to a more profound sense of gratitude for the small blessings, moments of peace, and acts of kindness that would have otherwise gone unnoticed.

Reordering Priorities and Valuing What Truly Matters

Loss has a unique way of clarifying what truly matters in life. Stripped of the distractions and superficialities, we are left to contemplate what is essential. For many in the camp, including myself, loss prompted a reordering of priorities. Material possessions, status, and external validation lost their significance. Instead, relationships, spiritual well-being, and personal integrity became the core focus.

The absence of freedom and the constrictions of camp life highlighted the value of inner freedom—the freedom to choose one's attitude and response to circumstances. Viktor Frankl, a Holocaust survivor, once said, "When we are no longer able to change a situation, we are challenged to change ourselves." This principle resonated deeply with me, prompting a shift in how I viewed loss. Instead of seeing it solely as a deprivation, I began to view it as an opportunity to cultivate qualities that truly mattered—faith, compassion, humility, and resilience.

Embracing the lessons of loss is not merely a survival strategy but a powerful approach to navigating the complexities of life. Loss, in its many forms, is an inevitable part of our human experience. However, by viewing losses as opportunities for growth and learning, we can transform these painful experiences into valuable lessons that shape our character and deepen our faith. This perspective allows us to approach loss not with a sense of defeat but with an attitude of resilience and hope. Through faith and resilience, every loss can be seen as a stepping stone towards greater maturity and spiritual depth, knowing that God has the power to use even the most difficult circumstances for our ultimate good.

The good news about loss is rooted in the nature of God as a redeemer. The concept of redemption is central to the Christian faith, offering a profound assurance that God can bring something beautiful out of what seems irreparably broken. Even when something is lost or appears to be beyond recovery, God promises a form of resurrection—a renewal that restores, replenishes, and revitalizes. Isaiah 61:3 captures this beautifully, reminding us that God bestows "a crown of beauty instead of ashes, the oil of joy instead of mourning, and a garment of praise instead of a spirit of despair." This promise does not erase the pain of loss but provides a framework of hope that empowers us to endure and to believe in the possibility of renewal.

By holding onto this assurance, we are encouraged to face our losses with a spirit of trust and expectation. The temporary nature of loss becomes a bridge to the eternal promises of God. It is through this divine perspective that we find the strength to endure, knowing that each loss is a thread in the larger tapestry of God's plan. It is not the end of the story but a chapter in the ongoing narrative of redemption and restoration. This mindset allows us to see beyond our immediate circumstances and to trust in God's ability to bring beauty from ashes and joy from mourning.

In essence, the true power of loss lies not in the loss itself but in our response to it. By embracing the lessons of loss, we open ourselves up to the possibility of transformation. Our pain becomes a catalyst for growth, our despair a pathway to deeper faith, and our grief an opportunity to experience God's grace in new and profound ways. Through the lens of faith, we learn that nothing is truly lost when it is entrusted into the hands of the One who holds all things together.

Strategies for Redeeming Loss

Redeeming loss means transforming the pain and hardships from loss into valuable, meaningful outcomes. It involves finding purpose and growth in difficult experiences, trusting that God can bring good from every situation. Rather than seeing loss as an end, it's about recognizing it as a part of a larger story where healing, restoration, and even joy can emerge. By shifting perspectives, developing resilience, and seeking the deeper lessons within the struggle, redeeming loss turns setbacks into opportunities for personal transformation and hope.

1. **Shift Your Perspective:** See loss not just as a setback but as an opportunity for growth and transformation. By changing how you view your circumstances, you can discover new paths and possibilities that may have been overlooked.
2. **Find Meaning in the Experience:** Look for lessons and insights within your losses. Reflect on what the situation taught you about yourself, others, or life in general. Finding meaning can bring purpose and a sense of peace, even in difficult times.
3. **Lean on Faith:** Trust that God has a plan for your life, even in the midst of loss. Draw strength from scripture and prayer, believing that God can use your circumstances to bring about good and fulfill His purposes.
4. **Embrace Vulnerability:** Allow yourself to feel and process the pain of loss. Being open and honest about your emotions can lead to healing and deeper connections with others who may share similar experiences.

5. **Seek Community Support:** Surround yourself with supportive people who can offer encouragement, prayer, and perspective. Sharing your journey with others can provide comfort and remind you that you are not alone.
6. **Practice Gratitude:** Focus on what you still have rather than what you've lost. Cultivating gratitude helps shift your mindset from one of lack to one of abundance, fostering hope and positivity.
7. **Take Small Steps Forward:** Start with manageable actions that help you move beyond your loss. Whether it's engaging in a new hobby, volunteering, or setting small goals, these steps can help rebuild a sense of purpose and momentum.
8. **Reflect on God's Promises:** Remind yourself of scriptures that speak of hope, restoration, and God's faithfulness. Verses like Isaiah 61:3 and Romans 8:28 can reinforce the belief that God can bring beauty from ashes and good from all situations.
9. **Use Your Experience to Help Others:** Sharing your story and supporting others who face similar challenges can bring healing and create a sense of purpose. By helping others, you turn your loss into a source of strength and encouragement for those in need.

These strategies are meant to help you not just endure loss but to grow and find meaning through it, believing that God's redemptive power can transform even the most painful experiences into a source of hope and joy.

Conviction Checkpoints

- **Self-Examination:** Reflect on a significant loss in your life. What lessons did you learn from this experience? How did it shape your character and deepen your faith?

- **Actionable Step:** Identify someone in your life currently experiencing loss. Offer your support and share your experiences of learning from loss to help them find strength and understanding.
- **Conviction Affirmation:** "Every loss I encounter carries a lesson that can strengthen my character and deepen my faith."
- **Prayer Focus:** Ask God for the wisdom to learn from losses and the strength to support others in their times of loss.

Profile in Conviction

Horatio Spafford

Horatio Spafford, a 19th-century American lawyer, businessman, and devout Christian, serves as a compelling example of enduring conviction in the face of unimaginable loss. Spafford's life, marked by both financial success and devastating personal tragedy, demonstrates how profound faith can transform even the darkest circumstances into a testimony of grace and resilience.

Spafford's early life in Chicago was prosperous—he was a successful lawyer and a dedicated church elder. However, in 1871, tragedy struck when the Great Chicago Fire destroyed much of his real estate investments, severely impacting his financial standing. As he and his family sought to rebuild, an even more catastrophic loss followed. In 1873, Spafford's wife and four daughters were en route to Europe on a ship when it collided with another vessel and sank. His four daughters perished, leaving his wife as the sole survivor.

Upon receiving the heartbreaking telegram from his wife—"Saved alone"—Spafford immediately set sail to join her. During the voyage, as his ship passed over the very waters where his daughters had drowned, Spafford penned the hymn "It Is Well with My Soul." This hymn, written in the wake of unthinkable grief, is a testament to his unshakable faith in God's sovereignty. The opening lines, "When peace like a river, attendeth my way; when sorrows like sea billows roll; whatever my lot, Thou hast taught me to say, it is well, it is well with my soul," reflect his profound ability to find peace in God's presence, even amid overwhelming sorrow.

Spafford's story did not end in despair. Rather than succumbing to bitterness or anger, he and his wife moved forward with a deepened sense of purpose. They later moved to Jerusalem, where they founded the American Colony, a Christian communal society dedicated to serving the poor and disadvantaged in the Holy Land. This legacy of service and grace continues to inspire people around the world today.

Spafford's life is a testament to the transformative power of faith and the strength of conviction in the face of profound loss. His ability to trust God in the midst of tragedy and to turn his grief into a source of inspiration for others has left an indelible mark on Christian history. Spafford's story reminds us that while suffering is inevitable, our response to it—rooted in faith and trust in God—can lead to a legacy of hope and redemption. His life, much like his hymn, affirms that peace is possible, even when the storms of life seem insurmountable.

As we conclude this chapter, it's essential to understand that loss, though inevitable and often painful, is not the end of our story. It offers profound opportunities for growth, resilience, and deeper understanding. Just as Horatio Spafford, in the depths of his personal tragedy, penned the timeless hymn "It Is Well with My Soul," we too can find strength in our faith, transforming our grief into a powerful testimony of grace and endurance.

Loss teaches us that life is not defined by what we accumulate, but by how we respond when those things are taken away. It reminds us that our true power lies not in controlling our circumstances, but in choosing our response to them. This perspective empowers us to turn adversity into strength, shaping us into more compassionate, empathetic, and resilient individuals.

Through the lens of faith, loss is not seen as a permanent defeat but as a temporary challenge with the potential for divine redemption. Scriptures like Isaiah 43:2 remind us that, even in the midst of trials, God is with us: "When you pass through the waters, I will be with you; and when you pass through the rivers, they will not sweep over you." This promise invites us to trust in God's purpose, even when the way forward is unclear.

In our journey through loss, we learn invaluable lessons about letting go, humility, and the significance of inner freedom. We discover that true liberation comes from within and that no external circumstance can confine a heart and mind anchored in faith and grace. By embracing the lessons of loss, we rise above our challenges, find joy in our resilience, and move forward with hope.

Ultimately, loss reminds us of our shared humanity and the importance of connection. Whether through personal reflection, support from loved ones, or the guidance of faith, we find the strength to face loss with courage and transform it into an opportunity for growth. In this way, we honor the legacy of those like Horatio Spafford, whose faith amid tragedy became a beacon of hope, and we, too, can inspire others navigating their own seasons of loss.

Let us embrace loss as a powerful teacher and a refining fire that shapes us into who we are meant to be. With faith as our foundation and grace as our guide, we can find meaning in every loss, knowing that each experience is a stepping stone on the journey toward purpose, peace, and fulfillment.

CHAPTER 10
FORGIVENESS FREES US

Forgiveness is one of the most profound and liberating choices we can make. It has the power to release us from the grip of anger, bitterness, and resentment, opening the door to healing and inner peace. Throughout my journey, I came to understand firsthand just how transformative forgiveness can be—not only for our own well-being but also for those we choose to forgive. It has the capacity to ripple outward, fostering reconciliation and grace in even the most difficult circumstances.

Forgiveness is not just a choice; it is a command woven deeply into the fabric of our faith. The Gospel of Matthew offers a powerful reminder: "For if you forgive other people when they sin against you, your heavenly Father will also forgive you. But if you do not forgive others their sins, your Father will not forgive your sins" (Matthew 6:14-15). This teaching became a guiding principle for me, revealing that forgiveness is not only an act of grace extended to others but also essential for our own spiritual well-being. It's a reflection of God's grace toward us, a necessary step in our journey toward inner peace and healing.

I still remember that day vividly. My heart was pounding, and my hands clenched into fists as I stared at the van driver. His words cut deep, and every fiber of my being wanted to lash out. Yet, as I stood there, something unexpected happened. A quiet voice whispered to my heart, 'Forgive.' I didn't want to hear it, but I knew that voice. It was the still, small voice that had guided me through so many storms before. At that moment, I faced a choice that would define not just my day but my very soul. More on this story later.

The Challenge of Forgiveness

Forgiveness is often one of the hardest things to embrace, especially when the wounds run deep. In an environment like the camp, where trust was fragile and tensions ran high, the idea of forgiveness seemed nearly impossible at times. The daily injustices, the harsh interactions with some correctional officers, and the betrayals from fellow campers created a breeding ground for bitterness and resentment. It was easy to let these experiences build up emotional walls, hardening the heart in an attempt to shield against further pain. Each slight felt like another layer of armor, making it more difficult to consider forgiveness as an option.

Forgiving someone who has caused us pain often feels counterintuitive. The natural human response to being wronged is to hold onto anger, using it as a shield to protect against further hurt. Anger can provide a sense of power and control, especially in situations where we feel powerless. It creates a barrier between us and the vulnerability of being hurt again. Forgiveness, by contrast, feels like an act of vulnerability—it means letting go of our defenses and risking further pain.

There is also the fear that forgiving someone equates to condoning their actions. In the camp, I often felt that by forgiving those who lied, distorted, and misrepresented facts for their own benefit, I was somehow justifying their behavior. This fear of letting the offender "off the hook" can make forgiveness seem like a betrayal of our own sense of justice. It's a common struggle to equate forgiveness with forgetting the wrongs done to us, or pretending that they didn't matter. This misunderstanding often leads us to cling to resentment as a way of acknowledging our pain and the injustice we've experienced.

Another challenge of forgiveness is the sense of injustice that accompanies it. When we are wronged, especially in significant ways, there is a deep desire for justice, for wrongs to be made right. The thought of forgiving those who have hurt us can feel like surrendering to the injustice, accepting that no reparation or acknowledgment will be made. This internal conflict can create a barrier to forgiveness, making it feel like an impossible task.

The emotional wounds inflicted by others can also leave lasting scars, and the idea of forgiveness might feel like dismissing the reality of those wounds. In the camp, the betrayal by fellow campers who prioritized their own safety and comfort over truth left a deep sense of betrayal. The unjust treatment from those in authority was like a daily reminder of my perceived helplessness. Forgiveness, in these circumstances, required me to look beyond the immediate pain and seek a higher understanding of what it meant to truly let go.

One of the hardest truths about forgiveness is that it often must be granted in the absence of an apology. Many times, those who hurt us are not sorry or may never even realize the depth of the pain they caused. In the camp, there were many who, driven by self-preservation, never acknowledged their wrongdoing. Waiting for an apology that may never come can keep us trapped in a cycle of resentment. Forgiveness, then, becomes an act of grace that we extend, not because the other person deserves it, but because we deserve peace.

The challenge of forgiveness is not just about the other person; it's also about confronting our own fears and vulnerabilities. It involves acknowledging that holding onto bitterness only prolongs our suffering.

> *"Resentment is like drinking poison and then hoping it will kill your enemies."* - NELSON MANDELA

This powerful statement captures the reality that harboring unforgiveness only harms ourselves, keeping us chained to past hurts and preventing us from moving forward.

Forgiveness challenges us to rise above our pain, to seek healing over retribution, and to find strength in grace rather than anger. It is a journey of releasing the grip of negative emotions that bind us to past wounds. While it may not be easy, forgiveness is essential for true freedom and peace. It is a decision to trust that God's justice is greater than our own, and that He is the ultimate healer of our hearts.

Personal Stories of Forgiveness

There were many instances in the camp where I had to confront the challenge of forgiveness. One such instance involved a fellow camper who had wronged me in a significant way. Initially, I was consumed with anger and a desire for revenge. I felt justified in my resentment and believed that holding onto it would somehow protect me from further harm.

During my time at the camp, the way we were transported to our jobs was through the "van driver." I had a standing appointment to be taken to the Power House around 3:30 after the early dinner but before the 4pm count. I did not know this at the time, but my commitment to working seven days a week was a thorn in many people's sides—especially on the weekend when only kitchen people worked. On one occasion, the van driver was upset about having to take me to work, and he made sure I knew it. He cussed, yelled, and called me all sorts of names. He had formed his words to call me the "N-word." I said, "Go ahead and say it; you've called me everything else. That's what you are building up to!" He caught himself and remained quiet the rest of the ride.

As he yelled, I could feel the heat rising in my chest, spreading like wildfire. I wanted to shout back, to let him know that I wasn't some helpless victim. The sound of his voice echoed in the van, bouncing off the metal walls, each word a dagger. But then, a different thought broke through the noise, as clear and as pure as a bell. 'Forgive.' It wasn't just a word; it was a command, a release. I had a choice: to escalate the anger or to let it dissolve into the air. Slowly, I unclenched my fists, feeling the tension ease out of my body like a sigh. This may have happened on a Saturday after our weekly service, as I recall. So when he came to pick me up at 10 pm, he was contrite.

As I reflected up in the Power House, I realized I had seen a side of this person I didn't recognize. This was a side of him I had never seen, though I had heard he could be this way. This is one of those instances when my old nature tried to arise, and anger almost overtook me. I can't say I prayed because I didn't. However, a sense of forgiveness overtook me even as I protested silently during my shift. "How could he talk to me like that? I don't even cuss, and he said all that stuff to me! I know how to get him. He'll rue the day he spoke to me in that manner!"

You see, I knew a lot of secrets because I'm observant and, as my grandmother used to say, "Every shut eye isn't sleep!" So much happened around my bunk at night, and they thought I didn't hear it or see it, but I did. I thought, "I am going to tell it all!" I could drop hints to the CO about where to look for contraband and when certain activity took place. This is called "dry snitching." You don't tell but you actually tell. It would be something like this: "You know it's so hard to sleep at night because the unit door keeps opening and closing all night long and I don't even know who comes in or out." Or, "I just don't understand why the guys are always going behind the washing machines and dryers after the 9pm count." Campers are masters at "dry snitching" and straight-out snitching. Though in truth, there were always snitches. I learned later that many of the "white-collar" guys gained credibility with the CO's by snitching.

I felt convicted about this strategy for obvious reasons. It is true that snitching does not go over well—even in a camp. My head was filled with anger, but God placed compassion in my heart toward the van driver. He did bring himself to apologize—as best as he could, but I knew he struggled to do it.

This story is not to extol my virtue because I felt he deserved the most vicious tongue-lashing I could offer and to be "ratted out," but God had a different plan. To this day, this guy has remained close. Before he left the camp, he confided in me that his relationship with God had been impacted by me, and he asked for me to pray for him. He continues to walk with God as of this writing.

The Process of Forgiveness

Forgiveness is a process, and it often takes time. It begins with a decision to forgive, even if our emotions are not yet aligned with that decision. This initial choice to forgive is an act of will, rooted in our commitment to follow Christ's example and commands, rather than waiting for the feelings of forgiveness to spontaneously arise. In the prison camp, I found that journaling and prayer were invaluable tools in this process. Writing down my thoughts and feelings allowed me to process my emotions and gain clarity on the situation. These practices helped me see beyond my immediate anger and hurt, allowing me to consider the bigger picture of God's plan and purpose.

One of the most important steps in the process of forgiveness is acknowledging the hurt and allowing ourselves to feel the pain. This may seem counterintuitive, especially when we often hear the phrase "forgive and forget," but it is a crucial part of healing. By acknowledging our pain, we can begin to release it and move forward. It's not about denying or minimizing what happened; it's about facing it head-on, admitting that it hurt, and then deciding not to let it define us. Remembering isn't contrary to forgiveness. In fact, the act of remembering is what allows us to forgive genuinely. Forgetting may lead to suppressed anger or unresolved feelings, but remembering and choosing to forgive despite the memory is where true freedom lies.

Remembering does not mean clinging to bitterness; rather, it involves reflecting on past hurts with a heart reshaped by grace. When we remember an offense, it's not to let it breed resentment, but to hold it up to God's light and allow His grace to redefine it. In doing so, our memories of wrongs are transformed from wounds into testimonies of healing and growth. As Psalm 103:12 reminds us, "*As far as the east is from the west, so far has he removed our transgressions from us.*" This verse illustrates how God removes our sins and, though He does not forget, He uses those experiences for our redemption and transformation. In the same way, we should remember our hurts not to dwell in pain, but to celebrate the grace that empowered us to forgive and move forward.

Another key aspect of forgiveness is empathy. Trying to understand the other person's perspective and the reasons behind their actions can help us to see them with compassion rather than judgment. This does not excuse their behavior, but it can help us to let go of our anger and move toward forgiveness. When I thought about the van driver's apology and his subsequent vulnerability, it became easier to forgive because

I recognized his humanity and his own struggles. Empathy allows us to step into the shoes of the one who wronged us and see the pain or fear that may have motivated their actions.

Jesus' teaching on empathy and forgiveness is echoed in the story of Joseph and his brothers (Genesis 45:1-15). When Joseph finally revealed himself to his brothers, who had sold him into slavery, he chose not to exact revenge or hold onto his bitterness. Instead, Joseph empathized with his brothers, understanding their fear and guilt. He reassured them, saying, *"Do not be distressed or angry with yourselves because you sold me here, for God sent me before you to preserve life"* (Genesis 45:5). Joseph's ability to empathize and forgive was rooted in his understanding of God's greater plan. His perspective allowed him to see beyond the hurt, to view his brothers not as enemies, but as instruments in God's plan to save many lives.

By choosing to remember the grace extended to us and empathizing with those who have wronged us, we mirror God's own mercy. This approach not only releases us from the grip of bitterness but also demonstrates God's love and mercy to others. Forgiveness becomes a powerful testimony of faith, showing that God's love can overcome any hurt or injustice. Through the process of forgiveness, we become living examples of God's redemptive power, demonstrating that it is possible to move from pain to peace, from resentment to reconciliation, and from brokenness to healing.

In the end, forgiveness is not just about what we release but also about what we embrace. It is about embracing God's grace, His command to love, and the freedom that comes with living in alignment with His will. By choosing to forgive, we open ourselves up to the fullness of life that God intends for us, free from the shackles of bitterness and open to the possibilities of peace and renewed relationships.

The Freedom of Forgiveness

The freedom that comes with forgiveness is profound. When we forgive, we release ourselves from the chains of bitterness and resentment, and we open the door to peace and healing. In the prison camp, I experienced this freedom firsthand. By choosing to forgive those who had wronged me, I was able to let go of the negative emotions that were weighing me down. The weight of anger and bitterness was replaced by a sense of peace and a deeper connection to God. This peace, however, was not merely an emotional state—it was a spiritual liberation that came from surrendering my hurt to God. It was as if a heavy burden had been lifted, allowing me to walk with a lighter heart and a clearer mind. The act of forgiving others became a source of strength rather than a sign of weakness.

Forgiveness also has the power to transform relationships. In some cases, it can lead to reconciliation and a renewed sense of connection. In others, it simply allows us to move forward without carrying the burden of past hurts. Either way, forgiveness frees us to live more fully and authentically. The relationship with the van driver didn't just improve; it deepened. His apology and my forgiveness created an unspoken bond that was more genuine than any forced camaraderie could have achieved. This transformation of our relationship demonstrated that forgiveness doesn't just heal the person who offers it; it also touches the one who receives it. Forgiveness builds bridges over chasms of misunderstanding and hurt, allowing for new paths of understanding and respect.

> *"I destroy my enemies when I make them my friends."* - ABRAHAM LINCOLN

President Abraham Lincoln's approach to conflict during one of the most divisive periods in American history demonstrates the healing potential of forgiveness. By extending the hand of reconciliation rather than retribution, he was able to unify a fractured nation. His perspective reminds us that forgiveness has the power to turn adversaries into allies, transforming conflict into opportunities for peace and unity.

The wisdom of Leo Tolstoy, the renowned Russian author, offers a profound perspective on forgiveness. He wrote, "Let us forgive each other—only then will we live in peace." Tolstoy's insight underscores the idea that forgiveness is not just a personal act, but a communal necessity for peace. His words challenge us to see that holding onto grudges perpetuates cycles of conflict, preventing us from experiencing the harmony that true forgiveness brings. In letting go of our grievances, we break these destructive patterns, allowing peace to flourish both within ourselves and in the broader world around us.

Similarly, the French philosopher Voltaire offers another dimension to forgiveness, stating, "The more a man knows, the more he forgives." Voltaire's observation speaks to the deep connection between understanding and forgiveness. As we grow in wisdom and empathy, we recognize the inherent imperfections in ourselves and others, leading us to extend grace more freely. This understanding fosters a spirit of forgiveness, helping us realize that we are all in need of mercy and compassion, just as we are called to offer it to others. Through knowledge and empathy, forgiveness becomes not just an act of mercy, but a reflection of our shared humanity.

Additionally, Corrie ten Boom, a Holocaust survivor, once shared, "Forgiveness is the key that unlocks the door of resentment and the handcuffs of hatred." Though a survivor of unimaginable atrocities, ten Boom's commitment to forgiveness was a powerful testament to its liberating power. Her forgiveness wasn't just a personal act of grace; it was a testimony of God's power to heal even the deepest wounds. By choosing to forgive those who had inflicted so much pain, she freed herself from the bondage of hatred and opened the door to healing and reconciliation.

The freedom of forgiveness is not just about emotional release; it's about spiritual growth and alignment with God's will. It's a pathway to personal transformation and relational restoration. Forgiveness opens our hearts to receive God's healing and to extend His grace to others. In my experience, letting go of my grievances against those who lied, distorted, and misrepresented facts for their own benefit was not easy, but it was necessary. It allowed me to focus on what truly mattered—my relationship with God and the purpose He had for my life. Through forgiveness, I found a freedom that no prison could take away, a peace that surpassed understanding, and a strength that sustained me through every trial.

The freedom that comes with forgiveness, therefore, is a powerful testimony of God's work in our lives. It's a reminder that we are called to forgive because we have been forgiven much. It's a way to reflect God's love to a world in desperate need of healing and reconciliation. As we choose to forgive, we not only set others free but find freedom ourselves, living more fully and authentically in the light of God's grace.

Biblical Examples of Forgiveness

The Bible offers numerous examples of forgiveness that can inspire and guide us, showing the profound impact that grace and mercy can have even in the most trying circumstances. One of the most compelling stories of forgiveness is that of Joseph. Sold into slavery by his jealous brothers, Joseph's early life was marked by betrayal and injustice. He endured the hardships of slavery, false accusations, and imprisonment. However, through it all, Joseph maintained his faith in

God, trusting that there was a larger plan at work even when his circumstances seemed bleak.

Years later, when Joseph rose to a position of power in Egypt, he found himself face to face with the very brothers who had betrayed him. They came to Egypt seeking food during a time of famine, unaware that the brother they had sold into slavery now held their fate in his hands. Joseph had every reason to exact revenge. He could have used his authority to punish them for the wrongs they had done to him. Instead, Joseph chose a different path—one of grace and forgiveness.

Joseph's forgiveness of his brothers reveals Joseph's deep understanding of God's sovereignty and his ability to bring good out of evil (Genesis 50:20). Joseph recognized that while his brothers' actions were meant to harm him, God had used those very actions to position him where he could save not only his family but also an entire nation from starvation.

Joseph's forgiveness was more than just an act of mercy toward his brothers; it was a recognition of God's greater purpose. He saw that the pain and suffering he endured were not meaningless but were part of a divine plan to bring about a greater good. This realization enabled Joseph to let go of bitterness and embrace forgiveness, understanding that his trials had been used by God to prepare him for a role that would ultimately save many lives. Joseph's story teaches us that forgiveness is often intertwined with a recognition of God's overarching plan, even when we cannot fully understand it.

This perspective can be incredibly liberating for us today. Like Joseph, we may face situations where others have wronged us or where the circumstances of life seem unfair. In these moments, we have a choice: to hold on to anger and resentment or to trust that God can bring good out of even the most painful experiences. Joseph's example encourages us to choose forgiveness, trusting in God's ability to turn what was meant for evil into something good.

The Psalms offer profound wisdom on the nature of forgiveness, particularly in Psalm 103:10-12, which says, *"He does not treat us as our sins deserve or repay us according to our iniquities. For as high as the heavens are above the earth, so great is his love for those who fear him; as far as the east is from the west, so far has he removed our transgressions from us."* This passage powerfully captures the depth of God's mercy, showing how His forgiveness is total and unconditional. It paints a picture of divine grace that not only pardons but completely removes the stain of our wrongs. This boundless love serves as a model for how we are called to forgive others—with the same completeness and generosity that God extends to us.

Psalm 86:5 beautifully declares, *"You, Lord, are forgiving and good, abounding in love to all who call to you."* This verse highlights that forgiveness is at the very core of God's nature—He is always ready to extend grace to those who seek Him. It serves as a profound reminder that as we experience God's forgiveness, we are called to reflect His character by being quick to forgive others, showing love and compassion even when wronged.

In Psalm 32:1-2, the psalmist reveals the joy and peace that come with forgiveness: *"Blessed is the one whose transgressions are forgiven, whose sins are covered. Blessed is the one whose sin the Lord does not count against them and in whose spirit is no deceit."* These verses remind us of the profound relief that comes from being forgiven by God, a freedom that transforms us and invites us to offer the same grace to others.

The Apostle Paul reinforces this call in Ephesians 4:31-32, urging believers to live lives marked by forgiveness: *"Get rid of all bitterness, rage and anger, brawling and slander, along with every form of malice. Be kind and compassionate to one another, forgiving each other, just as in Christ God forgave you."* Paul's exhortation reminds us that forgiveness is not merely a suggestion but a central command of the Christian life. To live a life rooted in Christ is to forgive as He forgave us, creating a world shaped by kindness, compassion, and grace.

These biblical examples underscore that forgiveness is not merely about releasing others from their offenses; it is about aligning ourselves with God's redemptive plan. It is a recognition that God can take the worst situations and use them for His glory and our good. Like Joseph, we are called to trust in God's sovereignty, believing that He can bring beauty from ashes, joy from mourning, and redemption from brokenness. By embracing forgiveness, we open ourselves to the transformative work of God's grace, allowing Him to heal our hearts and guide us toward a future filled with hope and restoration.

The Role of Faith in Forgiveness

Faith is the cornerstone that empowers us to forgive, especially when the act feels beyond our natural capacity. It is through faith that we tap into a divine strength, enabling us to release the pain and bitterness that often accompanies hurt. Forgiveness, rather than being a sign of weakness, becomes a profound demonstration of trust in God's justice and His plan for our lives. In Matthew 6:14-15, Jesus directly addresses this connection, teaching, *"For if you forgive other people when they sin against you, your heavenly Father will also forgive you. But if you do not forgive others their sins, your Father will not forgive your sins."* This scripture makes it clear that forgiveness is not only a command but a reflection of our faith. It serves as both a gift we give and one we receive, mirroring the grace that God has extended to us.

Through faith, we recognize that forgiveness is not about condoning wrongdoings but about trusting in God's ability to bring justice and healing in His perfect time.

In the parable of the unmerciful servant (Matthew 18:21-35), Jesus vividly illustrates the essence of forgiveness. In the story, a king forgives a servant who owes him an enormous debt, demonstrating the vast mercy of God. However, that same servant refuses to forgive a fellow servant who owes him a much smaller debt. The parable shows that faith and forgiveness are intertwined. Our ability to forgive others stems from understanding and accepting the forgiveness God has extended to us. When we recognize the magnitude of God's grace in our lives, it becomes a source of strength that empowers us to forgive others, no matter how deeply they have wronged us.

Another powerful story Jesus shared is the parable of the prodigal son (Luke 15:11-32). In this parable, the father's unwavering love and willingness to forgive his wayward son reflect the heart of God towards us. Even after his son squandered his inheritance and lived a life of rebellion, the father's arms were open wide in forgiveness, ready to restore the broken relationship. This parable teaches us that forgiveness restores and heals relationships and that it is never too late to seek or offer forgiveness.

Faith not only enables us to forgive but also to release the burden of hurt and resentment that we may carry. Through faith, we trust that God is the ultimate judge, as Romans 12:19 reminds us: *"Do not take revenge, my dear friends, but leave room for God's wrath, for it is written: 'It is mine to avenge; I will repay,' says the Lord."* This scripture reassures us that God sees the injustices we face and is committed to bringing about justice in His time. By trusting God's sovereignty, we free ourselves from the weight of seeking revenge, allowing us to experience peace and healing.

"As We Forgive Those Who Trespass..."

Prayer is a crucial practice in fostering forgiveness. When we bring our pain and struggles before God, we invite His healing presence into our lives. One of the most profound teachings on forgiveness comes from the Lord's Prayer, where Jesus instructs us to pray, *"Forgive us our trespasses, as we forgive those who trespass against us"* (Matthew 6:12). This petition underscores the reciprocal nature of forgiveness in the Christian faith. It suggests that our willingness to forgive others is directly tied to our own experience of being forgiven by God.

This line from the Lord's Prayer encapsulates the heart of Christian forgiveness. It places the act of forgiveness within the framework of a relationship with God and others, making it a key element of spiritual life. To ask God to "forgive us our trespasses" is to acknowledge our own shortcomings, sins, and need for mercy. It is an act of humility that recognizes the perfection of God's holiness against the backdrop of human imperfection.

By linking our forgiveness to the forgiveness we extend to others, Jesus teaches that forgiveness is not merely a divine act but a communal one. This prayer suggests that forgiveness is a bridge that connects us to God and to each other. In asking God to forgive us in the same measure that we forgive others, we are acknowledging that forgiveness is a two-way street. It cannot flow from God to us if it is not flowing from us to others.

This teaching aligns with the broader biblical narrative that emphasizes the interdependence of divine and human relationships. Jesus' teaching here is not suggesting that God's forgiveness is conditional but rather that our experience and understanding of God's forgiveness are directly affected by our willingness to forgive. If our hearts are hardened by unforgiveness, we are unable to fully receive the grace that God offers. Forgiveness, therefore, becomes a spiritual practice that frees us from bitterness and aligns us with God's will, allowing His grace to flow through us and to us more abundantly.

My own journey in the prison camp was marked by moments of intense struggle with forgiveness, and these were not just abstract or distant feelings—they were raw, immediate, and deeply personal. Many days, I was confronted with situations and individuals that tested my capacity to forgive, pushing me to the limits of my faith and emotional endurance.

One of the most challenging aspects was dealing with the pervasive sense of betrayal. I had been sentenced for a crime I did not commit, which naturally led to feelings of deep injustice. Forgiving those who were responsible for my wrongful conviction was not something that came easily. The prosecutors who aggressively pursued my case, the judge who handed down a harsh sentence, and even the people who lied, distorted, and misrepresented facts for their own benefit—each represented a significant hurdle in my journey towards forgiveness. I felt anger and resentment toward these individuals, believing they had deliberately overlooked the truth. My heart was hardened by the thought that my life and freedom had been taken away by a system that was supposed to deliver justice.

One of the most unexpected lessons in forgiveness came through my experience as the town driver—a coveted position within the camp. Early on, I had been advised to bring my driver's license with me, a piece of advice that seemed insignificant at the time. It wasn't until much later that the reasoning became clear. The inmate who held the position of town driver was nearing release, and his role, which involved running errands and transporting inmates to the bus station, would soon be vacant. This job offered a rare degree of trust and freedom, allowing the driver to leave the camp without supervision—a privilege nearly everyone wanted. However, there was one crucial requirement: the person had to have a valid driver's license on record.

Taking the town driver job meant leaving the Power House, a place that had become more than just a job—it was my refuge, my routine in the midst of chaos, a place of purpose and camaraderie. Walking away from that stability was not easy. However, with most other candidates disqualified, I found myself unexpectedly called into the office and offered the role. It was an opportunity I couldn't pass up, but it also ignited intense resentment, particularly because I was breaking an unspoken rule: no Black person had ever held this position before. Historically, the job had been reserved for white inmates, and my appointment upset that established order.

At this point, I had already navigated a delicate balance within the camp. I had a chair in both the "White TV Room" and the "Black TV Room," something unheard of in camp culture. This acceptance into both spaces happened gradually, beginning when a close white inmate left and publicly declared that I should have his chair. Though this was meant as a gesture of friendship, it was controversial. And now, with my new job, the tension escalated. Many of the white inmates viewed me as receiving "special treatment" or disrupting their hierarchy, and the backlash was swift.

One of my responsibilities as town driver was to haul landscaping supplies using a flatbed truck. Upon my return, the landscaping crew was supposed to help unstrap and unload the crates, but their resentment boiled over, and they refused to assist until everything was unstrapped—an exhausting task for one person. They believed that my size and age would prevent me from completing the job, hoping I would fail. But, through God's grace, I managed, though the physical toll was significant. The soreness and pain lingered for days, but I pressed on.

Despite the animosity, driving off-campus offered me moments of freedom that felt like a brief return to normalcy, even in my green uniform. Yet, each of those moments required a decision: to forgive. I had to forgive the men who tried to make my job harder, not because they deserved it, but because holding onto their bitterness would only weigh me down. I understood their envy, though I had done nothing to provoke it. I hadn't lobbied for the job; I was simply the one who met the qualifications.

What I didn't realize at first was how much these men had benefited from the previous town driver, enjoying special privileges that disappeared with me in the role. That, combined with the fact that the job came with one of the highest salaries in the camp, only deepened their resentment (That meant it paid $100 per month).

Ultimately, I chose to forgive. I couldn't let their anger become mine. Forgiveness wasn't about excusing their actions; it was about liberating myself from their negativity. Over time, the hostility subsided, but the lesson remained clear. Forgiving them freed me to move forward, and in doing so, I found peace. Through this experience, I learned that forgiveness is not just a gift to others—it's a gift we give ourselves, allowing us to rise above the circumstances and continue with integrity and grace.

Even among those who were close to me, forgiveness was necessary. Some fellow campers whom I had considered friends turned their backs on me when situations became difficult. Their disloyalty stung, and I wrestled with feelings of betrayal. I was faced with the reality that trust is fragile and that people often act out of fear or self-preservation. Forgiving these individuals required me to dig deep into my faith, to remind myself that everyone is flawed and that expecting perfection from others was unrealistic. I had to learn to forgive and let go, understanding that holding onto these hurts would only prolong my suffering.

Grievance is the currency of life within prisons, where every slight, insult, or injustice seems to accumulate into a mountain of resentment. Each day brought new annoyances and challenges, each of which required a measure of forgiveness. Without it, the grievances could have easily solidified into a wall of bitterness, choking out any sense of peace or joy. But in the stillness of prayer, I found the strength to let go. In those quiet moments with God, I poured out my heart—my frustrations, my hurts, my deep sense of injustice. With each confession, I laid my burdens at His feet, and slowly, I began to notice a shift within. The spaces once filled with bitterness were replaced with God's peace, and His compassion began to soften the hardness that had taken root in my heart.

Faith became my anchor, reminding me that forgiveness was not just for the benefit of those who had wronged me; it was a gift I needed to give to myself. Holding onto anger and resentment would only serve to keep me chained to my pain, hindering my emotional and spiritual growth. Through the lens of faith, I understood that forgiveness was not about condoning the wrongs done to me or pretending they didn't hurt. It was about choosing to let go of the power those wrongs held over me. It was about reclaiming my freedom to live with peace and joy, unburdened by the weight of past offenses. I had literally seen guys ruin their lives because of the bitterness built on unforgiveness.

Forgiveness also allowed me to see my fellow campers, guards, and even those involved in my conviction through a different lens. I began to see them as individuals who, like me, were dealing with their own struggles, fears, and failures. Compassion replaced judgment, and understanding replaced animosity. I recognized that my capacity to forgive was a reflection of God's grace working in my life, teaching me to love as He loves—unconditionally, without reservation, and with a heart open to healing.

In this process, I discovered that forgiveness is not a one-time act but a continuous choice. There were days when old wounds would resurface, and I would feel the familiar sting of anger and hurt. It was in those moments that I would return to prayer, asking God to renew my heart and give me the strength to forgive once more. This ongoing journey of forgiveness brought a profound sense of freedom, allowing me to move forward without the chains of bitterness dragging me back. It taught me that true freedom is found not in external circumstances but in the state of one's heart—a heart willing to forgive, to heal, and to embrace the peace that comes from trusting in God's unfailing love.

By embracing forgiveness, I learned that I could walk in freedom even within the confines of a prison. I realized that my spirit was not bound by the physical walls around me but was liberated by the grace of God working through me. In this way, forgiveness became not only a means of personal healing but also a testimony of God's transformative power—a beacon of hope for others who might be struggling to let go of their own hurts and offenses.

Faith assures us that forgiveness is a divine act, empowered by God's grace. As we trust in His ability to bring justice and healing, we find the courage to forgive and let go. It is through faith that we can see forgiveness not as an obligation but as an opportunity to reflect God's love and mercy, both to others and to ourselves.

Strategies for Fostering Forgiveness

Forgiveness is not a one-time event but a journey—a deliberate and ongoing process that requires intentionality and effort. It involves releasing resentment, letting go of grudges, and embracing the freedom that comes with forgiveness. Fostering forgiveness means creating an environment within our hearts where grace can flourish and bitterness finds no room to take root. It is about allowing ourselves to be transformed by God's love and mercy, recognizing that we have been forgiven much and, therefore, must forgive others. The following strategies are designed to help you nurture and cultivate a forgiving spirit, enabling you to extend grace even when it feels most challenging.

1. **Acknowledge the Hurt:** Don't suppress or deny the pain you feel. Accept that you are hurt and allow yourself to feel the emotions associated with the experience. This is the first step toward healing. Think of a time when a close friend betrayed your trust. Instead of brushing it off, take a moment to sit with that feeling. Acknowledge the pain and disappointment. Write down your feelings. 'I felt betrayed because...' This simple act of naming the hurt can begin to ease the power it holds over you.

2. **Practice Empathy:** Try to understand the perspective of the person who wronged you. Ask yourself what might have led them to act in that way. This can help humanize them and reduce the intensity of your anger. Consider someone who cut you off in traffic, causing a near accident. Instead of reacting with anger, try to think of possible reasons for their behavior. Maybe they were rushing to a hospital or dealing with a personal crisis. This shift in perspective can help reduce the intensity of your emotional reaction.

3. **Journal Your Feelings:** Writing down your thoughts and emotions can help you process what happened. It allows you to express your pain and begin to see the situation more clearly.
4. **Pray for Guidance and Strength:** Turn to God in prayer, asking for the strength to forgive. Prayer invites God into your healing process and opens your heart to His peace.
5. **Seek Support:** Talk to a trusted friend, pastor, or counselor about your struggles with forgiveness. Sometimes, an outside perspective can offer clarity and encouragement.
6. **Take Small Steps:** Forgiveness doesn't have to happen all at once. Take small steps toward letting go of the anger and bitterness. Each step, no matter how small, is progress.
7. **Remember the Benefits of Forgiveness:** Reflect on the freedom and peace that come with forgiveness. Keeping the end goal in mind can motivate you to continue the process.

Conviction Checkpoints

- **Self-Reflection:** Reflect on a time when you struggled to forgive someone. What emotions did you experience? How did the process of forgiveness unfold for you? How do you feel now about that situation?
- **Actionable Step:** Identify someone in your life whom you need to forgive. Take a step toward forgiveness, whether through prayer, a conversation, or simply letting go of the anger you hold against them.
- **Conviction Affirmation:** "I choose to forgive, releasing anger and bitterness, and embracing the freedom and peace that forgiveness brings."
- **Prayer/Meditation Focus:** Pray for the strength to forgive those who have wronged you. Ask God to fill your heart

with compassion and to help you let go of any lingering bitterness or resentment.

Profile in Conviction

John Wesley

John Wesley, the founder of Methodism, stands as a powerful example of grace and forgiveness in action. Born in 1703 in England, Wesley's early life was steeped in faith, but his understanding of forgiveness deepened only after a series of personal failures and disappointments. After an unsuccessful mission trip to Georgia, where his attempts to spread the Gospel ended in rejection, legal troubles, and heartbreak, Wesley found himself in spiritual crisis. It was in this season of doubt that he came to a profound realization: forgiveness, both given and received, was central to his faith.

A transformative moment came in 1738 at a meeting on Aldersgate Street, where Wesley experienced what he described as his "heart strangely warmed." He came to understand that God's grace was not earned but freely given, and that this grace extended even in moments of personal failure. It was this deep sense of God's forgiveness that became the foundation of his renewed mission, fueling his lifelong commitment to preach about grace, love, and holiness.

Wesley's life was filled with moments that tested his ability to forgive. In personal relationships, particularly in the painful experience with Sophy Hopkey, Wesley faced betrayal and humiliation. Yet, instead of allowing bitterness to take root, Wesley chose to forgive and focus on his calling. Throughout his ministry, he faced opposition, mockery, and even physical attacks. One memorable instance saw him attacked by a mob while preaching in Wednesbury. Rather than respond with anger or revenge, Wesley remained committed to love and forgiveness, choosing to reflect Christ's grace to even his harshest critics.

Forgiveness, for Wesley, was not a passive act but a courageous decision. He saw forgiveness as central to Christian discipleship, preaching that believers must "love your enemies" and pray for those who wrong them. Wesley understood that while forgiveness was difficult, it was made possible by the transformative power of the Holy Spirit. He believed that just as God forgave us through Christ, we are called to extend the same grace to others.

Wesley's message reached beyond personal slights to address societal injustices. His ministry brought him into contact with the marginalized, the poor, and those deemed unworthy by society. He taught that God's grace was available to all, regardless of status or past mistakes. For Wesley, true holiness was rooted in love, and love was inseparable from forgiveness. He believed that living a holy life meant practicing forgiveness in every aspect, a teaching that continues to inspire Christians today.

In reflecting on Wesley's life, we are reminded that forgiveness is not just a one-time act but a lifelong practice. His legacy challenges us to forgive not because it is easy, but because it is essential to our spiritual growth. By choosing to forgive, we reflect the heart of God, and in doing so, we free ourselves from the weight of bitterness. Wesley's example encourages us to trust in the power of grace, knowing that through forgiveness, we not only heal ourselves but also extend Christ's love to the world.

Forgiveness is more than a moral obligation; it is a profound act of liberation that breaks the chains of anger, bitterness, and resentment. Through forgiveness, we are not only fulfilling a divine command but also releasing ourselves from the burdens that hinder our spiritual growth and personal peace. In the prison camp, I learned that forgiveness was not a sign of weakness but a testament to the strength and resilience of my faith. It was a daily practice, a conscious choice to let go of the pain inflicted by others and to embrace the healing grace of God.

Forgiveness transforms us from the inside out. It softens our hearts, opens us to compassion, and aligns us with God's will. By choosing to forgive, we mirror the character of Christ, who forgave even those who crucified Him. In doing so, we become agents of peace and reconciliation in a world that desperately needs both. The freedom that comes with forgiveness is unparalleled. It unburdens our hearts, clears our minds, and allows us to walk forward in life with a renewed sense of purpose and joy.

In forgiving, we not only free ourselves but also create a ripple effect that can transform our relationships, communities, and society at large. The power of forgiveness lies in its ability to heal wounds that seem irreparable and to restore hope where despair has taken root. It is a divine exchange where we offer our hurt and receive God's peace in return.

As you reflect on the people in your life who have wronged you, remember that forgiveness is not about condoning their actions but about choosing to be free. It's about trusting that God is the ultimate judge and that His justice and mercy are perfect. By letting go of the desire for revenge or retribution, you open your heart to receive the peace and joy that only God can give.

Embrace forgiveness as a way of life, a testament to your faith, and a reflection of God's love. In doing so, you will find that forgiveness is not just a pathway to freedom; it is the pathway to a life filled with grace, healing, and abundant blessings. Let forgiveness be the key that unlocks the door to a life of peace and fulfillment, allowing you to experience the fullness of God's love in every area of your life.

As I look back on my time in the prison camp, I see that forgiveness wasn't just about the van driver or the officials who wronged me—it was about finding my own freedom. It was about breaking the chains that held my heart captive to bitterness. Today, I encourage you to take a moment and think of the person you find hardest to forgive. Picture their face, and then, in your heart, release them. Let go of the anger that binds you. Offer the same grace that God extends to us every day. In doing so, you will not only set them free but will find your own soul soaring toward the peace that surpasses all understanding.

CHAPTER 11
RESILIENCE REDEFINES RESULTS

Resilience is the inner strength that empowers us to endure and rise above the harshest of circumstances. It is the steadfast capacity to confront adversity, withstand hardship, and emerge not only intact but stronger and wiser. During my time in confinement, where every day presented new challenges and uncertainties, I realized that resilience was not merely a tool for survival but a transformative force that reshaped my entire outlook. I came to see that resilience was the key to turning setbacks into opportunities, channeling pain into purpose, and uncovering growth and meaning even in the darkest moments. Through this strength, I found the ability to redefine my path and reclaim the narrative of my life.

Resilience is not just about enduring; it is about thriving amid adversity. It is a quality that allows us to adapt, grow, and become more than our circumstances. It is an act of defiance against the weight of despair, a declaration that we are more than what happens to us. In the bleak confines of the prison camp, where the walls seemed to close in and hope was a scarce commodity, resilience became my lifeline. It was the quiet voice that encouraged me to get up each morning, to face the challenges with courage, and to hold on to my faith when everything around me seemed to fall apart. Resilience taught me that while we cannot always control our circumstances, we can control our response to them. It showed me that the true measure of a person is not how they handle the good times but how they persevere through the trials.

In a world where setbacks are inevitable, resilience equips us to keep moving forward, even when the path is unclear and the outcome uncertain. It is the tenacity to pursue our goals despite the obstacles, to continue to strive for excellence even when success seems out of reach. My time in the camp taught me that resilience is about rising each time we fall, learning from our failures, and using those lessons to propel us towards a better future. It is about choosing hope over despair, strength over weakness, and faith over fear. It is the realization that our circumstances do not define us; rather, it is how we respond to those circumstances that shapes our character and our destiny.

Resilience is a choice, a daily commitment to push through pain, to embrace challenges as opportunities for growth, and to trust that every struggle has a purpose. It is a journey that begins in the mind and heart, a decision to face life's storms with the conviction that they will not last forever, and that we will emerge from them more refined, more focused, and more prepared for the journey ahead. As I navigated the trials of incarceration, I came to see that resilience was not just about personal strength but also about leaning on faith, community, and the understanding that no matter how dark the night, the dawn would come. This chapter explores the profound role that resilience plays in our lives, how it empowers us to redefine our outcomes, and how it is ultimately a testament to the enduring spirit of the human soul.

A Dark Day

I was in the middle of my usual routine when the announcement crackled over the camp's loudspeaker system, jolting me out of my thoughts like a clap of thunder in a clear sky.

"Rev, report to the office! Rev, report to the office!"

The words echoed through the concrete walls, bouncing off the steel and wire that had become the contours of my existence. My heart skipped a beat, my mind racing to fill in the blanks of what could possibly await me. In a place where routine was the lifeline, any disruption was a signal that something was out of order, and more often than not, it wasn't good. I stood frozen for a moment, trying to steady my breath, feeling a cold sweat break out on the back of my neck.

Every step toward the office felt like trudging through quicksand. My mind was a whirlwind of possibilities. What could this be about? News from the outside world always carried a weight here—whether it was good or bad, it was never neutral. The idea that my attorney was reaching out filled me with a mix of hope and dread. She wouldn't call without a reason, and every possibility my mind conjured seemed fraught with anxiety. Had the Supreme Court made a decision on my appeal? Was it the breakthrough I had been praying for, or another nail in the coffin of my dwindling hope?

The office door loomed ahead, a nondescript portal that suddenly felt like the threshold between fate and despair. My legs felt heavy, as though they were resisting what my heart already suspected. I took a deep breath, steeling myself for whatever awaited me on the other side.

Inside, the counselor's office was just as bleak as I remembered—drab walls, flickering fluorescent lights, a steel desk bolted to the floor. The counselor barely looked up as he nodded toward the phone. I could see the blinking red light, the silent harbinger of a conversation that might shatter me or save me.

I picked up the receiver, the plastic cool and hard against my ear. My attorney's voice came through the line, her tone measured, almost too careful.

"Trevon," he said, and just from the way he said my name, I knew. My heart sank like a stone. I braced myself against the desk, feeling the edges of my resolve begin to fray.

"We received the decision today," she said. "The Supreme Court..."

The pause stretched, each second an eternity, my heartbeat pounding like a drum in my ears.

"They have denied your appeal."

For a moment, I couldn't breathe. The room seemed to close in around me, the air thick and heavy. It felt like the walls themselves were pressing in, suffocating me. All the months of hope, the prayers whispered in the dead of night, the desperate belief that justice would somehow prevail—it all collapsed under the weight of those words. Denied. My last legal lifeline had been severed.

My attorney's voice was still talking, explaining the next steps, the possibilities of other legal avenues, but her words were a distant echo. All I could focus on was the finality of it. The door to freedom had been slammed shut, and I was still on the inside.

I managed to mutter a thank you before hanging up the phone, my hands trembling. I felt like I was standing at the edge of an abyss, staring into the darkness, unable to see the bottom. The counselor looked at me with a blank expression, offering no comfort, no words. This was just another day for him, another inmate receiving another piece of bad news.

Chapter 11: Resilience Redefines Results

I turned and walked out of the office, the door shut behind me, sealing me back into my reality. As I made my way to my bunk, each step felt like it was being guided by autopilot, my mind numb, my heart shattered. The familiar halls, the faces of fellow inmates, the smell of institutional food—everything seemed muted, like I was moving through a fog. My thoughts swirled in a storm of disbelief and despair.

How could this be happening? Every bit of hope I had carefully built up over the months, every prayer that had sustained me in the darkest hours, seemed to crumble into nothingness. I had believed so fiercely that God would intervene, that justice would prevail, and now that belief was hanging by a thread. I felt betrayed, not just by the legal system but by my own faith.

Back in my cube, I sat down on the edge of my bunk, the thin mattress sagging under my weight. The unit was quiet, but inside my mind, there was a raging battle between anger and sorrow. I had spent so much time trying to keep it together, to remain strong for myself and for my family. But now, in this moment, I felt like the foundation I had stood on was collapsing. My hands clenched into fists, my eyes stinging with the threat of tears I refused to let fall.

I needed to cry out, to scream, to release the overwhelming pain that was building up inside me like a pressure cooker ready to explode. I thought of my wife, Qwynn, her voice of reason, her unwavering support. She had believed in me when no one else did. She had held our family together while I was trapped in this place. How could I tell her that the last shred of hope we clung to had been ripped away? How could I face my children, knowing that they would continue to grow up with their father behind bars?

Resilience. It was a word that had been thrown around so often in my life. Be strong. Keep faith. Trust in God's plan. But right now, those words felt hollow, like platitudes spoken to someone else. I wasn't feeling resilient. I felt broken.

And yet, deep down, a small flicker of something stirred within me. It was barely there, but it was enough to stop the flood of despair from completely drowning me. I remembered the countless stories of others who had faced insurmountable odds, who had been denied justice, who had been wronged yet found the strength to keep going. Joseph, who was betrayed by his own brothers and unjustly imprisoned, but who ultimately rose to a position of great power because he refused to let bitterness and anger consume him. His story wasn't over when he was thrown into a pit. It wasn't over when he was sold into slavery or falsely accused by Potiphar's wife. God had a purpose for him, even when he couldn't see it.

Maybe, just maybe, God still had a purpose for me. Maybe this denial wasn't the end of my story, but a chapter in a book that was still being written. I didn't know what that purpose was, and I certainly didn't understand why this was happening to me, but I knew one thing: I couldn't give up. Not now, not ever.

I took a deep breath, trying to steady the storm inside. The road ahead was uncertain, and it was littered with challenges I couldn't yet see. But I had faced dark moments before and found the strength to rise again. I would do it once more. For myself. For my family. For the God who had never truly abandoned me, even if His presence felt far away at this moment.

I stood up from the bunk, the heaviness still pressing on my shoulders, but my resolve was beginning to harden. This battle wasn't over. I would continue to fight, not just for my freedom, but for the resilience that would see me through whatever lay ahead. As I walked out of my cell, I knew the day wasn't done breaking me. But I also knew I wasn't done rising.

The Importance of Resilience

Resilience is not about avoiding difficulties; it is about meeting them with courage, determination, and an unwavering spirit. It involves maintaining a positive outlook, staying adaptable, and using setbacks as stepping stones toward greater achievements. Resilience empowers us to confront life's challenges, to learn from them, and to rise stronger each time we fall.

> *"Although the world is full of suffering, it is also full of the overcoming of it."* - HELEN KELLER

Every challenge, no matter how daunting, can be overcome. This perspective shifts our focus away from life's inevitable trials and toward the potential for triumph. Resilience is more than just surviving hardship—it's about thriving in the face of adversity. It is a powerful force that shapes our future, allowing us to turn pain into strength and transform obstacles into opportunities for growth.

The act of being resilient is a testament to our inner strength and the human spirit's capacity to adapt and endure. It is a refusal to be defined by our circumstances, a declaration that we are more than the hardships we face. Resilience allows us to navigate the ups and downs of life with grace and determination, to weather the storms and come out the other side with renewed strength and purpose. This quality is not something we are born with but something we cultivate over time through our experiences, choices, and faith. As the ancient Greek philosopher Epictetus said, "It's not what happens to you, but how you react to it that matters." This quote highlights the power of our response to adversity, emphasizing that resilience is rooted in our perspective and our willingness to face challenges with a courageous heart.

Romans 5:3-4 offers profound insight into the value of resilience: *"Not only so, but we also glory in our sufferings, because we know that suffering produces perseverance; perseverance, character; and character, hope."* These verses remind us that resilience is not merely a coping mechanism but a pathway to spiritual and personal growth. Our struggles and hardships are not without purpose; they serve as a crucible that refines our character, molds our integrity, and deepens our capacity for empathy and compassion. Each trial we endure strengthens our ability to persevere, and each act of perseverance builds our character, which in turn fosters a hope that is resilient and steadfast.

Resilience, therefore, is a divine gift, a source of strength that God provides to help us navigate the trials of life. It is through resilience that we learn to trust in God's plan, even when we cannot see the way forward. It reminds us that our pain is not wasted; it has a purpose. The trials we face are not designed to break us but to build us up, to prepare us for the future that God has planned for us. As C.S. Lewis once said, "Hardships often prepare ordinary people for an extraordinary destiny." This quote captures the essence of resilience, highlighting how our challenges are often the very thing that equips us for the great purpose and impact we are destined to achieve.

Resilience is the bridge between the past and the future, the quality that allows us to carry forward the lessons learned from our hardships and apply them to the opportunities that lie ahead. It is the essence of hope, the belief that no matter how difficult the present may be, there is a brighter future waiting if we continue to press forward. It is a choice to see every setback as a setup for a comeback, to embrace each challenge as an opportunity for growth, and to trust that even in our suffering, God is working for our good. As we cultivate resilience, we discover that we are not defined by our trials but by our response to them. We find the strength to endure, the wisdom to learn, and the faith to keep moving forward, confident that God's purpose will prevail.

Resilience, Perseverance, and Persistence

Resilience, perseverance, and persistence are intricately connected, each playing a vital role in our ability to withstand and overcome adversity. While they share similarities, they are distinct in how they function and in the roles they play in our journey through life's hardships. Together, they form a formidable force that enables us to move forward, even when faced with the most daunting challenges.

Persistence is the unwavering dedication to a task or goal, regardless of the difficulties that arise. It is the determination to keep moving forward, even when the path is fraught with obstacles and progress is slow. Persistence is often characterized by a relentless, almost stubborn commitment to an objective, refusing to give up no matter how many setbacks one encounters. Albert Einstein, a figure synonymous with intellectual prowess, humbly attributed his success not to superior intelligence but to persistence. "It's not that I'm so smart," he said, "it's just that I stay with problems longer." This underscores the power of persistence—it's not necessarily about outsmarting a problem, but about outlasting it. Persistence is the act of consistently pushing against barriers, believing that each effort brings us closer to a breakthrough.

Perseverance takes persistence to a deeper level. It is the ability to remain steadfast in a prolonged effort, especially when the path is difficult and success feels distant or uncertain. Perseverance is about maintaining hope and continuing forward, even when circumstances seem bleak and there is little visible evidence that progress is being made. It demands not only effort but also patience and unwavering faith. As 1 Peter 5:10 (NLT) reminds us, *"In His kindness God called you to share in His eternal glory by means of Christ Jesus. So after you have suffered a little while, He will restore, support, and strengthen you, and He will place you on a firm foundation."* This scripture beautifully captures the essence of perseverance. It is through enduring suffering and remaining committed that God strengthens us, restores us, and places us on solid ground. Perseverance refines our character, deepens our faith, and ultimately leads to a life marked by resilience and purpose.

Resilience is the overarching quality that encompasses both persistence and perseverance. It is the capacity to not only endure hardship but to bounce back and recover stronger. Resilience is the ability to adapt to changing circumstances, to bend without breaking, and to maintain one's sense of purpose and hope, even in the face of severe adversity. It is the quality that allows a person to withstand not just a single setback, but an ongoing barrage of challenges, emerging not unscathed but transformed, stronger, and more capable.

These qualities were not merely theoretical concepts; they were essential for survival and well-being in the camp. Each day presented its own set of challenges, from the emotional toll of being separated from loved ones to the mental and physical rigors of adapting to the prison environment. The confinement, the loss of freedom, and the uncertainty about the future could easily erode one's spirit. It was persistence that kept me going when I felt like giving up, reminding me that each day of survival was a victory. It was perseverance that enabled me to maintain my faith and my commitment to personal growth, even when the days seemed long and the prospect of release felt like a distant dream.

The day I received the devastating news about my appeal was one of the hardest I've faced. I had placed so much hope in the legal process, truly believing that justice would prevail, that my case would be reviewed fairly, and that my time in the camp would be cut short. But when the news came that the appeal had been denied, it felt as though the ground had been ripped out from beneath me. The weight of disappointment was immense, and I felt like giving in to despair. In that moment, it seemed natural to question the point of holding on to hope. But resilience stepped in, offering a quiet, unwavering assurance that this setback did not define my story.

I recalled the words of Helen Keller: "Although the world is full of suffering, it is also full of the overcoming of it." That reminder helped me shift my perspective. This defeat was not the end—it was merely one chapter in a larger narrative still being written by a sovereign God. Proverbs 19:21 came to mind: *"Many are the plans in a person's heart, but it is the Lord's purpose that prevails."* Even in my disappointment, I realized that God's purpose was still at work, and that no denial or delay could thwart His ultimate plan for my life. Resilience allowed me to press on, trusting that this temporary defeat was part of a bigger journey toward victory.

This notion of resilience is evident in Joseph's life as we've seen from the Book of Genesis, a narrative teeming with lessons on resilience, perseverance, and persistence. Joseph's life journey is a testament to the power of these three virtues, and without them, he would have never risen to the position of power that he ultimately held in Egypt. His story began with betrayal—sold into slavery by his own brothers, stripped of his family, and thrust into a life of servitude in a foreign land. This betrayal could have easily shattered his spirit, leading him to a life of bitterness and resentment. Instead, Joseph chose resilience. He adapted to his new circumstances, maintaining his faith and integrity even as a slave. His resilience in the face of such adversity is evident as he quickly rose to a position of trust and responsibility in the house of Potiphar, his Egyptian master.

However, Joseph's trials did not end there. Despite his faithful service, he was falsely accused of attempting to violate Potiphar's wife, leading to his unjust imprisonment. For many, this would have been the final blow, a point at which hope would have been extinguished. But Joseph's perseverance shone through even in the darkest dungeon. He did not succumb to despair; instead, he continued to trust in God's plan, using his God-given gifts to interpret the dreams of his fellow prisoners. His ability to see beyond his immediate suffering and to remain steadfast in his faith is a powerful example of perseverance. Joseph's response to his imprisonment was not to give up but to keep believing that God was with him, even in the midst of his suffering. His enduring commitment to his faith, despite the bleakness of his circumstances, refined his character, shaping him into a leader capable of wisdom and grace.

Joseph's persistence, his continuous effort in the face of adversity, is further exemplified when he interpreted the dreams of Pharaoh's cupbearer and baker. Even then, he displayed a willingness to serve others, using his gifts to bring clarity and hope to those around him. He did not allow the confines of the prison to limit his impact or to dim his faith. It was Joseph's persistent faithfulness in small things that prepared him for greater responsibilities. When he was finally called upon to interpret Pharaoh's dreams, his persistence paid off. His accurate interpretation and wise counsel during a time of crisis catapulted him from the prison to the palace, making him second only to Pharaoh in power over all of Egypt.

Joseph's resilience is most profoundly illustrated in his response to his brothers when they came to Egypt seeking food during a famine. By this time, Joseph had every human right to retaliate, to hold a grudge, or to exact revenge. Yet, he displayed a remarkable level of grace and understanding. Joseph recognized that every betrayal, every hardship, and every injustice was part of a divine tapestry that God was weaving, not just for Joseph's benefit, but for the preservation of many.

Joseph's journey from the pit to the palace is far more than a tale of vindication; it's a profound testimony to how God's purposes unfold through the resilience, perseverance, and persistence of His people. Despite the betrayal of his brothers, the injustice of his imprisonment, and the seeming futility of his circumstances, Joseph's unwavering faith and steadfast trust in God enabled him to rise above every challenge. It wasn't merely his trials that shaped his destiny, but his response to them—his ability to remain resilient in the face of adversity, to persevere when hope seemed lost, and to persist in using his God-given gifts, even in the most unlikely places.

Joseph's life illustrates a divine truth: our circumstances do not define us, but our faith-filled response to them does. His journey shows that trusting in God's overarching plan, even when the path seems obscured, leads to a fulfillment greater than we could imagine. The story challenges us to reflect not only on how we endure our trials but on how those very trials might be the catalyst for fulfilling God's purpose in our lives. As we reflect on Joseph's rise, we might well ask, "Was his ascent to power achieved because of his hardships or in spite of them?" The answer reveals the mystery and power of God's providence: our trials are not obstacles to His plan but essential instruments in shaping it.

Resilience was not just about surviving; it was about thriving amidst adversity. It was about finding ways to turn challenges into opportunities, to see each obstacle not as a setback but as a stepping stone. Robert Jordan's metaphor, "The oak fought the wind and was broken, the willow bent when it must and survived," resonates deeply with this approach. The strength of resilience lies not in rigidity, but in flexibility. The ability to bend, to adapt, and to remain rooted despite the storm was essential.

There were moments when the monotony of camp life seemed unbearable, when the days blurred together and hope felt distant. In those moments, it was the small acts of persistence—getting up each day, maintaining a routine, engaging in meaningful conversations, praying, and reflecting—that built the foundation for resilience. It was the quiet perseverance, the daily commitment to stay true to my values, to support my fellow campers, and to maintain my faith, that allowed me to weather the storm.

Resilience, perseverance, and persistence are not just abstract concepts; they are lived realities, essential tools that empower us to navigate life's greatest challenges. They remind us that we have the power to redefine our circumstances, to transform setbacks into opportunities for growth, and to trust that God's plan for our lives is greater than the trials we face. Through resilience, we learn that we are not defined by our hardships but by how we respond to them, and that every challenge is an opportunity to grow, to learn, and to emerge stronger.

Personal Story of Resilience

One of the lowest points in my journey came when my appeal to the Supreme Court was denied. It felt like the final nail in the coffin of hope. Up to that moment, I had restricted my family from visiting me, thinking that in my isolation, I could shield them from the pain I was enduring. This decision, looking back, was purely selfish. I convinced myself that my suffering was greater than theirs because my liberty had been stripped away, while they still had the freedom to live their lives. I rationalized that focusing solely on surviving my incarceration was the only productive way forward. Allowing myself to feel sadness or longing for home seemed counterproductive. I observed how other men, after their weekly visits, often came back hollowed out, the pain of parting etched on their faces. I wanted no part of that agony. Saying goodbye to my wife the day I self-surrendered had been hard enough; reliving that kind of heartache regularly felt unbearable.

Then came the blow that shattered my fragile emotional defenses. My final appeal had been denied. My last shred of legal hope had been crushed under the weight of a system I felt was unjust and unrelenting. In that moment, I felt my heart crack wide open. The walls I had built around my pain could no longer contain the flood of sorrow and despair. Thankfully, I married a woman who has always been attuned to the things I try hardest to hide. My wife, Qwynn, heard the defeat in my voice, the silent cries I was trying to suppress. She said, "I'm coming to visit you this weekend, and I don't care what you think." Hearing her words, I broke down. I cried on the phone, unable to muster even a word of protest. She knew I needed her presence more than I needed my self-imposed isolation. Her visit became a lifeline, a rope tossed into the dark well of my despair, pulling me back to the surface. That weekend, her touch, her voice, her unwavering love reminded me that resilience isn't merely about standing tall on your own—it's also about leaning on the support of those who love you.

Each time I filed an appeal, I held onto the belief, "This is it. This is when God will come through and end this nightmare." But as my last appeal was denied, that fragile belief crumbled. It felt like a betrayal, not just by the justice system but by God Himself. Every suppressed negative thought and emotion erupted like a dormant volcano. I was overwhelmed by sadness—not just sadness, but a deep, consuming sorrow. Sorrow over what my life had become, sorrow over not understanding why God had allowed this to happen, sorrow over serving a God who seemed to allow injustice to prevail. I felt abandoned, lost, and utterly defeated.

Sharing this memory is not about recounting my suffering but about illustrating a vital truth: no one is impervious to life's pain and sorrow. Even the strongest among us will encounter moments when we can't make it on our own. This vulnerability is not a sign of weakness or a lack of faith; it is a testament to our humanity. We are designed to need each other, to find strength in community. I have always known my family was my home team, but it was in the midst of that painful phone call with Qwynn that I truly understood how much I needed them. I had always measured my worth by how much my family depended on me, but that moment taught me how much I depended on them. It wasn't just that they needed me to come home; I needed them to keep me whole while I was away.

In August 2019, more than a year and a half into my five-year sentence, I finally saw my wife again, and then my children. That visit was the medicine my soul desperately needed. As they sat across from me, their smiles lit up the dim visiting room, and for the first time in months, I felt the clouds of despair begin to part. When the visit ended, and they left, I cried like a baby. The pain of saying goodbye was intense, but the love and connection we shared fortified my spirit. I knew then that I could face whatever the future held. Those visits became my anchor, my reminder that I was not alone. Before COVID restrictions put a halt to all visits, those precious moments with my family provided the strength and resilience I needed to endure.

The Role of Faith in Building Resilience

Faith is the bedrock of resilience. It's the unshakable confidence in God's Word and His promises that equips us to stand firm, even when the world around us is crumbling. Faith is not just a passive belief; it's an active, dynamic force that propels us forward. It has been said, "Faith begins where the will of God is known." Knowing God's will, as revealed in His Word, gives us the boldness to face every trial with the assurance that we are not fighting alone.

The Bible tells us in Philippians 4:13, *"I can do all things through Christ who strengthens me."* This isn't just a nice saying to put on a refrigerator magnet; it's a divine promise from the Creator of the universe. This verse means that no matter how fierce the storm, no matter how high the mountain, God's strength is available to us. It's His power that enables us to persevere, to press on, and to overcome. When we meditate on this truth, it becomes a spiritual weapon, a shield of faith that quenches every fiery dart the enemy throws at us.

Faith is like a muscle; it grows stronger through resistance. As we face trials, we meet those trials by intensifying our reliance on God's Word. Each trial, each challenge is an opportunity for our faith to develop. The Apostle Paul faced countless hardships—imprisonment, beatings, shipwrecks—but he never lost sight of God's promises. He knew that faith was the victory that overcomes the world (1 John 5:4). We, too, must develop the mindset of a conqueror, believing that with God, we are always on the winning side.

Prayer and meditation are vital tools in building and maintaining our faith. Through prayer, we tap into the supernatural power of God. Prayer isn't just a religious ritual; it's a lifeline to Heaven. It's where we receive divine strategies, encouragement, and strength. When we pray, we are not just speaking words into the air; we are entering into a conversation with the

Almighty. We are laying hold of His promises and pulling them into our reality. The more time we spend in God's presence, the more His resilience rubs off on us.

John Osteen used to teach that meditating on the Word of God is like planting seeds in the soil of our hearts. As we meditate on God's promises, those seeds begin to grow, producing a harvest of faith, hope, and resilience. Joshua 1:8 instructs us to meditate on the Word day and night, for then we will make our way prosperous, and then we will have good success. When challenges come—and they will—we need to be so rooted in the Word that nothing can shake us. Our faith must be so deeply embedded that it becomes our first response to every trial.

It was this deep-seated faith that kept me going. I would wake up each morning and declare, *"This is the day that the Lord has made; I will rejoice and be glad in it"* (Psalm 118:24). Even in a place designed to break my spirit, I chose to stand on God's Word. I knew that my circumstances didn't define me—God's promises did. His Word became my anchor in the storm, my refuge in the time of trouble.

There were moments when despair threatened to overwhelm me, when the weight of my circumstances felt impossible to bear. In those dark times, I found comfort in the words of Psalm 34:17-18: *"The righteous cry out, and the Lord hears them; he delivers them from all their troubles. The Lord is close to the brokenhearted and saves those who are crushed in spirit."* This scripture reminded me that even in the depths of my pain, God was near, listening to my cries and working to deliver me. It became my anchor, reassuring me that no matter how heavy the burden, God was always present, offering His comfort and strength.

It was through faith and prayer that I found the peace that surpasses all understanding. In the stillness of my heart, I would hear the gentle whisper of the Holy Spirit saying, *"Be still, and know that I am God"* (Psalm 46:10). It was in these sacred moments of communion with God that my spirit was renewed, my hope rekindled, and my resilience fortified. I learned that no matter how dire the situation, God was my rock, my fortress, and my deliverer.

Resilience is built not in the absence of challenges, but in the midst of them, through a steadfast faith in God's unchanging promises. It's the unwavering belief that *"no weapon formed against us shall prosper"* (Isaiah 54:17) and that *"we are more than conquerors through Him who loved us"* (Romans 8:37). With faith as our foundation and prayer as our practice, we can rise above any adversity and stand victorious, knowing that God is with us, for us, and working all things together for our good.

The Power of Community in Fostering Resilience

Community is not just a comforting presence; it is a lifeline that breathes resilience into our spirits when we feel like we can't go on. In the prison camp, community was not a luxury; it was a necessity. The bonds formed within those walls created a network of support that was as essential as food and water. Together, we forged an unbreakable chain of encouragement and accountability. When one of us faltered, the others would lift him up, reminding him that he was not alone. It was this shared strength that enabled us to keep moving forward, no matter how insurmountable the obstacles seemed.

The African proverb wisely states, "If you want to go fast, go alone. If you want to go far, go together." We understood that resilience is not built in isolation; it flourishes in the soil of shared experience and mutual support. Each of us brought our own unique story, our own battle scars, and our own victories. By coming together, we created a tapestry of hope and strength that was far more powerful than anything we could achieve individually.

The prison camp, in many ways, was an extreme example of the group development theory often described as forming, storming, norming, and performing. Initially, when new inmates arrived, there was a period of forming—an introduction phase where men were getting to know each other and establishing the unspoken rules of engagement. This was followed by storming, a phase marked by conflicts, power struggles, and the testing of boundaries. Differences in background, beliefs, and attitudes often led to tensions. But just like any group dynamic, we moved through this phase, slowly finding common ground. The next stage, norming, involved the creation of unwritten codes of conduct, shared values, and mutual respect. It was here that a true sense of community began to form. We came to understand that despite our differences, we were all in this together, facing the same daily challenges and fears. Lastly, we reached the performing stage, where we functioned as a cohesive unit, supporting each other and working towards common goals of resilience, survival, and personal growth.

In this environment, resilience was not an abstract concept but a lived reality. It was during these times that the men showed their true colors. When resilience was needed most, it was often those who had once seemed the most hardened or detached who came forward with words of encouragement, a pat on the back, or a shared prayer. As I went through one of my darkest moments—the denial of my appeal to the Supreme Court—I saw this theory of group development come to life in the most powerful way. News of my appeal spread through the camp, and almost immediately, men from all walks of life approached me with words of comfort and solidarity. Some of these men had themselves experienced the sting of a denied appeal, while others simply understood the weight of the disappointment. In those moments, our differences faded away, and what remained was a collective strength, a mutual resilience that transcended individual pain.

One of the most profound elements of our community was the practice of sharing our stories. Storytelling became a sacred ritual, a way to connect on a deep, soulful level. When we gathered to share our journeys, it wasn't just about recounting past events—it was about weaving together our collective resilience. Each story shared was a thread that strengthened the fabric of our community. Listening to the experiences of my fellow campers, I found new perspectives that illuminated my own path. Their courage fueled my courage; their hope rekindled my own. In a place designed to strip away our humanity, our shared stories reminded us of our intrinsic worth and the power we held within.

The Apostle Paul, in his letter to the Corinthians, spoke of the body of Christ, where each part is essential and interdependent: *"If one part suffers, every part suffers with it; if one part is honored, every part rejoices with it"* (1 Corinthians 12:26). This was our reality in the camp. We were different parts of the same body, feeling each other's pain and celebrating each other's victories. This spiritual connection was more than camaraderie; it was a divine fellowship that reflected the heart of God. We learned that our resilience was not just about personal endurance but about standing strong together, holding each other up, and moving forward as one.

In moments of deep despair, it was often the encouragement of a fellow camper that reignited my hope. A simple, "You can get through this," or a shared prayer could turn a day of darkness into a day of possibility. The communal meals, the Bible study groups, and even the casual conversations in the yard were more than just activities—they were lifelines. They were acts of defiance against the despair that sought to consume us, acts of faith that declared, "We are in this together, and we will rise above it."

In this crucible of adversity, I came to understand that resilience is contagious. When you see someone else face their giants with grace and courage, it inspires you to do the same. It's like the embers of a fire; when brought together, they burn brighter and stronger. This collective resilience became a beacon of light in the darkness, guiding us all towards a brighter future.

The power of community in fostering resilience cannot be overstated. It is a force that transforms individual survival into collective thriving. In a world that often emphasizes self-reliance, the prison camp taught me that our greatest strength lies in our connections with others. We are designed to live in relationship, to bear each other's burdens, and to celebrate each other's victories. In doing so, we find the strength to endure, the courage to persevere, and the resilience to redefine our outcomes. As I reflect on my time in the camp, I am grateful not only for the resilience I found within myself but for the resilience we found in each other. Together, we learned that while life may knock us down, we do not have to rise alone.

Strategies for Developing Resilience

1. **Set Small Goals**

    Facing overwhelming challenges can often feel paralyzing, but setting small, achievable goals can provide a sense of direction and purpose. Breaking down larger obstacles into manageable tasks not only makes the path forward clearer but also allows for frequent celebrations of progress, no matter how small. These small victories serve as stepping stones, boosting confidence and building momentum, gradually transforming seemingly insurmountable challenges into attainable goals.

2. **Stay Positive**
Adopting a positive outlook in the face of adversity is more than just an optimistic mindset; it's a powerful tool for resilience. By choosing to focus on the potential for growth and learning in every situation, we cultivate a sense of hope that drives us forward. This doesn't mean ignoring the difficulties but rather reframing them as opportunities for development. A positive attitude can act as a buffer against stress, making it easier to cope with setbacks and maintain a hopeful perspective even when circumstances are challenging.

3. **Practice Self-Care**
Resilience is deeply connected to our physical, mental, and emotional well-being. Prioritizing self-care is crucial, as it ensures that we are equipped to handle life's challenges. This means engaging in regular exercise to keep the body strong, eating nutritious foods to fuel our minds, and ensuring adequate rest to recharge our spirits. Self-care also includes activities that nourish the soul, such as meditation, prayer, or hobbies that bring joy. When we take care of ourselves, we build a solid foundation that supports our resilience.

4. **Connect with Others**
Human beings are inherently social creatures, and our connections with others play a vital role in building resilience. Strong relationships provide emotional support, encouragement, and a sense of belonging. Whether it's family, friends, or community groups, these relationships remind us that we are not alone in our struggles. Sharing our experiences and listening to others can offer new perspectives

and practical advice, helping us navigate tough times with the combined strength of community.
5. **Embrace Flexibility**
Life is unpredictable, and the ability to adapt to changing circumstances is a key aspect of resilience. Embracing flexibility means being open to new ideas, willing to adjust plans, and finding creative solutions when faced with unexpected obstacles. It involves letting go of rigid expectations and learning to flow with the changes, trusting that each new challenge offers an opportunity to grow and develop. By cultivating a flexible mindset, we become more resilient in the face of uncertainty, better equipped to handle whatever life throws our way.

Conviction Checkpoints

- **Self-Examination Question:** Reflect on a time when you faced a significant challenge. How did you demonstrate resilience? What strategies helped you overcome the difficulty?
- **Actionable Step:** Identify a current challenge in your life. Break it down into smaller manageable tasks and create a plan to address each step. Seek support from a trusted friend or community member.
- **Conviction Affirmation:** "My resilience, strengthened by faith and community, empowers me to redefine outcomes and transform challenges into opportunities."
- **Prayer/Meditation Focus:** Pray for strength and resilience in the face of current and future challenges. Ask God to help you see opportunities for growth and to provide the courage to persevere.

Profile in Conviction

Winston Churchill

Winston Churchill, the iconic British Prime Minister during the harrowing years of World War II, stands as a timeless symbol of resilience and unyielding leadership. His ability to inspire a nation teetering on the brink of despair and rally it against the overwhelming might of Nazi Germany is a testament to the indomitable spirit he embodied. Faced with the threat of invasion, the bombardment of British cities, and the immense pressure to negotiate a peace deal with Adolf Hitler, Churchill's resolve never wavered. His unwavering determination and refusal to surrender, encapsulated in his legendary rallying cry, "Never, never, never give up," fueled the spirit of resistance across Britain and beyond.

Churchill's resilience was not merely rhetorical; it was a lived experience. He had faced political failures, personal setbacks, and public criticism throughout his career. Yet, each failure seemed to fortify his resolve rather than diminish it. When the fate of the world hung in the balance, Churchill's speeches infused the British people with hope and courage, galvanizing them to endure the hardship of war with stoic determination. His declaration during the darkest days of the Blitz, "We shall fight on the beaches, we shall fight on the landing grounds, we shall fight in the fields and in the streets, we shall fight in the hills; we shall never surrender," was more than just words; it was a battle cry that resonated deeply within the hearts of a nation under siege.

Churchill's ability to maintain a vision for victory, despite the near-impossible odds, underscores the transformative power of resilience. His leadership was a beacon of hope, not just for the United Kingdom, but for the entire free world. His unwavering belief in the eventual triumph of good over evil played a pivotal role in the defeat of the Axis powers, securing freedom and democracy for future generations. Churchill's life is a profound reminder that resilience, when coupled with conviction and unwavering faith in a righteous cause, has the power to change the course of history.

Churchill's story is a masterclass in the art of resilience. His ability to stand firm in the face of adversity, to inspire a beleaguered nation, and to never lose sight of the greater purpose serves as a powerful lesson for us all. His life demonstrates that resilience is not simply about enduring hardship, but about rising above it, refusing to yield, and forging a path to victory no matter the obstacles. His legacy teaches us that, in the darkest of times, it is resilience that lights the way to hope, purpose, and ultimately, triumph.

As we reflect on the powerful example set by Winston Churchill, it becomes clear that resilience is an essential ingredient for overcoming life's greatest challenges. It is this same resilience that we must cultivate in our own lives, allowing us to face adversity with courage, to hold steadfast to our convictions, and to transform our trials into triumphs. The following conclusion brings together the insights gained from this chapter and offers a final reflection on the enduring power of resilience.

Resilience is not just a personal attribute; it is a collective strength built through faith, community, and persistence. By embracing resilience, we can redefine our outcomes, turning obstacles into opportunities for growth and transformation. As we face the challenges of life, let us remember the words of Winston Churchill and the strength found in our faith and community. With resilience, we can navigate any storm, emerging stronger and more determined than before.

CHAPTER 12
INTEGRITY GUIDES

Integrity is more than just a trait; it is the foundational cornerstone of a person's character. It is the quality of being honest and adhering to strong moral principles that are unshakable, regardless of the circumstances. Integrity acts as an internal compass, constantly guiding us to navigate through life's complexities and make the right decisions, even in the face of adversity. It requires a commitment to truthfulness and ethical behavior, holding oneself accountable to the highest standards of conduct.

Integrity shapes our interactions with the world, influencing how we respond to challenges, how we treat others, and how we perceive ourselves. It is not just about avoiding dishonesty or wrongdoing; it's about being consistently true to one's values and ethical beliefs. This consistency fosters trust, not only from others but within oneself. A life marked by integrity is one that is steady and secure, like a ship with a reliable anchor in the midst of a storm.

In the camp, where everyday decisions were often shaded by desperation and moral compromise, I discovered that integrity was not only crucial but necessary for survival. It was through maintaining integrity that I was able to preserve my self-respect and dignity, even in a setting designed to strip these away. My commitment to integrity became a beacon that guided my actions and decisions, helping me to build trust with those around me. In an environment where trust was scarce and suspicion was abundant, integrity became the bedrock upon which I could stand firm. It did not just keep me morally aligned; it steered me toward positive outcomes, proving that holding fast to one's principles, even when it is the hardest path, ultimately leads to true success and peace.

The Importance of Integrity

Integrity is more than just a commitment to honesty or ethical conduct; it is a way of life that demands unwavering consistency in actions, values, and principles, regardless of the audience or situation. It's about making the right choices not just when others are watching but even more so when no one is around to hold us accountable. This consistency forms the bedrock of trustworthiness and respect, both from others and within ourselves.

> *"Integrity is doing the right thing, even when no one is watching."* - C.S. LEWIS

Regardless of external pressures or temptations, It's about aligning one's conduct with one's core beliefs and values. Integrity involves a conscious decision to act ethically and morally, even when it's challenging or unpopular. It's this consistency that builds a solid reputation, making a person reliable and worthy of trust.

Proverbs 10:9 underscores the value of integrity, stating, *"Whoever walks in integrity walks securely, but whoever takes crooked paths will be found out."* This verse captures the essence of integrity's protective power. Living a life marked by integrity provides a profound sense of security and inner peace. When our actions align with our values, there is no fear of exposure or the anxiety that comes from living a double life. Integrity eliminates the need for deception and pretense, allowing us to live openly and authentically.

Integrity is like a shield, safeguarding us against the pitfalls of dishonesty and deceit. A life lacking integrity may achieve short-term gains, but it is built on shaky foundations that will eventually crumble. As integrity provides a clear conscience and stable footing, it guards against the eventual downfall that comes with dishonesty. "The truth may hurt for a little while, but a lie hurts forever," goes the old adage. This wisdom highlights how a lack of integrity may provide temporary relief or gain, but the repercussions of deceit and betrayal lead to long-term damage and ruin.

Looking back through history, one compelling example of integrity is found in the life of George Washington. As the first President of the United States, Washington was known for his unwavering commitment to honesty and ethical leadership. Faced with the temptation to seize more power and become a monarch, Washington chose to step down after two terms, setting a precedent for future presidents. His actions demonstrated that true leadership is grounded in integrity, prioritizing the welfare of the nation over personal ambition.

Similarly, the story of Sir Thomas More, a renowned English statesman, and author of *Utopia*, exemplifies integrity. More served as a counselor to King Henry VIII, but when the king demanded his endorsement of the Act of Supremacy, declaring Henry as the head of the Church of England, More refused. His commitment to his principles and faith led to his execution, but his legacy of integrity has endured for centuries. More's unwavering stance reminds us that integrity sometimes requires great personal sacrifice but ultimately leads to a legacy of honor and respect.

Another historical figure known for his integrity was the Roman philosopher and statesman Marcus Aurelius. In his *Meditations*, Aurelius wrote extensively about living a life of virtue, emphasizing honesty, humility, and justice. Despite being an emperor with immense power, he consistently upheld his ethical values, demonstrating that integrity transcends status and power. His reflections continue to inspire people to live with moral clarity and consistency.

Ultimately, integrity is about being true to oneself. It is about having the strength to adhere to one's principles and values, regardless of external pressures or the cost involved. It is a commitment to personal authenticity, ensuring that our public persona is a true reflection of who we are privately. Integrity brings coherence to our lives, a unity between what we believe and how we act, making us individuals of character and purpose.

Integrity in Action

In the camp environment, where trust is scarce and suspicions run high, integrity becomes a vital currency. It's more than just about telling the truth; it's about consistently aligning actions with personal values, even when faced with temptations or pressures that make compromising seem like the easier path. Upholding integrity in such an environment demands a constant commitment to one's principles, especially when the path of least resistance appears so inviting.

Every day presented new challenges to maintaining integrity. The temptation to bend the rules for personal gain or to fit in with certain groups was ever-present. Whether it was witnessing minor infractions like bending the rules for convenience or being aware of larger, more serious schemes that pushed the boundaries of legality, the question was always the same: How much could I tolerate without compromising my own sense of right and wrong?

There were times when turning a blind eye seemed not only wise but necessary for peace of mind and self-preservation. In a place where alliances shifted quickly, and minor misunderstandings could escalate into significant conflicts, maintaining a strict black-and-white view of morality was neither practical nor safe. This realization didn't mean abandoning principles but rather choosing battles wisely, understanding that every situation didn't require a reaction or intervention.

However, there were lines that I could not, in good conscience, allow myself to cross. In moments where the integrity or well-being of others was at stake, I had to weigh the risks and decide how best to navigate the situation. This often involved quietly encouraging others to rethink their actions or offering subtle advice that promoted peace and fairness without directly confronting the issue or escalating it. Integrity, in these cases, was about influence rather than control—finding ways to uphold my values without putting myself or others at unnecessary risk.

Maintaining integrity also meant resisting offers that would compromise my moral standing, even if they came with the allure of making life a bit more bearable. There were always opportunities to take shortcuts, to engage in activities that could provide immediate benefits but at the cost of long-term self-respect. These choices required a conscious commitment to the values that I held dear, even if saying "no" sometimes led to misunderstanding or distrust from others. I found that staying true to my principles earned a different kind of respect, one based on consistency and reliability, even among those who didn't share my views.

Living with integrity in the camp was not about being perfect or never making mistakes. It was about recognizing my own humanity, understanding my limits, and continuously striving to make decisions that aligned with my core beliefs. It was about the small, everyday choices that defined my character and kept me grounded, even in an environment designed to erode personal values.

In this way, integrity became a quiet force, guiding my actions and decisions without needing to make a show of it. It wasn't about grandstanding or proving moral superiority; it was about maintaining a sense of self that couldn't be easily swayed by the changing tides of the camp's social dynamics. Integrity was my anchor, providing a sense of stability and self-respect amidst the uncertainty and volatility of life inside.

This nuanced approach to integrity allowed me to navigate the camp's complex environment without becoming hardened or cynical. It gave me the inner strength to endure, knowing that while I couldn't control everything that happened around me, I could control how I responded to it. My integrity wasn't defined by the opinions of others but by my own ability to look in the mirror each day with a sense of peace and self-respect. It was about staying true to who I was, even when doing so required quiet courage and a strong sense of self-awareness.

Personal Stories of Integrity

In the camp, where the walls seemed to close in a little tighter each day and the air was thick with the unspoken rules of survival, my integrity faced its fiercest tests. There were countless moments when the line between right and wrong blurred under the pressure of confinement, the scarcity of resources, and the hunger for acceptance. But there is one moment that stands out more vividly than the rest, a moment that nearly shook the foundation of who I believed myself to be.

There was an unspoken code in the camp, a tacit understanding that certain behaviors would be overlooked as long as they didn't upset the fragile equilibrium of our lives. Among these behaviors, the smuggling of contraband was a silent, shadowy practice that everyone knew about but rarely spoke of openly. It was a lifeline for some—a means to gain a sliver of control, to barter for favors, or simply to make the harsh conditions more bearable.

One day, a fellow camper approached me, his eyes sharp with the glint of secrecy and opportunity. He offered me a role in smuggling a small item, promising certain privileges and a more secure position within the camp's social hierarchy. For a fleeting moment, the offer was tantalizing. I could see the allure of the advantages it might bring—the small comforts, the protection, the acceptance that seemed always just out of reach. In a place where every day was a struggle for dignity and respect, these offers felt like a shortcut to a semblance of normalcy.

The temptation gripped me, a whisper in the back of my mind suggesting that maybe, just maybe, this was a way to make my life a little easier. But beneath the surface of that temptation lay a deeper voice, quieter but resolute. It was the voice of my upbringing, my faith, and the principles I had spent a lifetime cultivating. I knew that compromising my integrity, even for something that seemed so minor, would be like opening a door to a darkness I couldn't close.

With a steady breath, I looked him in the eye and declined. My voice was calm but firm, "I can't do that. It goes against everything I believe in." The reaction was immediate and varied. Some campers nodded with a glimmer of respect in their eyes, recognizing the quiet strength it took to stand by one's principles in a place designed to strip you of them. Others shook their heads, muttering about missed opportunities and foolish idealism.

As the days passed, I wondered if I had made the right choice. The allure of those small comforts and the promise of security gnawed at the edges of my resolve. But I knew that my decision had to be about more than just surviving each day; it had to be about living in a way that allowed me to hold my head high, even when no one was watching.

Over time, my unwavering commitment to integrity began to earn me something far more valuable than any material gain—trust. Both campers and correctional officers came to see me as someone who could be relied upon, someone who wouldn't shift with the winds of convenience or succumb to the pressures of the moment. It wasn't an easy path. There were days when the isolation of standing alone felt heavier than the walls around me. But with that burden came a profound sense of inner peace, a self-respect that no one could take from me.

The same man who had approached me with the offer to smuggle contraband came to me later, a smile playing on his lips. "You know, Rev.," he said, almost conspiratorially, "I only asked you to see if you were the real deal. I wanted to see if you'd bend." His words stayed with me, not just because of the relief they brought, but because of the stark truth they revealed. Integrity wasn't just about avoiding the big mistakes; it was about the thousand little decisions we made every day.

Reflecting on my journey, I realized that much of my resolve came from an unexpected place—fear. As a child, I had learned quickly that wrongdoing came with serious consequences. In my household, the line between right and wrong was drawn in bold, unmistakable strokes. (Strokes that were distributed from the switches we had to get from the oak tree in the backyard.) The phrase "If you can't do the time, don't do the crime" wasn't just a saying; it was a way of life, a mantra that had been etched into my conscience. I avoided many temptations not out of some lofty sense of morality but because I was genuinely afraid of the consequences. I hope you can handle this level of transparency.

And perhaps, that fear wasn't such a bad thing. It was a fear that had kept me out of trouble, that had guided my steps when the right path wasn't clear. It was the kind of fear that forged integrity not out of weakness but out of a recognition of the power that comes from living a life aligned with one's principles. It was this fear—this respect for the weight of consequences—that had kept me standing, even when the winds of temptation blew hardest.

In the end, my integrity was not a banner I waved to showcase my righteousness. It was a quiet, steadfast anchor that held me in place, a beacon that guided my choices, and a shield that protected my soul. And in a place where everything else was stripped away, it was enough to remind me of who I was and who I wanted to be.

Integrity and Building Comfort

Integrity is a trait that provides a sense of comfort and safety to those around you, knowing that your principles and actions will remain consistent regardless of the situation. In an environment like a prison camp, where uncertainty, fear, and distrust are rampant, integrity is a beacon of stability. It's like a lighthouse that cuts through the darkness, offering direction and hope. People are drawn to those whose words align with their actions, whose promises are not just empty rhetoric, but a bond that can be relied upon. When you demonstrate unwavering integrity, you create an atmosphere where others feel secure, respected, and valued.

In the camp, integrity was not just a matter of moral high ground; it was a vital survival tool. People quickly learned who could be trusted and who would flip under pressure. Maintaining integrity meant that my fellow campers knew where I stood at all times. There were no hidden agendas, no secret maneuvers. This consistency allowed me to form authentic relationships based on mutual respect. When people know that you won't change up on them, that you won't compromise your values for the sake of convenience or personal gain, it builds a kind of invisible armor around you—one that repels deceit and fosters genuine connection.

The comfort that comes from integrity isn't just a one-way street; it also flows back to the person who practices it. Living with integrity means that I never had to second-guess my decisions or worry about being caught in a lie. There was a profound inner peace that came from knowing I was being true to my beliefs, regardless of the circumstances. This self-assuredness acted as a pillar of strength, helping me navigate through the maze of camp politics and power dynamics. In a place where alliances were often fragile and shifting, my integrity became a constant—an unchanging anchor that held fast even when the tides were at their strongest.

In an environment where deception and manipulation were common survival tactics, maintaining integrity set me apart. It meant that others could approach me without fear of betrayal or exploitation. It meant that when I gave my word, it was as solid as any written contract. This reliability fostered deeper connections, as people found comfort in knowing that they could count on me. Integrity built bridges where there might otherwise have been walls, opening doors to conversations and relationships that may not have been possible otherwise.

Integrity also became a teaching tool, a silent example that spoke louder than any sermon. People observed my actions, and slowly, some began to adopt similar principles. In this way, integrity didn't just benefit me; it had a ripple effect, contributing to a more stable and respectful community within the camp. It created a kind of moral ecosystem, where trust and honesty could take root and flourish, even in the most inhospitable conditions.

The comfort and security that integrity provides are invaluable, particularly in a setting where trust is scarce and every interaction could be laden with hidden motives. People in the camp began to recognize that my integrity wasn't just about avoiding trouble or maintaining a reputation. It was about creating a space where honesty and authenticity could thrive. It was about showing that even in the darkest places, light could still shine through. And as that light shone, it brought comfort not only to those who sought it but to everyone within its reach.

In this way, integrity became more than just a personal virtue; it was a communal one. It was a force that brought people together, fostering an environment where openness and honesty were the norms rather than the exceptions. And in a place defined by confinement and restriction, this sense of communal integrity was a breath of fresh air, a reminder that even in the hardest of places, there was room for hope, trust, and the quiet comfort that comes from knowing that no matter how much the world around you may change, your principles remain steadfast and true.

The Role of Faith in Maintaining Integrity

Faith played a pivotal role in helping me maintain my integrity, acting as both a compass and a source of strength. It grounded my actions and decisions, providing a steadfast foundation that held firm even in the most trying circumstances. Faith wasn't just a belief; it was an active force that shaped my thoughts, guided my steps, and fortified my resolve. The teachings and principles I had absorbed over the years became a lifeline, anchoring me to a higher purpose and helping me stay true to my values.

The words of Ephesians 6:14 became particularly meaningful during my time in the camp: *"Stand firm then, with the belt of truth buckled around your waist, with the breastplate of righteousness in place."* This scripture vividly illustrates the protective nature of integrity, likening truth to a belt that holds everything together and righteousness to a breastplate that guards the heart. In an environment where lies, deceit, and moral ambiguity were rampant, these spiritual tools provided a sense of armor. They shielded me from the corrosive effects of dishonesty and compromise, ensuring that my character remained intact.

Living with integrity meant constantly choosing the path of righteousness, even when it was the harder road to walk. There were moments when taking shortcuts or bending the truth could have provided temporary relief or gain. However, my faith reminded me that the easy way is not always the right way. I held fast to the belief that God honors those who walk in truth and uprightness. This conviction gave me the strength to make decisions that aligned with my faith, rather than succumbing to the pressure to conform or take the path of least resistance.

Prayer and meditation were essential practices in reinforcing my commitment to integrity. They served as my daily check-in with God, moments of introspection where I could align my thoughts and actions with His will. Through prayer, I found the strength to resist temptation and the clarity to see beyond the immediate circumstances. Meditation allowed me to quiet my mind, to listen for God's voice, and to find peace in His presence. These spiritual disciplines were not just rituals; they were lifelines that kept my spirit strong and my conscience clear.

In the stillness of prayer, I would often find reassurance that God was with me, guiding my steps and protecting me from harm. This sense of divine companionship made it easier to stand firm in my convictions, knowing that I was never alone. Faith taught me that integrity is not just about what we do when others are watching, but about who we are when no one is around. It's about being true to ourselves and to God, even when no one else would know the difference.

There were times when maintaining my integrity came at a cost—social isolation, missed opportunities, or increased scrutiny. But my faith provided a broader perspective, reminding me that earthly gains are fleeting, while spiritual integrity has eternal value. The words of Proverbs 11:3 echoed in my heart: *"The integrity of the upright guides them, but the unfaithful are destroyed by their duplicity."* This verse served as a constant reminder that integrity leads to life and peace, while deceit ultimately leads to ruin.

Faith also provided me with the strength to face the consequences of my choices with grace and courage. It reassured me that, even if my integrity led to temporary hardship, God's justice would prevail. I held onto the promise found in Psalm 37:28: *"For the Lord loves the just and will not forsake his faithful ones."* This assurance gave me the courage to endure challenges with dignity, knowing that my integrity would ultimately be rewarded.

Faith, prayer, and meditation became the bedrock of my commitment to integrity. They enabled me to navigate the moral complexities of the camp with a steady heart and a clear conscience. In a place where moral compromises were often the norm, my faith was the guiding light that kept me on the right path. It reminded me that true strength comes not from outward success or approval but from a heart aligned with God's will. Through faith, I found the courage to stand firm, to speak truth, and to live with honor, no matter the cost.

The Impact of Integrity on Relationships

Integrity is the bedrock of meaningful and lasting relationships. It not only guides our actions but also profoundly influences the way we interact with others. By consistently demonstrating honesty and adhering to strong moral principles, we build trust and credibility—essential elements that form the foundation of genuine connections. In the prison camp, an environment often characterized by suspicion and mistrust, integrity served as a powerful force for good, enabling the formation of meaningful bonds and a sense of community.

Choosing to live with integrity was not only countercultural but also transformative. It sent a clear message to others that there was a different way to live, one that did not require compromising one's values for temporary gain. By consistently embodying integrity, I became a beacon of reliability in a place where stability was rare. Fellow campers knew that my word was trustworthy and that I would stand by my principles, regardless of the circumstances. This reliability made me a confidant for many, someone they could turn to for honest advice or simply a listening ear.

The trust that was built through integrity had a ripple effect, influencing not only my direct relationships but also the broader community within the camp. Trust is a rare commodity in environments where survival often depends on secrecy and alliances are formed out of necessity rather than genuine connection. Maintaining integrity helped break down some of these barriers, fostering an atmosphere where open communication and mutual respect could thrive. When people feel that they can trust one another, even in small ways, it changes the dynamics of a community, making it possible for cooperation and support to replace suspicion and rivalry.

One of the most profound impacts of maintaining integrity was the influence it had on others. When people observe someone consistently living by their principles, it challenges them to reflect on their own actions and behaviors. Integrity can serve as a mirror, prompting others to evaluate their own choices and consider the impact of their actions. In the camp, I noticed that my commitment to honesty and moral principles inspired others to think more deeply about their own values. Some fellow campers began to emulate the behavior they saw, choosing to act with greater honesty and integrity in their own interactions. It was a reminder that integrity is not just a personal journey but a social one, with the power to inspire change beyond ourselves.

By standing firm in my beliefs, I was able to contribute to a more respectful and supportive environment. This was not achieved through grand gestures or public declarations but through the quiet, consistent practice of integrity. Whether it was returning a borrowed item on time, speaking truthfully even when it was uncomfortable, or refusing to participate in unethical activities, each act of integrity reinforced the values I held dear and subtly influenced the camp's culture. Over time, these small, consistent actions created a ripple effect that fostered a greater sense of accountability and mutual respect among the campers.

The relationships I built on the foundation of integrity were marked by depth and authenticity. People knew that I was not interested in superficial alliances or manipulative games. My integrity created a safe space where genuine friendships could develop—relationships based not on what could be gained or exploited but on mutual respect and shared values. These connections were a source of strength and encouragement, providing emotional support that was vital for navigating the challenges of camp life.

Integrity also had a powerful impact on how I was perceived by the correctional officers. In a place where authority figures often viewed inmates with skepticism and distrust, maintaining integrity helped to establish a different kind of rapport. The consistency of my actions and the respect I showed to both fellow campers and officers alike did not go unnoticed. It earned me a level of trust that led to more open communication and, at times, more lenient treatment. While this was not the primary motivation for maintaining my integrity, it was a natural outcome of living in alignment with my values.

Ultimately, integrity builds a legacy that endures beyond individual interactions. It leaves a mark on the hearts and minds of those we encounter, influencing how they perceive themselves and the world around them. In the camp, my adherence to integrity served as a silent witness to the power of living a principled life, even in the most challenging circumstances. It demonstrated that integrity is not a burden to be carried but a gift to be shared—a guiding light that can illuminate the darkest of places and inspire hope in the hearts of others.

The impact of integrity on relationships cannot be overstated. It builds bridges where there might otherwise be walls, creates trust where there is doubt, and fosters understanding in the place of misunderstanding. In a world where integrity is often seen as negotiable, choosing to live with unwavering moral principles is a revolutionary act that has the power to change lives—starting with our own.

Leading with Integrity: Building Trust, Loyalty, and Community

Leading with integrity is about more than just doing the right thing; it's about setting a powerful example that can inspire and transform those around us. True leadership grounded in integrity cultivates trust, loyalty, and a strong sense of community. It is a guiding force that creates a lasting impact, not only on the individuals being led but also on the leader themselves. This form of leadership encourages authenticity, fosters collaboration, and promotes a culture where ethical behavior is the norm, not the exception.

Psalm 78:72 beautifully captures the essence of integrity in leadership: *"And David shepherded them with integrity of heart; with skillful hands he led them."* This scripture illustrates how David's leadership was marked by a genuine commitment to his people, fueled by an unyielding sense of integrity. His leadership was not merely about strategy or military might; it was deeply rooted in moral character and a heartfelt desire to serve those he led. David's integrity brought about security, prosperity, and a sense of unity among his people, showing that leadership is most effective when it is grounded in ethical principles and compassion.

Leading with integrity means consistently aligning actions with values, even when faced with immense pressure or adversity. It requires the courage to stand firm in one's convictions, to make difficult decisions, and to uphold ethical standards, regardless of the consequences. This is not an easy path to take. The pressure to compromise, to take shortcuts, or to prioritize personal gain over the welfare of others is often intense. However, true leaders understand that integrity is not a choice made in isolation; it is a commitment that shapes every aspect of their leadership.

Integrity in leadership is about transparency and accountability. It involves being honest and open with others, owning up to mistakes, and taking responsibility for one's actions. Leaders who practice transparency build a foundation of trust, making it easier for others to place their confidence in them.

This trust is essential for creating a sense of loyalty and commitment within a team or community. When people see that their leaders are willing to be honest, even when it is uncomfortable or when it exposes their own vulnerabilities, it inspires them to act with similar honesty and integrity.

Consider the difference between a leader who leads with integrity and one who does not. A leader without integrity might manipulate information, make decisions based solely on personal gain, or prioritize their own success over the well-being of others. While this may bring short-term success, it often leads to long-term failure—eroding trust, creating division, and ultimately leading to a breakdown in relationships and effectiveness. In contrast, a leader who embodies integrity prioritizes the collective good over personal ambition. They are willing to make sacrifices for the betterment of the team, community, or organization. This selflessness fosters a culture of mutual respect and collaboration, where individuals feel valued and motivated to contribute their best.

Integrity in leadership also means being consistent. A leader's actions, words, and decisions should align with their stated values and principles. This consistency builds credibility, making it clear to others that the leader can be relied upon to act with fairness and justice. When leaders are consistent in their integrity, it removes uncertainty and creates a stable environment where people feel safe and secure. In such an environment, creativity and innovation flourish because individuals know that their contributions will be judged based on merit and not on favoritism or deceit.

One of the most powerful aspects of leading with integrity is its ability to inspire others. When leaders demonstrate integrity, it sets a standard for everyone else to follow. It encourages a culture where ethical behavior is celebrated, and unethical behavior is not tolerated. This influence extends beyond the immediate team or organization; it has a ripple effect that can impact entire communities or even societies. People are more likely to emulate leaders they respect and admire, which means that the integrity of a single leader can inspire countless others to act with integrity in their own lives.

In the camp, the impact of leading with integrity was evident. When those in leadership positions—whether formal or informal—demonstrated integrity, it created a positive environment where trust could flourish. People knew where they stood, and this predictability reduced conflict and fostered cooperation. Leaders who acted with integrity were able to mediate disputes, offer guidance, and provide support in ways that others could not. Their integrity made them approachable, and their decisions were trusted because they were rooted in fairness and concern for the well-being of all.

The legacy of integrity in leadership is enduring. It is not measured by the titles one holds or the accolades one receives, but by the lives one touches and the positive change one brings about. Integrity leaves a lasting imprint, shaping not only the present but also influencing future generations. When leaders act with integrity, they contribute to building a culture that values honesty, respect, and ethical behavior. This culture becomes a powerful force that sustains organizations, communities, and societies, enabling them to thrive even in the face of challenges.

Integrity in leadership is not just a moral obligation; it is a strategic asset that builds trust, fosters loyalty, and creates a sense of community. By leading with integrity, we set a powerful example that encourages others to do the same, creating a positive cycle that benefits everyone involved. Integrity is the bedrock of effective leadership, providing the stability, credibility, and ethical foundation necessary to navigate challenges and inspire lasting change. It is a commitment that requires strength and courage but yields immeasurable rewards, both for the leader and those they lead. As we strive to lead with integrity, we not only honor our values but also leave a legacy that can inspire and uplift others for years to come.

As we consider the profound impact that integrity has on our leadership and our relationships, it becomes clear that maintaining such a high standard of ethical conduct requires intentional effort. Integrity, like any virtue, must be nurtured and developed. It is not a one-time decision but a continual commitment to act in accordance with our deepest values, regardless of the circumstances we face. The question then arises: How do we cultivate and sustain integrity, especially in environments that challenge us to compromise? The answer lies in adopting practical strategies that help us stay grounded in our principles and guide our actions with consistency and purpose. Here are some strategies for developing and maintaining integrity in all areas of life.

Strategies for Developing Integrity

1. **Reflect on Core Value**
   Regularly take time to reflect on your core values and principles. This helps reinforce your commitment to integrity and provides a clear foundation for decision-making.

2. **Seek Accountability**
   Surround yourself with individuals who share your commitment to integrity and can hold you accountable. This support system can provide encouragement and guidance when faced with difficult decisions.

3. **Stay True to Yourself**
   Avoid compromising your values for temporary gains or to fit in with others. Staying true to yourself ensures that your actions are aligned with your beliefs.

4. **Practice Honesty**
   Make honesty a habit in all interactions, regardless of the circumstances. Consistent honesty builds trust and credibility over time.
5. **Pray and Meditate**
   Regularly seek guidance and strength from your faith. Prayer and meditation can provide clarity and reinforce your commitment to integrity.

Integrity is a guiding force that shapes our actions, decisions, and relationships. By upholding integrity in all aspects of life, we build trust, foster respect, and navigate through challenges with a clear conscience. Embracing integrity allows us to live authentically and honorably, ultimately leading to positive outcomes and a sense of fulfillment.

Conviction Checkpoints

- **Self-Examination Question:** Reflect on a time when your integrity was tested. How did you respond, and what was the outcome? What did you learn from the experience?
- **Actionable Step:** Identify an area in your life where you can demonstrate greater integrity. Take a specific action this week to uphold your values and build trust with those around you.
- **Conviction Affirmation:** I commit to living a life of integrity, making decisions that align with my core values, and setting an example for others to follow.
- **Prayer/Meditation Focus:** Pray for strength and wisdom to maintain integrity in all aspects of your life. Ask God to help you stay true to your values and make decisions that honor Him.

Profile in Conviction

Immanuel Kant – A Life of Integrity

Immanuel Kant, a German philosopher born in 1724, is often regarded as one of the most influential thinkers in Western philosophy. Kant's philosophy centered on the importance of duty, moral law, and the categorical imperative—a principle that asserts one should act only according to that maxim which they can at the same time will to become a universal law. This emphasis on universal morality reflects Kant's deep commitment to integrity, both in thought and in action.

Throughout his life, Kant was known for his unwavering adherence to principles. He believed that integrity required not just acting according to moral laws but doing so out of a sense of duty rather than personal gain or emotion. For Kant, integrity was the cornerstone of a moral life, guiding individuals to act consistently with their values, regardless of external pressures. Kant's personal life mirrored his philosophical beliefs. He was known for his disciplined and structured lifestyle, reflecting his commitment to the principles he espoused. His dedication to integrity influenced his academic work, as he refused to compromise his philosophical positions even when they were unpopular or misunderstood.

Kant's legacy serves as a powerful reminder that true integrity involves consistency in both thought and action. His life exemplifies the belief that acting with integrity is not just about making the right choices in difficult moments but living in a way that consistently reflects one's deepest moral convictions. Through his philosophical teachings and personal example, Kant continues to inspire individuals to lead lives grounded in integrity and moral responsibility.

Integrity is more than just a personal virtue; it is the cornerstone of a life well-lived, a legacy built to endure, and the foundation upon which true leadership stands. In the challenging environment of the prison camp, integrity was not just a moral compass—it was a lifeline, guiding me through the darkest valleys and helping me navigate a landscape fraught with temptation, mistrust, and despair.

Integrity is not about perfection; it's about authenticity and consistency. It's about making the choice, day after day, to live according to your values, even when no one is watching and especially when the stakes are high. It is in those moments of testing that the true measure of one's character is revealed. Like a fortress, integrity protects us from the internal erosion of self-betrayal and the external pressures to compromise. It is a shield against the consequences of deception and the hollow victories of self-serving shortcuts.

The ripple effect of integrity extends far beyond personal benefit. It influences others, inspiring them to hold themselves to higher standards. It builds bridges of trust in environments where suspicion reigns. It strengthens the fabric of communities by providing a foundation of reliability and respect. Integrity sets the stage for genuine relationships, authentic leadership, and lasting impact.

Reflecting on the role of integrity in my own journey, I realize that it was not the absence of trials that defined my path, but rather how I chose to face those trials. Integrity was the steady hand that guided me, the inner voice that reassured me, and the constant companion that reminded me of my purpose. It was my commitment to integrity that allowed me to emerge from the prison camp not just as a survivor, but as a stronger, wiser, and more compassionate leader.

Integrity demands courage, for it often requires us to stand alone. It demands humility, for it acknowledges our flaws and the continuous work needed to align with our values. Most of all, it demands resilience, for integrity is not a shield from hardship but a tool to navigate through it. In the end, a life of integrity is not just a life of doing what is right; it is a life of being who we are truly meant to be. It is the path to peace, purpose, and profound impact.

As we strive to lead with integrity, let us remember that every decision we make, no matter how small, is a step on a journey. With each choice, we write the story of our lives, and through our integrity, we ensure that it is a story worth telling—a story of unwavering commitment to what is right, a story that inspires others, and a story that leaves a legacy of honor and respect for generations to come.

CHAPTER 13

GREATER THINGS ARE STILL TO COME

When I first entered the prison camp, I resolved to trust God and never lose hope despite the circumstances. However, as the days turned into months and the months into years, my faith was tested in ways I had never imagined. One of the most challenging moments came when my attorney informed me that my final appeal to the Supreme Court had been denied. This was my last legal hope, and I had convinced myself that this would be the moment God would come through and end this nightmare. But it didn't happen, and I was broken.

Thankfully, I married the right woman. My wife, Qwynn, heard something in my voice that I was desperately trying to hide. She said, "I'm coming to visit you this weekend, and I don't care what you think." All I did was cry on the phone. I could not even talk. But she knew she needed to be with me, and God knows I needed her.

The Test of Faith and Patience

After that visit, I was frustrated. I still could not fathom what God was doing and what the purpose of all this was. Yes, I had glimpses of what God was doing through me in the camp, but I still could not get over my feeling that God could have used anybody else other than me.

I couldn't wait to get to the Power House so God and I could really talk. These talks were often, and they usually involved my waiting until the machines were at their loudest, and I would just scream, "Why?" I knew enough not to verbally express all my feelings because I knew my words mattered, even when I didn't understand.

Let me say something about my heart... My heart was polluted by all my questions. I knew that God could handle the questions, but none of the answers comforted me. I bring this up because many of us have mastered the formula of our words so we make sure we never utter a word out of place, yet all we've done is master duplicity because our hearts are the most important. I was not hearing from God clearly because I was so broken internally by my questions. In the quietness after all my screaming, all I could say was, "Come on, God, help me understand this!" Nothing came.

There was a song that had ministered to me when I was in my worst moods—which were surprisingly often. It was a song called, "In Good Hands." Oh, how this song ministered to me. Even now, while I'm writing, I'm listening to it and crying. At a fundamental level, when I could not trace His hands, I had to trust God's heart toward me. I could not have made it this far without the strong hands of God. He was the one who had upheld me this entire time—even my family. Here are the lyrics as sung by Angela Primm:

*"In good hands, I'm in good hands,
I'm in the hands of Jesus.
Winds may blow, but this I know:
I'm in the good, good hands of Jesus.*

*Now I cannot answer every question,
And I cannot know what life will bring.
But this I know: my Lord is faithful,
And to this clear hope my spirit clings.*

*I may not know the seas He's charted;
I may not know how long the storm may rage.
But this I know: I trust the Captain.
My anchor holds secure and safe!*

*In good hands, I'm in good hands,
I'm in the hands of Jesus.
Winds may blow, but this I know:
I'm in the good, good hands of Jesus."*

When I got to that second verse, and tears were streaming down my face, I felt the calming presence of God come over me. In response, all I could do was repent for my arrogance in questioning His goodness based on what had happened to me. I just whispered, "I trust the Captain!" When I gave my life to Jesus as a young boy, I gave Him complete control over my life—I hadn't realized until that moment that in everything I had been through for my entire life, God had protected me on so many levels. Things I should have been caught doing, I hadn't been, and now I was enduring the punishment for something I didn't do, and I had to conclude God was no less good now than He had been when I was wrong, and He protected me. In that moment, I asked God to forgive me—I know it was a little late, but that was a destiny moment in the Power House that night. An unknown burden had lifted from me that I didn't even know I was carrying. I felt lighter and was determined that if

God's plan was for me to spend three more years in this place, I would give Him the glory each day. I returned to the unit that night as a new man.

Renewed Hope and Divine Assurance

The following morning during my devotions, I completed the day's reading from my one-year Bible and felt an unexpected urge to journal. Journaling wasn't something I typically did, but on this day, I knew I needed to capture what was stirring in my spirit. It was December 1, 2019—my 658th day in the camp. As I quieted myself, I sensed God's voice speaking clearly to me: "Six more months. Get ready. I am giving you a platform. Be prepared."

If I had heard this prior to my "come to Jesus moment" in the Power House, I would have dismissed it because my heart was not ready for this. The statement on its face was farcical! I had exhausted all my appeals. There was only one other motion to file, which was ineffectiveness of counsel, and, even though my attorney said, "Do it, throw me under the bus," I had no qualms about her representation. She fought for me even when I was numb from the fight. But I knew how to hear God's voice. I knew this was God, and I also had no idea how it could happen!

Around that same time, guys started getting sick in the Unit. Mysteriously, guys would fall ill and couldn't get out of bed. It was not a new thing because when sickness went through the unit, it usually hit a bunch of guys at once. Thankfully, it hit me, and I was sluggish for a day or so but kept going. That was the first and only time I had gotten ill inside.

The Season of Unexpected Change

We all looked eagerly for spring to come, as that winter was especially brutal. Also, I saw many of the guys with whom I had

Chapter 13: Greater Things Are Still to Come

been inside getting their dates to go home. We had formed a community, and while I was happy about them leaving, there was a sadness that went along with it. I kept hope in the Word I heard from God: "Six months..." How could that be?? Right as the winter months faded and Spring was blooming, the news of a strange virus called COVID was occupying the news. There were more questions than answers concerning this illness. I didn't think much of it. However, I should have because it changed the entire dynamic within the camp. Guards started wearing masks. They even tried to persuade us to wear them, but that was not successful. Twice a day, the medical team came through to take temperatures. All activities and jobs were canceled. We were effectively quarantined.

The camp, which had been a comfortable place to be, suddenly became a "real" prison. We were effectively stuck in the unit 24 hours a day. Except for the count, we couldn't go anywhere or do anything. Even walking outside was discouraged. In late March, we heard that COVID was taking its toll, and people were dying. In response, Congress passed the CARES Act, which was signed into law by President Donald J. Trump on March 27, 2020. It contained a provision that gave the Attorney General the prerogative to release inmates whose time was nearing completion and who were over the age of 50. The administration produced a list of inmates who were recommended for release. I was not on it. In my old frame of mind, it would have been another blow, but I was unmoved. Strangely, those who were recommended for release had to be quarantined for at least 21 days before their release. Since the camp had no segregated place for quarantine, campers were put in the SHU (Special Housing Unit) for 21 days. I said to God, "Please don't let that be my experience." God knew I couldn't handle that level of confinement.

While the guys were gathering their belongings, ready to be taken up for quarantine, I was called to the office because my attorney was trying to reach me.

I thought that was strange since there was nothing left for her to do. When I finally spoke to her, she said that she was concerned about my health and was going directly to the judge to request my release. This is the same judge who had denied EVERY motion we offered and had shown herself particularly predisposed against me. I said, "It didn't matter," and questioned why she would waste her time since we knew the answer would be "no." She persisted, and I said, in essence, "Do what you think, but I'm not holding out hope!"

An Unexpected Release

Much to my surprise, the judge agreed that I should be released, but the Bureau of Prisons had dissented because it would break their administrative process, which the judge was bound to respect. They had a time limit to consider any request, and I think it was 30 to 45 days. The judge was so determined to get me out that she said if I wasn't out by the end of the administrative review period, she would order my release the very next day. That would have put me towards the middle of May, which would have been more than six months—but don't get me wrong, I was willing to take it. My lawyer continued to push! Conditions in the camp deteriorated even more with new restrictions, new testing, and temperatures. With about one-third of the camp in quarantine in the SHU, it was a ghost town. Even our religious services were canceled. We did manage to hold Easter Service in the Greenhouse before all access was cut off.

My wife was unaware of the legal issues swirling around, but she received a call from my attorney that I was ordered by the judge to be released "forthwith," which meant immediately.

It was during our regularly scheduled evening call that she told me I was being released the next day and that she was leaving first thing in the morning to get me. Could it be that this part of the nightmare was really coming to an end? It appeared so!

The next morning, I was in a state of disbelief. Could this really be happening? After so many setbacks and disappointments, it seemed surreal that I would be going home. My mind was racing as I packed my belongings. I had made peace with my situation, and now, suddenly, everything was changing.

As I waited in the holding area, memories of the last two years flooded my mind. I thought about the men I had met, the lessons I had learned, and the ways I had grown. Despite the hardship, I knew that my time in the camp had a purpose. I had been tested and refined, and now I was being released into a new chapter of my life.

When the guard finally called my name, I felt a rush of emotions. Relief, gratitude, and even a sense of sadness. The camp had been a difficult place, but it had also been where I found a deeper connection with God and a renewed sense of purpose.

The New Beginning

The drive home was quiet. My wife and I didn't need to say much. We both knew that our journey was far from over, but we were ready to face whatever came next—together.

Once I got home, I realized that my experience in the camp had changed me in ways I hadn't anticipated. I was more aware of the importance of trust, the power of community, and the need for resilience. Most importantly, I had learned that God's plans are often beyond our understanding, but they are always for our good.

As I settled back into life outside the camp, I reflected on the words God had spoken to me: "This is just the beginning." I knew that my time in the camp was not the end of my story, but the start of something new. God had given me a platform, and I was determined to use it to share the lessons I had learned and to help others who were going through their own trials.

Strategies for Developing Hope

1. **Focus on the Bigger Picture:** Remember that your current circumstances do not define your future. Keep your eyes on the greater plan that God has for you.
2. **Practice Gratitude:** Cultivate a habit of gratitude by focusing on the blessings in your life, no matter how small. This can shift your perspective and foster hope.
3. **Surround Yourself with Positive Influences:** Build a support system of people who encourage and uplift you. Positive relationships can reinforce hope and resilience.
4. **Stay Connected to God:** Regular prayer, meditation, and reading Scripture can help you maintain a hopeful outlook and stay grounded in your faith.
5. **Take Small Steps Forward:** Even when the path seems unclear, take small steps in the right direction. Progress, no matter how incremental, can build momentum and hope.

Better Tomorrows

As I close this chapter of my life, I am filled with hope and anticipation for what lies ahead. The journey I have undertaken has been marked by trials and triumphs, lessons and growth, but most importantly, it has been a testament to the power of resilience, faith, and integrity. I am convicted that this is just the beginning of a new and exciting chapter, one filled with endless possibilities and opportunities for growth and impact.

Philippians 3:13-14 says, *"Brothers and sisters, I do not consider myself yet to have taken hold of it. But one thing I do: Forgetting what is behind and straining toward what is ahead, I press on toward the goal to win the prize for which God has called me heavenward in Christ Jesus."* With this conviction, I press on, ready to embrace the new beginnings that await and am committed to continuing to lead a life of purpose, faith, and integrity.

I want to implore you that our trials and hardships are not the end, but often the beginning of something greater. It's about trusting that God is always working behind the scenes, even when we can't see it, and that His plans for us are good. My time in the prison camp was an uncomfortable season, but it was also a time of growth and transformation. It taught me that no matter what we go through, God is always with us, guiding us, and preparing us for what's next. I can truly say that **my tomorrows will be better than my yesterdays.**

Conviction Checkpoints

- **Self-Examination Question:** Reflect on a time when you faced a significant trial. How did this experience shape your faith and perspective on life?
- **Actionable Step:** Identify an area in your life where you need to trust God more. Commit to praying and seeking His guidance in that area daily.
- **Conviction Affirmation:** I trust in God's plans for my life, knowing that He is always in control and working for my good.
- **Prayer/Meditation Focus:** Pray for the strength to trust God in every situation, especially when the path is unclear. Ask Him to give you peace and assurance that He is with you every step of the way.

Profile in Conviction

Richard Wurmbrand

Richard Wurmbrand, a Romanian Christian pastor, was a beacon of hope and resilience during one of the darkest periods of the 20th century. Arrested in 1948 by the Communist regime for preaching the Gospel, Wurmbrand was subjected to 14 years of imprisonment and brutal torture. Despite the harsh conditions, including years in solitary confinement, his faith never wavered. Instead, he saw his suffering as a way to share in the sufferings of Christ, maintaining his commitment to God and the message of salvation even when it meant facing severe physical and psychological torment.

Throughout his imprisonment, Wurmbrand found ways to continue his ministry, preaching to fellow prisoners through Morse code tapped on the walls of his cell. His ability to hold onto hope in such dire circumstances was a testament to his deep faith and his belief in the power of God's love to transcend even the most oppressive forces. Wurmbrand's resilience was not just about surviving; it was about thriving spiritually, even when the world around him was designed to crush his spirit.

After his release, Wurmbrand did not allow bitterness or despair to take root in his heart. Instead, he used his experience to advocate for persecuted Christians worldwide, founding The Voice of the Martyrs, an organization dedicated to supporting believers facing persecution. His story, detailed in his book *Tortured for Christ*, serves as a powerful reminder that hope, grounded in faith, can sustain us through any trial and that God's light can shine even in the darkest of places.

Richard Wurmbrand's life is a profound example of hope and resilience in the face of unimaginable adversity. His unwavering faith and commitment to spreading the Gospel, even under the threat of death, inspire us to remain steadfast in our convictions, no matter the challenges we face. Wurmbrand's story encourages us to draw strength from our faith, trusting that God's purposes will prevail, and to remember that hope, when anchored in Christ, is a force that can endure any storm.

EPILOGUE:
D. QWYNN GROSS

Before my ears heard the allegations against my husband, an ominous weight surrounded me. I wasn't familiar with the feeling, nor could I put my finger on what or where the problem was, but I knew something wasn't right. My discernment never came with immediate answers; it just kept me in my prayer closet. No relief seemed to be in sight as I rose early morning to pray, felt pressure in the middle of the day to pray, stopped to pray before going to bed, and was interrupted throughout the night to get up and pray. Prayer was constant.

By the time my husband broke the news that charges were brought against him, my disposition looked and sounded the same as always though shock, disappointment, anger, humiliation, uncertainty, and instability would all begin to brew slowly, then surge and retreat like waves on the shoreline, each wave bringing in one feeling or the other as decisions were made that affected so many—it wasn't just his life now grossly affected—we had college-bound children, family, a church, respect, dreams, vision—even more, I had a vow; a promise to God made years prior that I would be an example of Christianity that anyone could follow; and now, not only was it all threatened at the very least and tarnished in my mind, but I would have to honor this commitment to Him despite this woeful breach to my desired ideals.

Blindsided by the events during that time is an understatement as the implications of impending humiliation and potential ruin were disorienting; and while time seemed to stand still, matters would escalate until I was found seated in a courtroom with his family on the opposite side of the room, along with church leaders scattered within, and our eldest child in the space though now a blur of where, as a judge would sentence "my" husband to sixty months in federal prison for a crime he did not commit and for a duration incommensurate for the crime if he did. Nevertheless, he was convicted. And, quite honestly, it didn't matter to me what his convictions were, or what was broken in the judicial system, or the motives of a judge, or how incompetent the jurors appeared, or how efficient our attorney was or was not, or the jarring wail from his sister after the verdict, or what those present to support were now thinking and feeling. It was all inconsequential as the gavel hit. I sat dumbstruck. Stunned by a metaphorical sucker punch that marked the beginning of a new and sobering reality, punctuated only by the day that I would drive the man I married to a facility where he would spend life as a common criminal while I was this naive woman now fully awake and aware that my only option as a Christian was to do my very best to please God regardless and have something to offer my husband when the nightmare was over.

And so, the balancing act began. I knew I would not make it without our Father, so He was the constant priority. I devoted much time in His presence, holding onto my confession of hope and inviting specific others to join me while trusting that He would build His church and that He could use me because I was determined to be found faithful. Faithful in my private devotion and public ministry, lest I risk a heart of duplicity. Faithful as a wife because this was a part of the covenant, for better or worse. Faithful as a mother because they would need stability now more than ever. Faithful to the church so there would be no need to scatter and no reason to stumble in faith. And faithful to who I claimed to be as a believer because I didn't want to disappoint my Father in any of it. I wanted to honor God with all of my heart and in every way.

And, while it was a noble commitment in theory, in reality, I now had a husband whose dignity was assaulted in ways that seemed to debatably exceed physical pain as he would manage the throes of inexplicable disgrace, and defamation of character with a determination to showcase strength based upon principle alone, all while assuring me and everyone around him that he was "fine," "alright" and "at peace." He claimed to be "fine" from the beginning and "fine" while inside, yet his ego, I presumed, was bruised, if not completely broken based upon how detached he was and seemingly on his own journey. From the beginning to the end, he seemed to resign from his need for family while distancing himself from the family's need for him. Graciously, he would hand over his life—transferring power of attorney, and management of our household and the church, while refusing visitation. In light of this, it made a part of my job to honor him and his role in my life and our family necessary, more than ever, because he *was* still valued, and would have to feel needed, I thought.

So, I did my best to follow his counsel and wisdom for the church because it seemed all he had left to offer, and yet, in his absence, there came a time when he was no longer in position because obscure changes were happening incrementally but quickly; it became like driving a bus with him in the very last row, blindfolded but giving passive-aggressive instructions as if behind the steering wheel himself. And, after a night in the ER from the stress of wanting and failing to please him, I was left with a new determination to remove the training wheels, accept change, make decisions, and literally expect God to be with me through the waters and protect me from rivers that *could* overtake me (Isaiah 43:2). He would have to be God or everything would fall apart.

To be sure, it was a difficult time for several reasons, but I realized very quickly that I could not afford the distraction of feelings, nor did I have the bandwidth for hollow issues or tolerance for pessimism. The devil could not win. I needed to produce. Administrative decisions had to be made, people had to be pastored, church leaders would need direction, my daily job description for work would have to be fulfilled, and somehow, my children would have to know that they were loved and that all was well. With everything and everyone being a priority, robotic rhythms from morning to nightfall would become natural, even safe. Nevertheless, abrupt moments of overwhelm would snatch the REM from my sleep, or I'd have to vigorously evict the spirit of loneliness that would jump into my car as I traveled home to an empty house, while those removed and unable to absorb my reality avoided the obvious, evasively inquired, empathized with distrust, or showed glib indifference.

But as much as there were superficial or questionable people, there were also genuine ones. From the beginning, my employer supported my family which relieved my mind when thinking about job security. In the thick of it, an unknown couple would press an average person's savings into my hands for legal fees—so needed and so refreshing at that time; a pastor I didn't consider myself necessarily close to would send random texts asking if I needed "Ice-cream money." To God be the glory, I never did, but when the heating unit blew out in our Children's Church building, I reached out to this same pastor, and money was sent the next day. When repayment was mailed, it was also returned. In addition, my husband's spiritual father was available for him in ways that brought peace of

Epilogue: D. QWYNN GROSS

mind on varying occasions. Interestingly, my mentor from before marriage would randomly reach out from another country, saying, "I promised your mother I would keep you in my prayers; now what is going on?" He knew nothing of our family's plight before that call, and he became a great blessing as he affirmed me and voiced his confidence in me and my ability to lead God's people—his words were invaluable as I latched onto whatever he and my mother saw.

Though few in number, altogether, these people remind me of Acts 18, where God spoke to Paul in a vision and said, *"Do not be afraid; keep on speaking, do not be silent. For I am with you, and no one is going to attack and harm you because I have many people in this city."* Indeed, God has people—and those who allowed Him to use them for my family and me were indeed momentary respites and encouragement during the entire ordeal. They were light in my life, but they were also a perk to my husband as he would talk about the handful of people who wrote him letters or placed money in his commissary account while he gave sacrificially to other inmates who had no one to care, or no money to give. It would serve as the healthiest of our nightly 10-minute phone conversations after rehearsing the well-being of our own children and those within our church.

By the time my husband and I established this pattern to communicate, and two years were over, the plague of COVID became headline news, the university where I worked shut down abruptly, and churches were required to close; but I can say thanks be to God because my employer kept me on staff, though seven from our team of nine were let go; and, our church remained in operation because we followed God's leading before the world was quarantined, and years in advance, my husband had the wherewithal to set the church up to meet virtually, which made Sunday morning worship possible without interference. Not only did God sustain and protect both my natural family and the entire church family from lack and premature death, but amazingly, the turmoil in the world became the surprising catalyst for my husband's early release. It was a whirlwind.

By his return, he was different, but he had the time and privacy needed to reacclimate to home life and reassume his role and responsibilities as lead pastor. The church was different, as new faces that included many men now filled vacant seats. (I mention men because they were my barometer to determine the strength of the church). My family was different, as my young adult children were now in a new stage of life, resilient, and very adept at independence in ways that I could lament. Marriage was different, as a strained relationship was now held together by what I presume to be loyalty alone. Life was and is different, as people were no longer a source or resource of "feeling" safe. But then, I am different. Different in some ways that I fully appreciate and in other ways that I continue to process. Yet, I can say I'm grateful for an experience that allowed me to grow as a person, completely dependent upon God, and be the desired example of how to stand, how to endure, how to fight, and to overcome, even more, how to follow Jesus even when expectations are dashed, love is hard, and life hurts. I'm grateful because through it all, the true meaning and purpose for life was distilled in Christ alone, and my life is what it is, not because I'm so strong, but because our God is so faithful.

The Gospel of Matthew, chapter 7 includes a story of how we're all building our house using either rock or sand as a foundation, and there is a storm that will come to each, where the rain will descend, the flood waters will rise, and the wind will beat against the house. If we've built our house on the sand, it will fall, but if we've built our house on the rock, it will remain. Thus, I can close this chapter of my life, and close this chapter in my husband's book by admonishing you, reader, to do the Word of God now so that when unexplainable crises and/or distasteful events happen in your life, you too will experience His faithfulness and will be able to comfort others with the comfort you yourself received.

"Blessed be the God and Father of our Lord Jesus Christ, the Father of mercies and God of all comfort, who comforts us in all our tribulation, that we may be able to comfort those who are in any trouble, with the comfort with which we ourselves are comforted by God." 2 Corinthians 1:3-4 NKJ

ABOUT THE AUTHOR

Trevon Gross, PhD, is a devoted husband, father, and spiritual leader who has dedicated his life to serving others and spreading the message of God's love. Through his experiences, he has gained a profound understanding of resilience, faith, and the transformative power of grace. Trevon's story is one of redemption and triumph, inspiring countless individuals to find their own paths to victory.

For more information, visit TrevonGross.com

Convicted

www.ingramcontent.com/pod-product-compliance
Lightning Source LLC
Chambersburg PA
CBHW050852160426
43194CB00011B/2119